HISTORY COMICS

ROSA PARKS & CLAUDETTE COLVIN

CIVIL RIGHTS HEROES

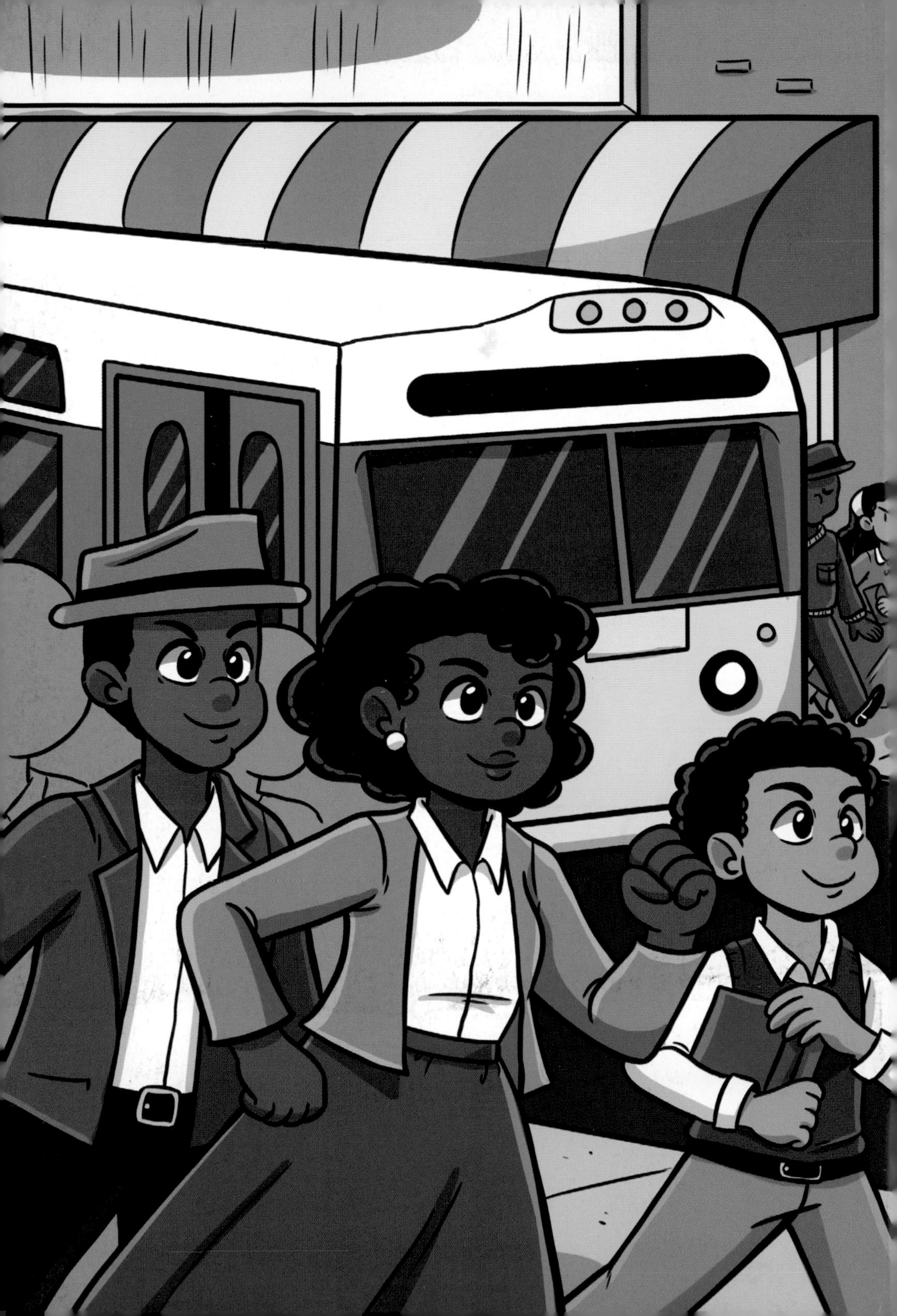

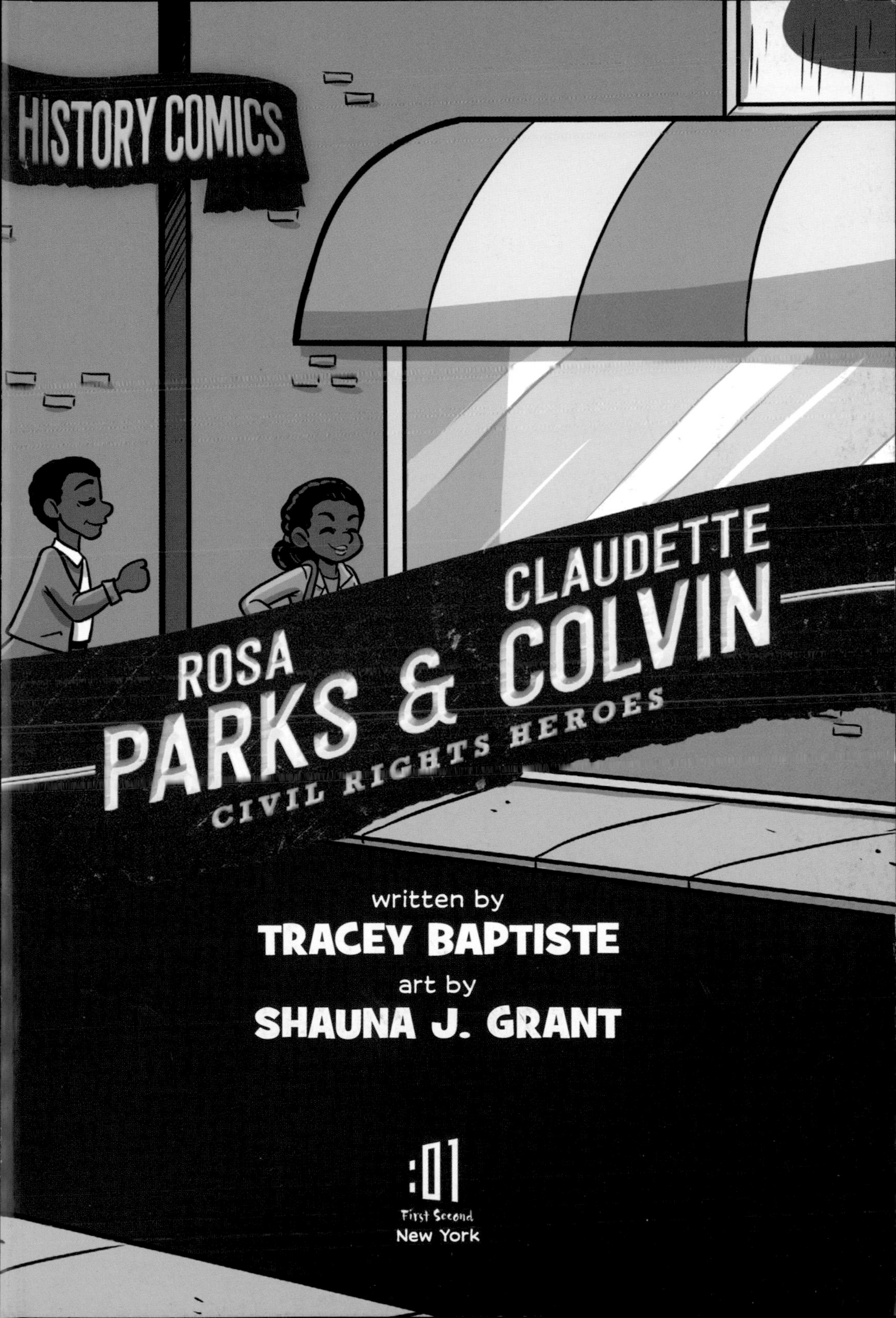
HISTORY COMICS

ROSA PARKS & CLAUDETTE COLVIN

CIVIL RIGHTS HEROES

written by
TRACEY BAPTISTE
art by
SHAUNA J. GRANT

:01
First Second
New York

First Second

Published by First Second
First Second is an imprint of Roaring Brook Press,
a division of Holtzbrinck Publishing Holdings Limited Partnership
120 Broadway, New York, NY 10271
firstsecondbooks.com
mackids.com

Library of Congress Cataloging-in-Publication Data is available.

Our books may be purchased in bulk for promotional, educational, or business use. Please contact your
local bookseller or the Macmillan Corporate and Premium Sales Department at (800) 221-7945 ext. 5442
or by email at MacmillanSpecialMarkets@macmillan.com.

First edition, 2023
Edited by Dave Roman and Benjamin A. Wilgus
Cover design by Andrew Arnold and Molly Johanson
Series design by Andrew Arnold
Interior book design by Sunny Lee and Madeline Morales
Production editing by Avia Perez
Color by Jessie Cooke
History consultant: Jeanne Theoharis
With special thanks to Francesca Lyn

Digitally penciled, inked, and colored in Clip Studio Paint and Photoshop on a Wacom Cintiq Pro.
Lettered with Soliloquous font from Comicraft.

Printed in China by Toppan Leefung Printing Ltd., Dongguan City, Guangdong Province

ISBN 978-1-250-17422-2 (paperback)
10 9 8 7 6 5 4 3 2 1

ISBN 978-1-250-17421-5 (hardcover)
10 9 8 7 6 5 4 3 2 1

Don't miss your next favorite book from First Second! For the latest updates go to
firstsecondnewsletter.com and sign up for our enewsletter.

The past is filled with heroes who don't make history. Traditionally, heroes are pedestaled as flawless, fearless, extraordinary people who single-handedly save the world. But those heroes don't exist, and those standards only make it harder for many of us to see ourselves as leaders capable of effecting change.

Heroes are not born, they are nurtured. They are curious, critical, and even uncertain in the face of adversity. They are motivated by a deep concern for the well-being of our shared humanity, and most importantly, they are supported by and embedded in a community working toward liberation.

Although most heroes never make it into our history books or onto big screens, their stories matter because they challenge dominant narratives about how change is made and who has the power to make it happen. By shedding limiting beliefs about who is capable of being a hero, we make room in our consciousness, our narratives, our history for young people, people in poverty, disabled people, queer people, ordinary people, *more* people to transform this world.

Respectability politics, ageism, and colorism nearly erased Claudette Colvin's powerful contributions from history. By telling her story and Rosa Parks's story, not in competition with each other but as two strands in a large tapestry of ordinary people fighting for freedom, we can learn to recognize that heroic people live among us—they are us. After all, the perfect hero is not coming to set us free. *We* are the ones we've been waiting for.

—*Kadiatou A. Tubman*
Schomburg Center for Research in Black Culture

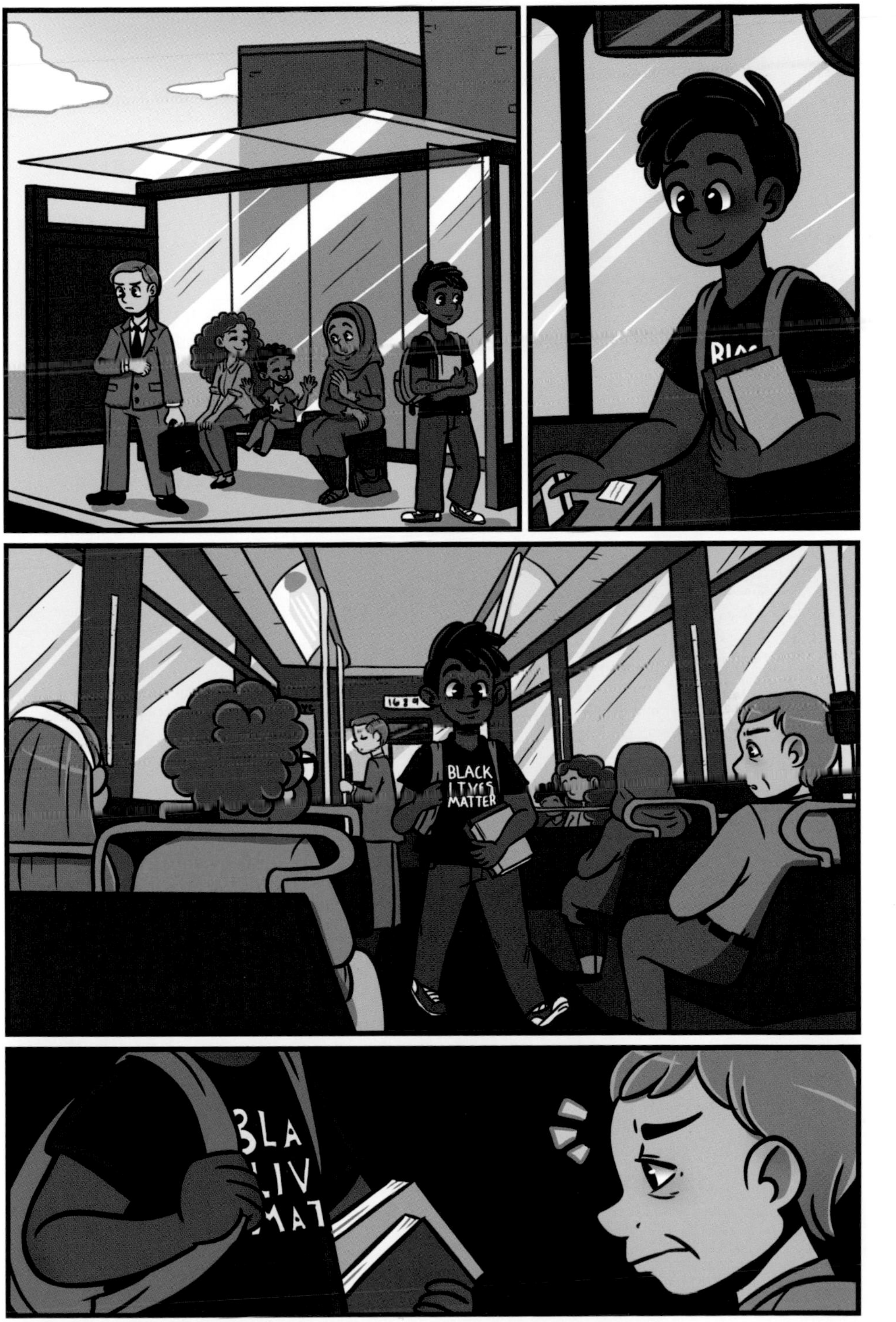
BLACK LIVES MATTER

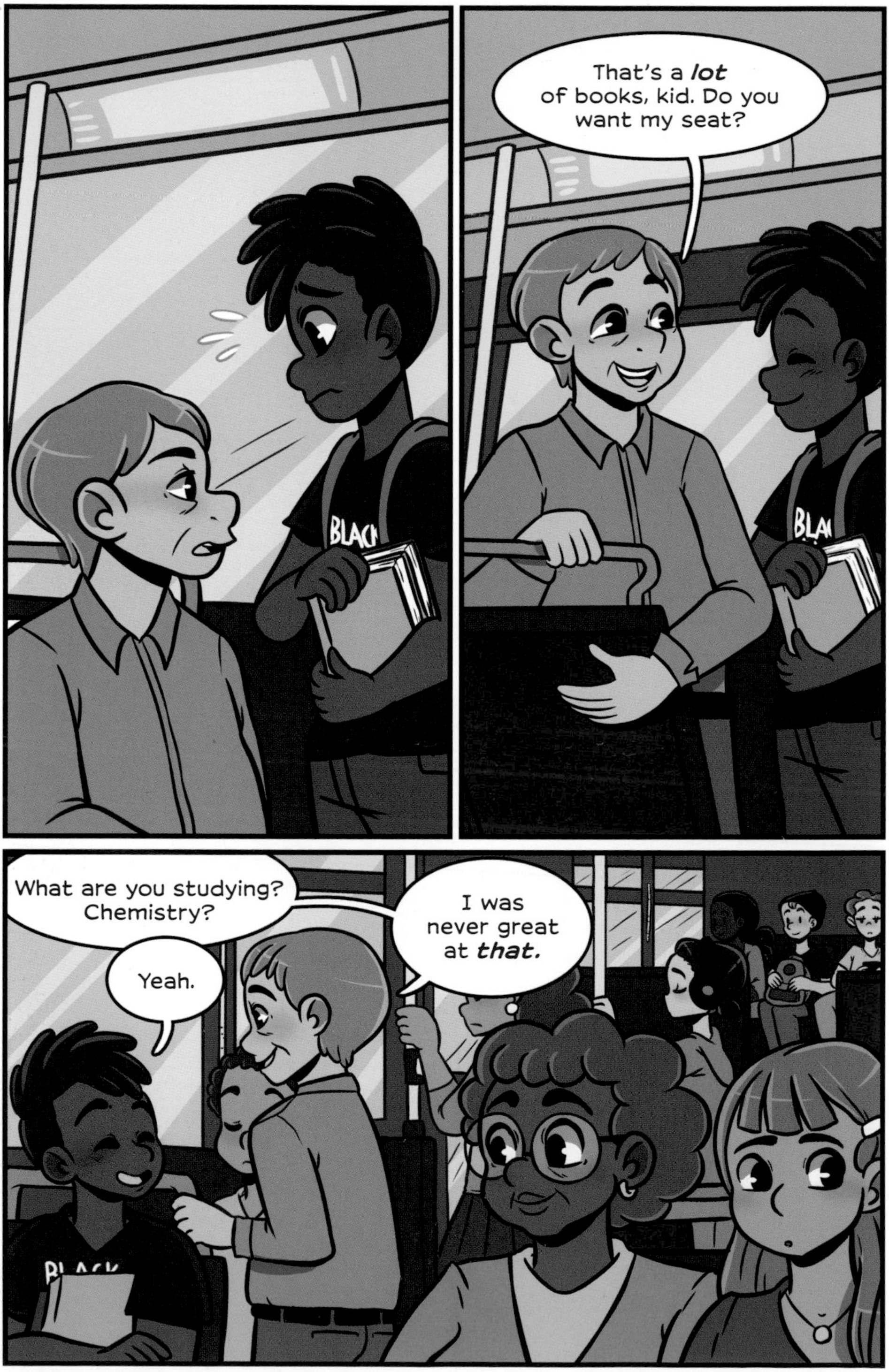
BLACK
That's a *lot* of books, kid. Do you want my seat?
What are you studying? Chemistry?
Yeah.
I was never great at ***that.***

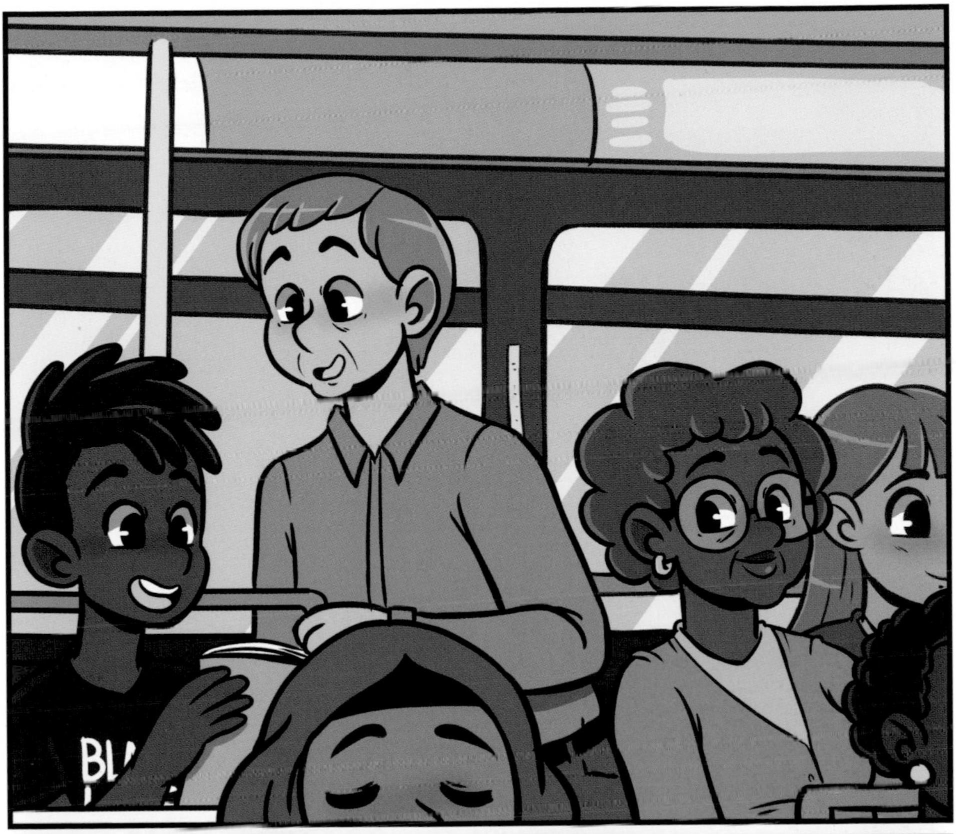

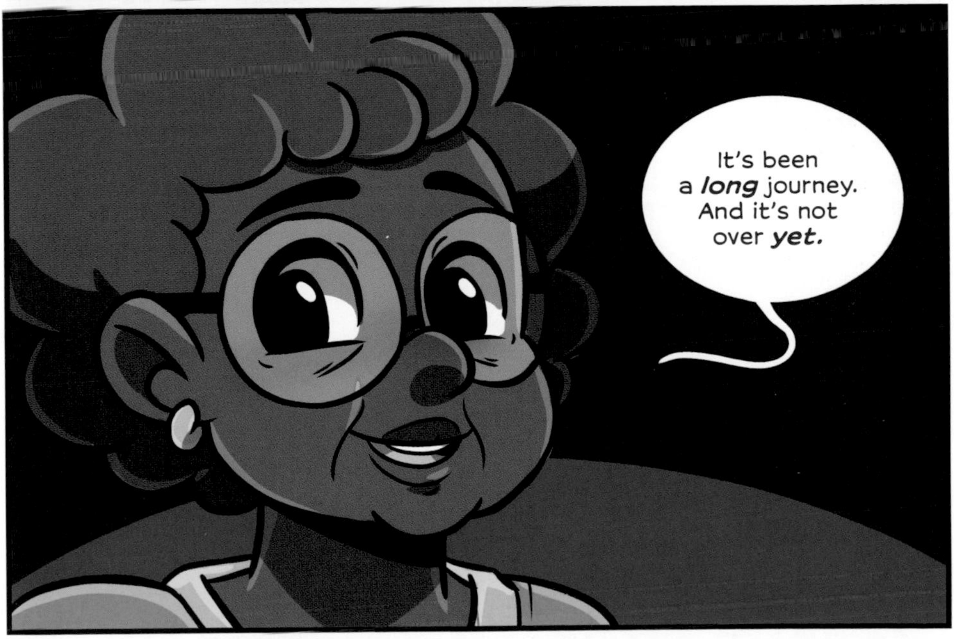
It's been a *long* journey. And it's not over ***yet.***

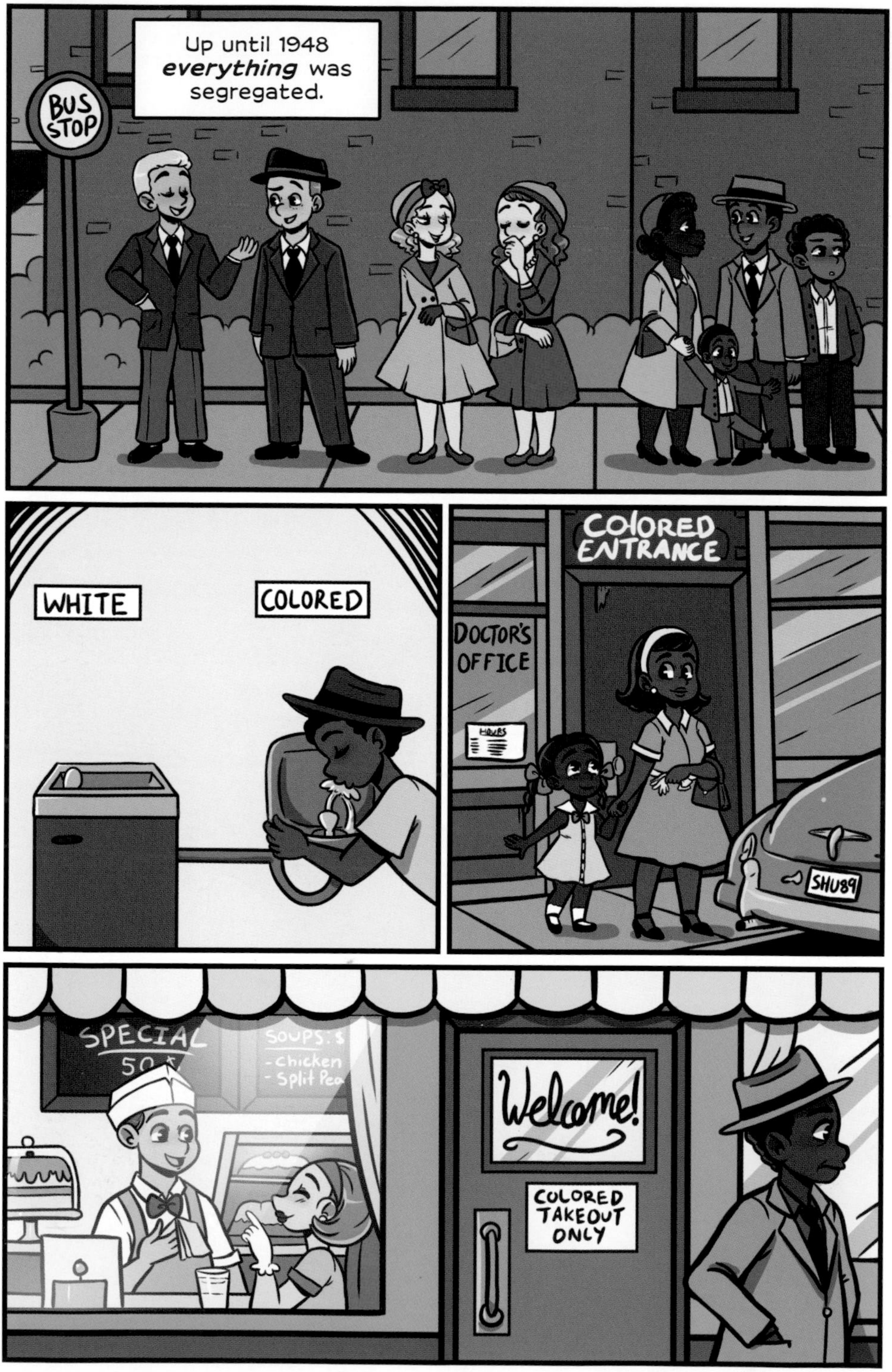
Up until 1948 *everything* was segregated.
BUS STOP
WHITE
COLORED
COLORED ENTRANCE
DOCTOR'S OFFICE
HOURS
SHU89
SPECIAL
-Chicken
Welcome!
COLORED TAKEOUT ONLY

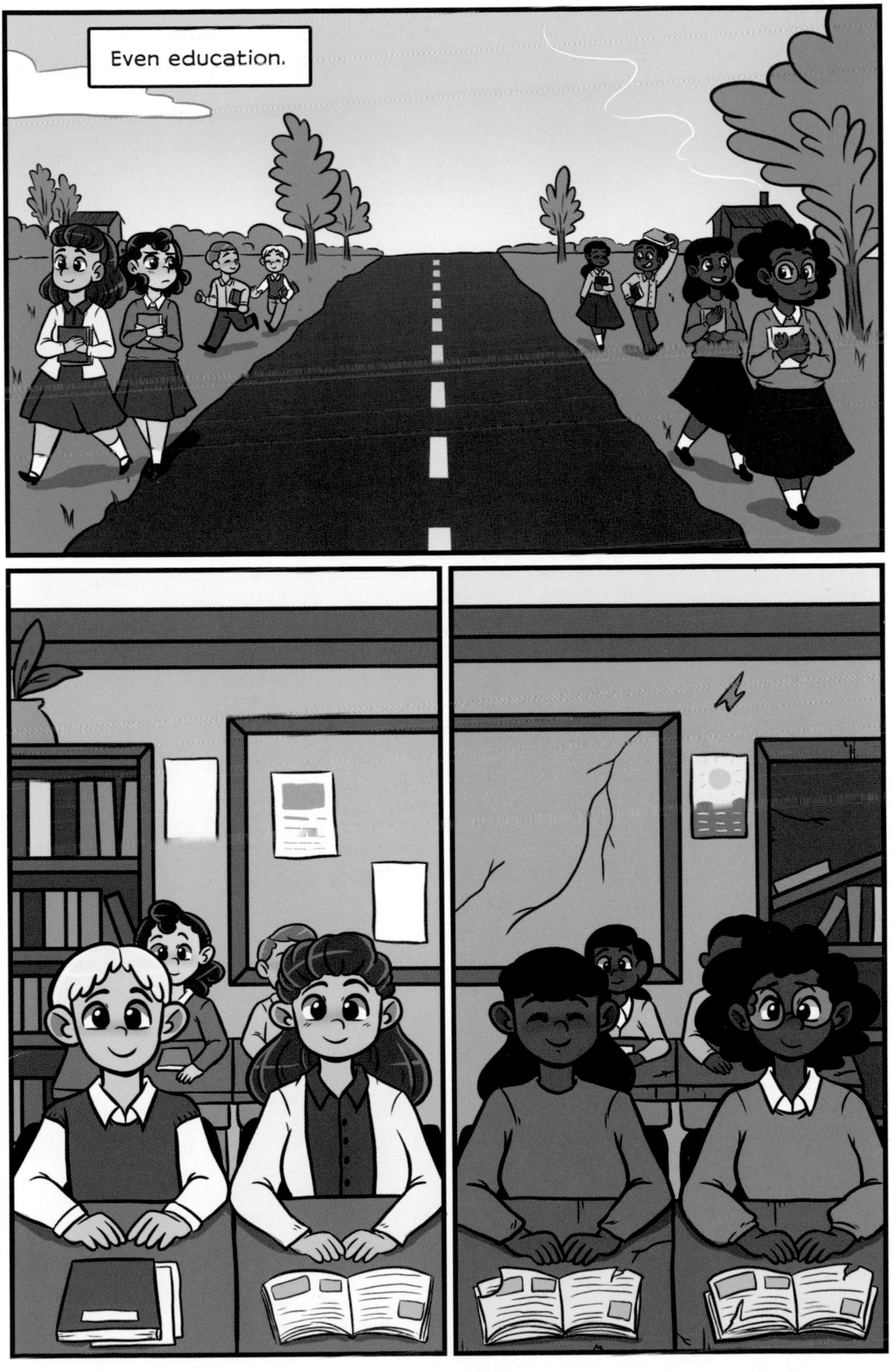
Even education.

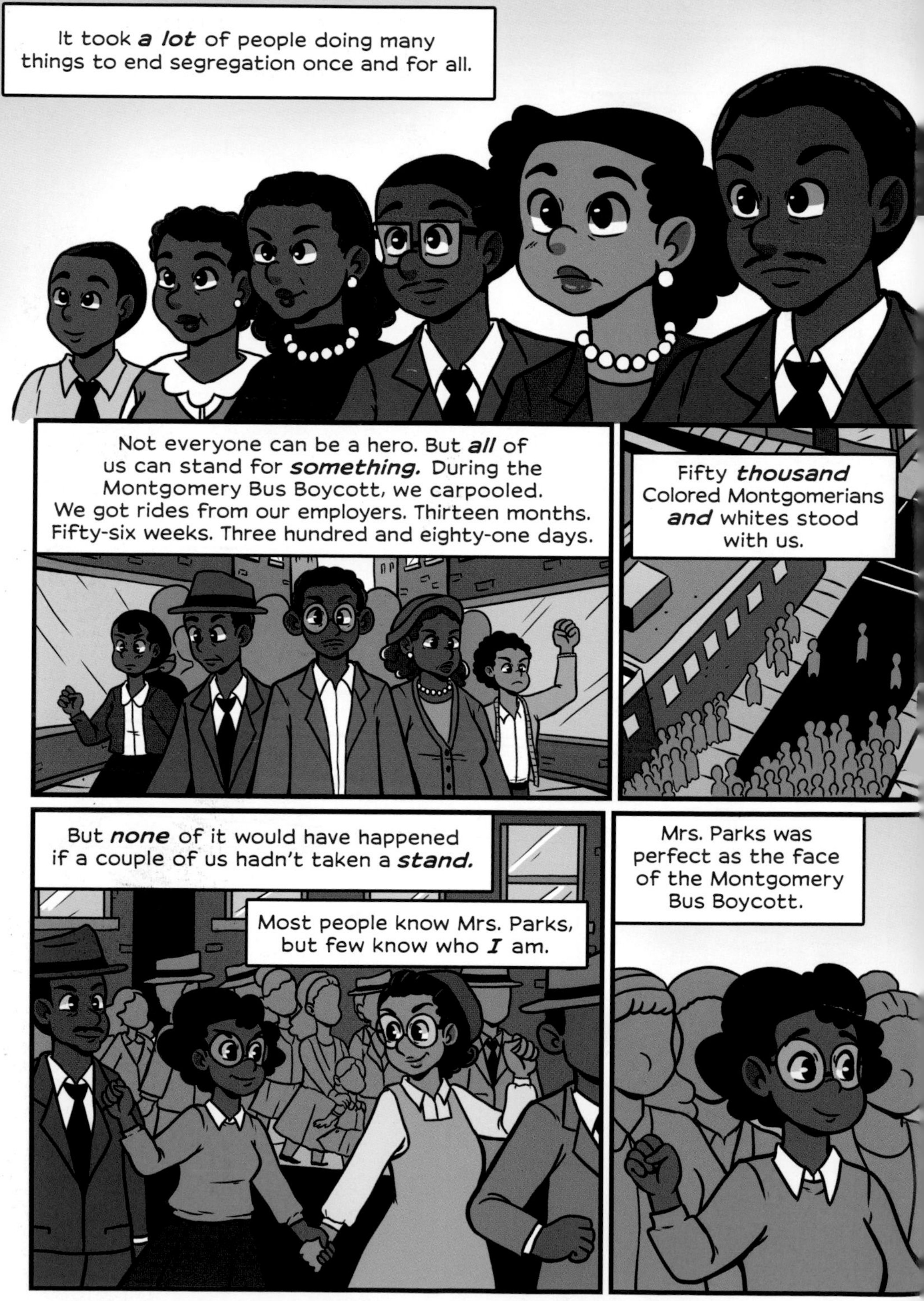
It took *a lot* of people doing many things to end segregation once and for all.
Not everyone can be a hero. But *all* of us can stand for *something.* During the Montgomery Bus Boycott, we carpooled. We got rides from our employers. Thirteen months. Fifty-six weeks. Three hundred and eighty-one days.
Fifty *thousand* Colored Montgomerians *and* whites stood with us.
But *none* of it would have happened if a couple of us hadn't taken a *stand.*
Most people know Mrs. Parks, but few know who *I* am.
Mrs. Parks was perfect as the face of the Montgomery Bus Boycott.

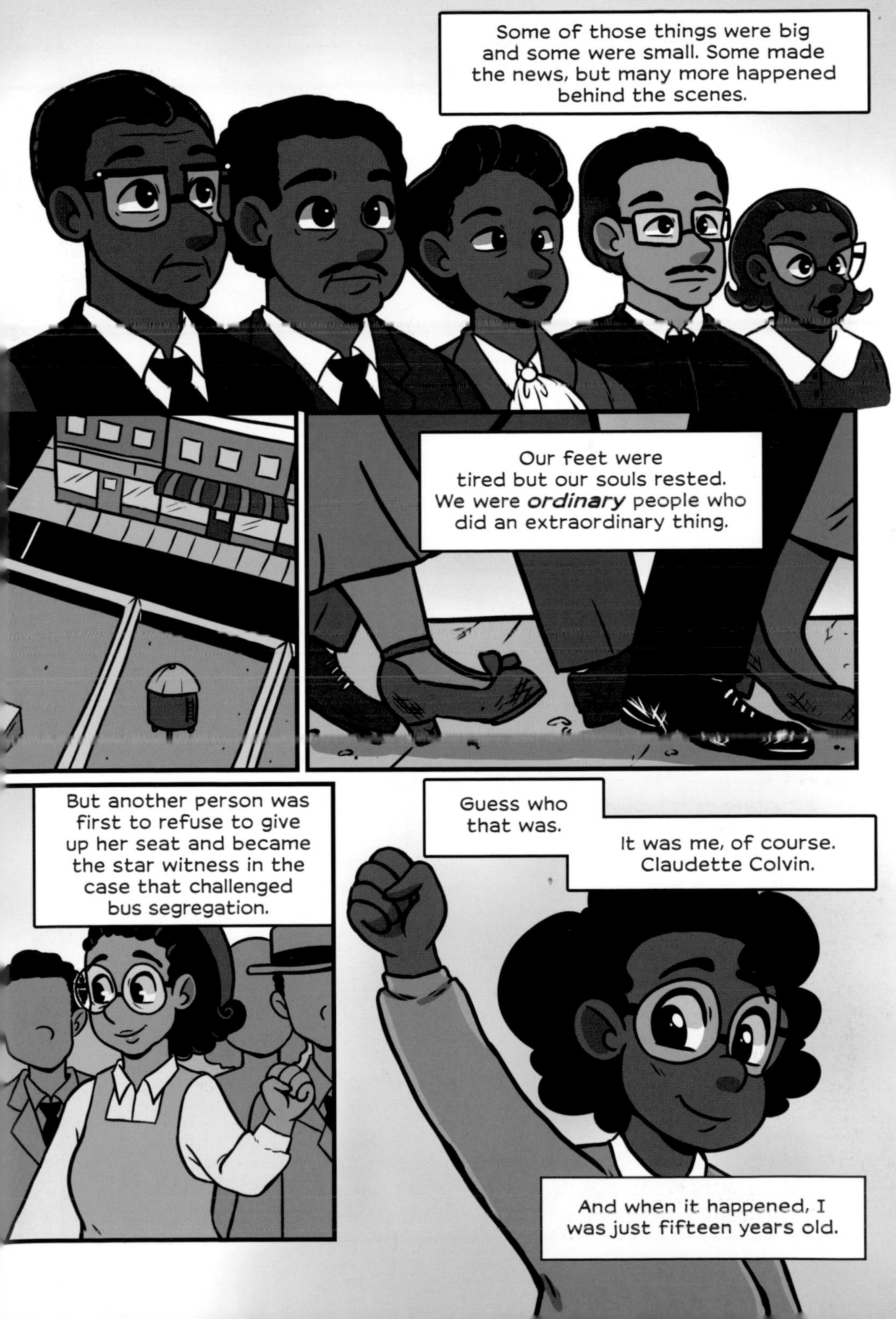

Some of those things were big and some were small. Some made the news, but many more happened behind the scenes.
Our feet were tired but our souls rested. We were *ordinary* people who did an extraordinary thing.
But another person was first to refuse to give up her seat and became the star witness in the case that challenged bus segregation.
Guess who that was.
It was me, of course. Claudette Colvin.
And when it happened, I was just fifteen years old.

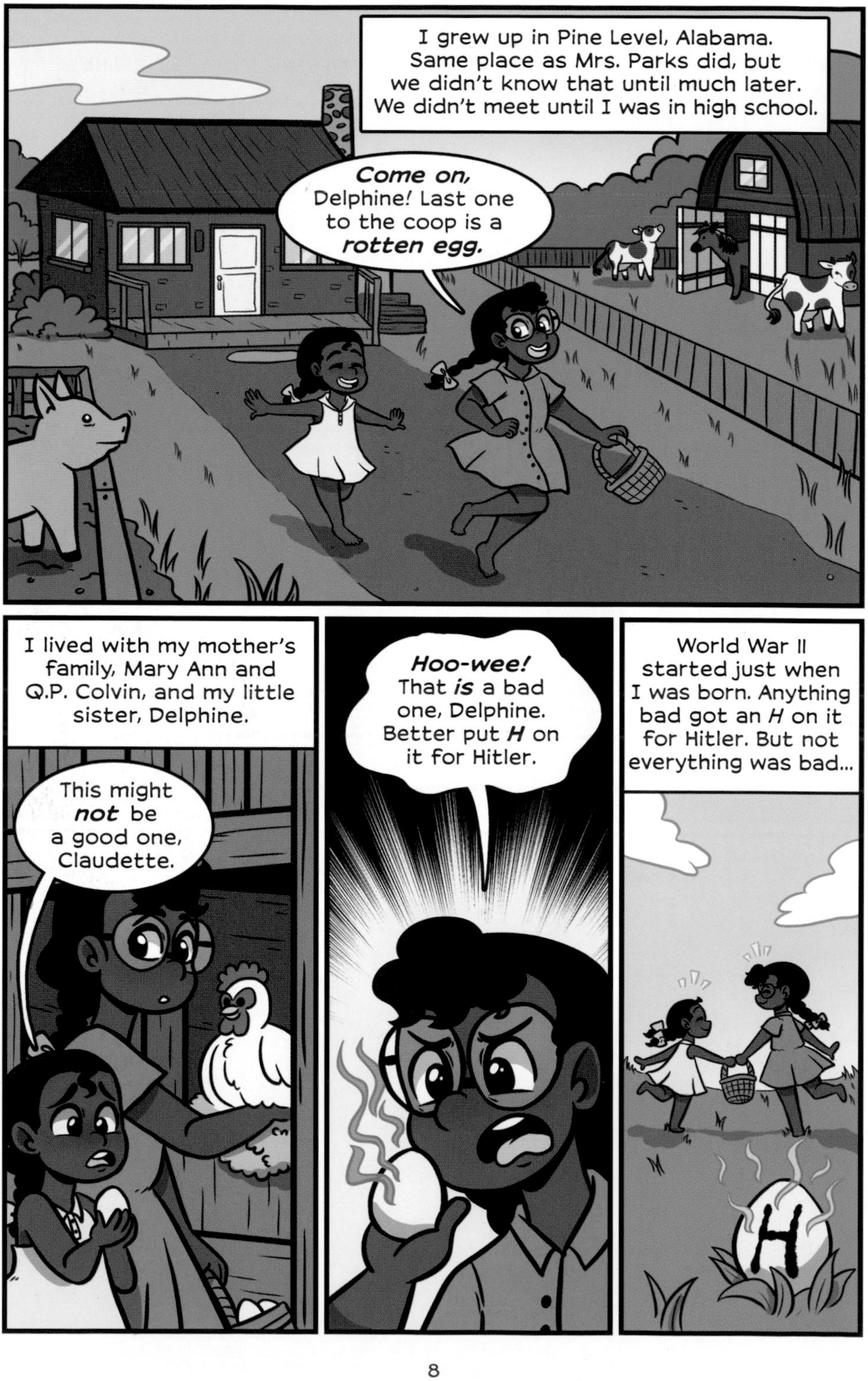
I grew up in Pine Level, Alabama. Same place as Mrs. Parks did, but we didn't know that until much later. We didn't meet until I was in high school.
Come on, Delphine! Last one to the coop is a *rotten egg.*
I lived with my mother's family, Mary Ann and Q.P. Colvin, and my little sister, Delphine.
This might *not* be a good one, Claudette.
Hoo-wee! That *is* a bad one, Delphine. Better put *H* on it for Hitler.
World War II started just when I was born. Anything bad got an *H* on it for Hitler. But not everything was bad...
H

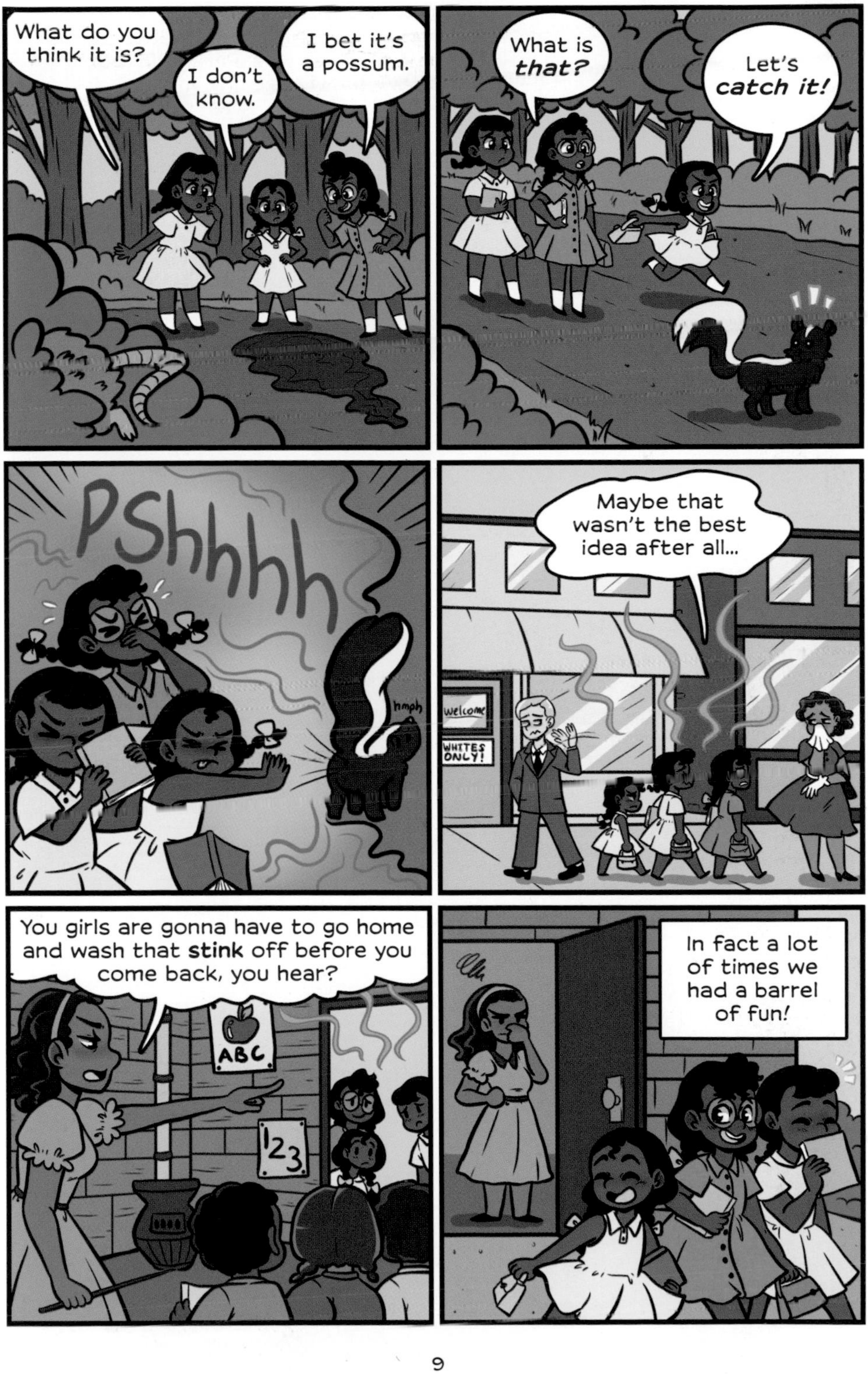
What do you think it is?
I don't know.
I bet it's a possum.
What is *that?*
Let's **catch it!**
PShhhh
hmph
Maybe that wasn't the best idea after all...
welcome
WHITES ONLY!
You girls are gonna have to go home and wash that **stink** off before you come back, you hear?
ABC
123
In fact a lot of times we had a barrel of fun!

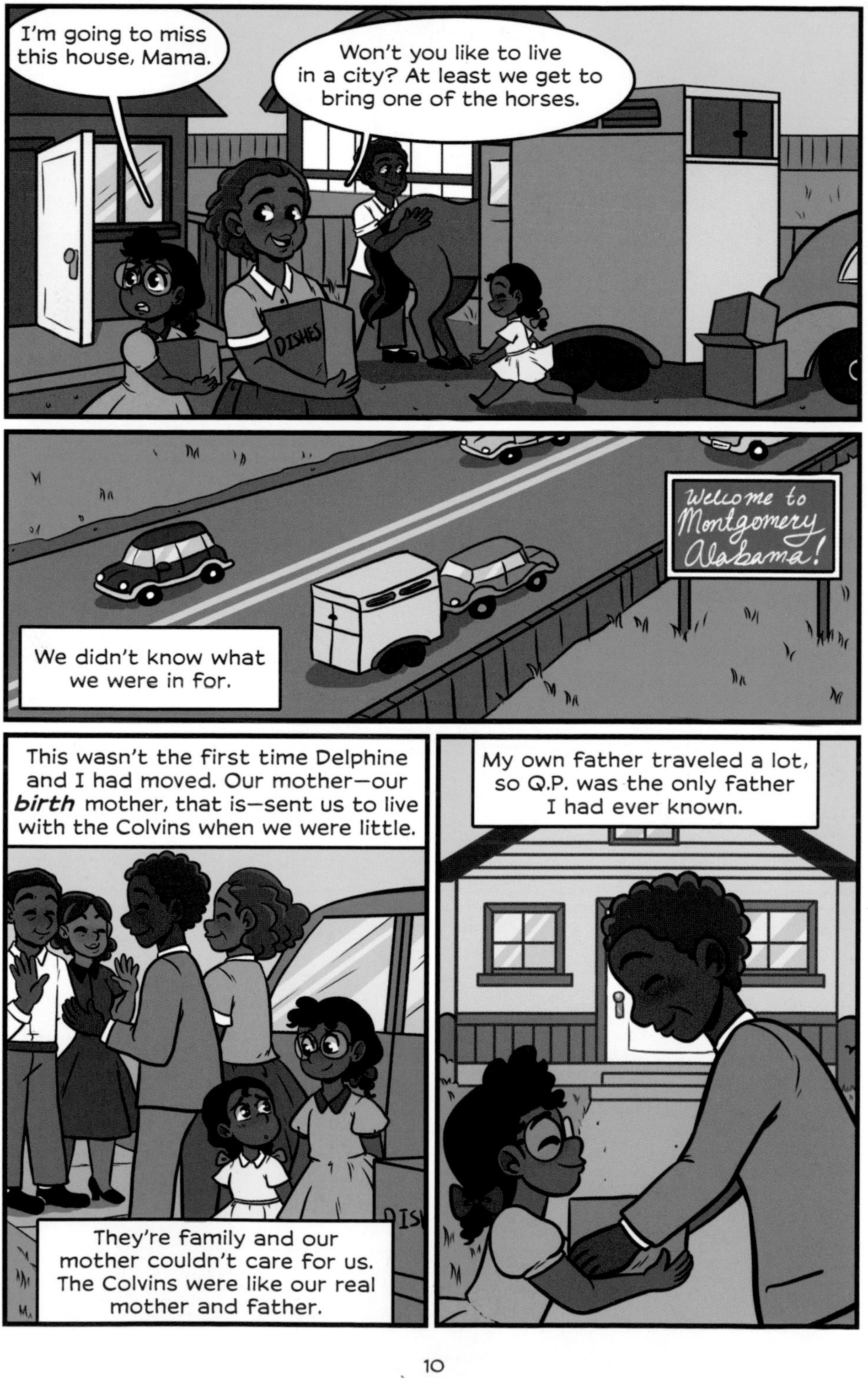
I'm going to miss this house, Mama.
Won't you like to live in a city? At least we get to bring one of the horses.
DISHES
Welcome to Montgomery Alabama!
We didn't know what we were in for.
This wasn't the first time Delphine and I had moved. Our mother—our ***birth*** mother, that is—sent us to live with the Colvins when we were little.
My own father traveled a lot, so Q.P. was the only father I had ever known.
They're family and our mother couldn't care for us. The Colvins were like our real mother and father.

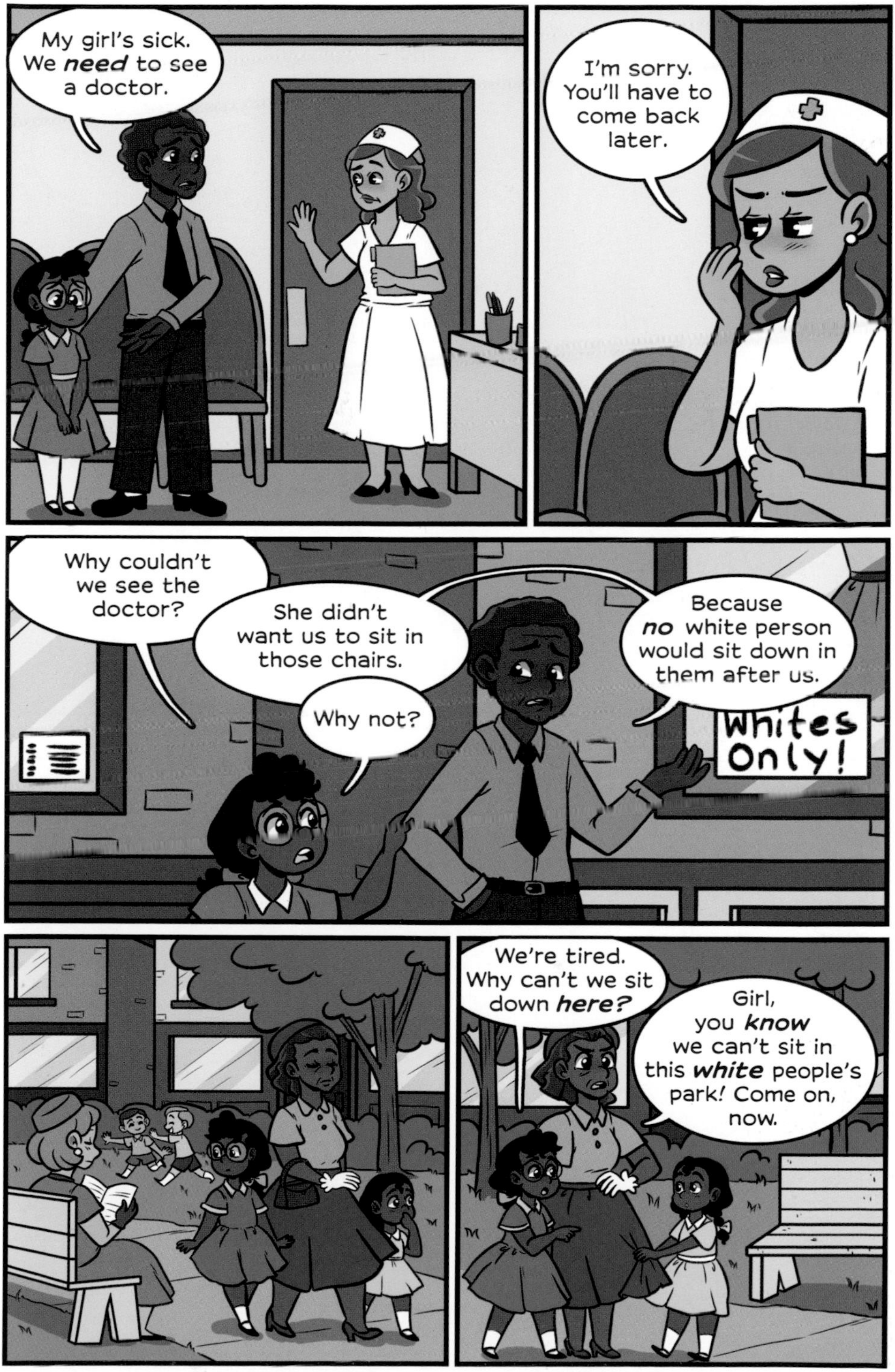
My girl's sick. We *need* to see a doctor.
I'm sorry. You'll have to come back later.
Why couldn't we see the doctor?
She didn't want us to sit in those chairs.
Why not?
Because *no* white person would sit down in them after us.
Whites Only!
We're tired. Why can't we sit down *here?*
Girl, you *know* we can't sit in this *white* people's park! Come on, now.

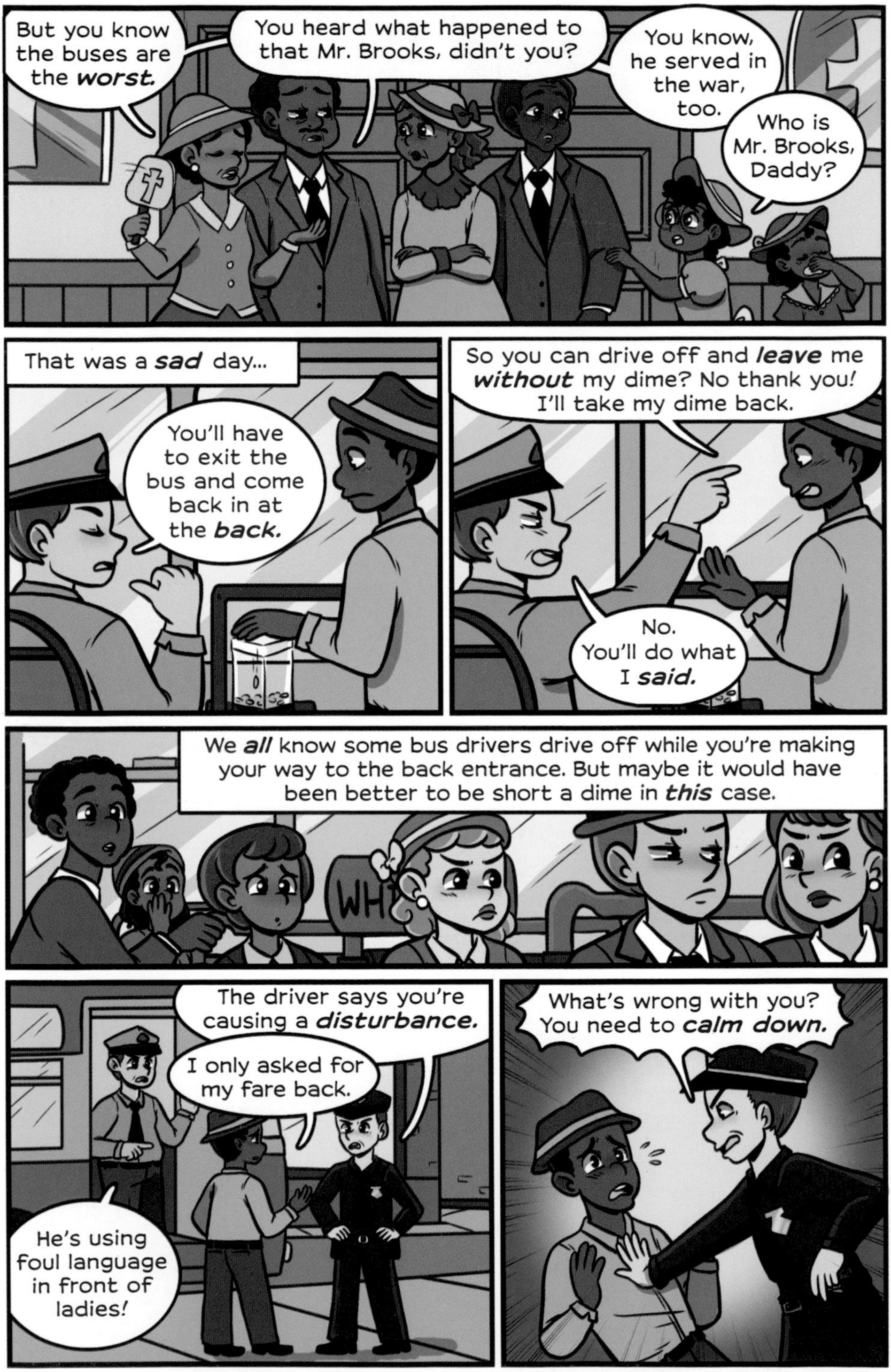

But you know the buses are the *worst.*
You heard what happened to that Mr. Brooks, didn't you?
You know, he served in the war, too.
Who is Mr. Brooks, Daddy?
That was a *sad* day...
You'll have to exit the bus and come back in at the *back.*
So you can drive off and *leave* me *without* my dime? No thank you! I'll take my dime back.
No. You'll do what I *said.*
We *all* know some bus drivers drive off while you're making your way to the back entrance. But maybe it would have been better to be short a dime in *this* case.
The driver says you're causing a *disturbance.*
I only asked for my fare back.
He's using foul language in front of ladies!
What's wrong with you? You need to *calm down.*

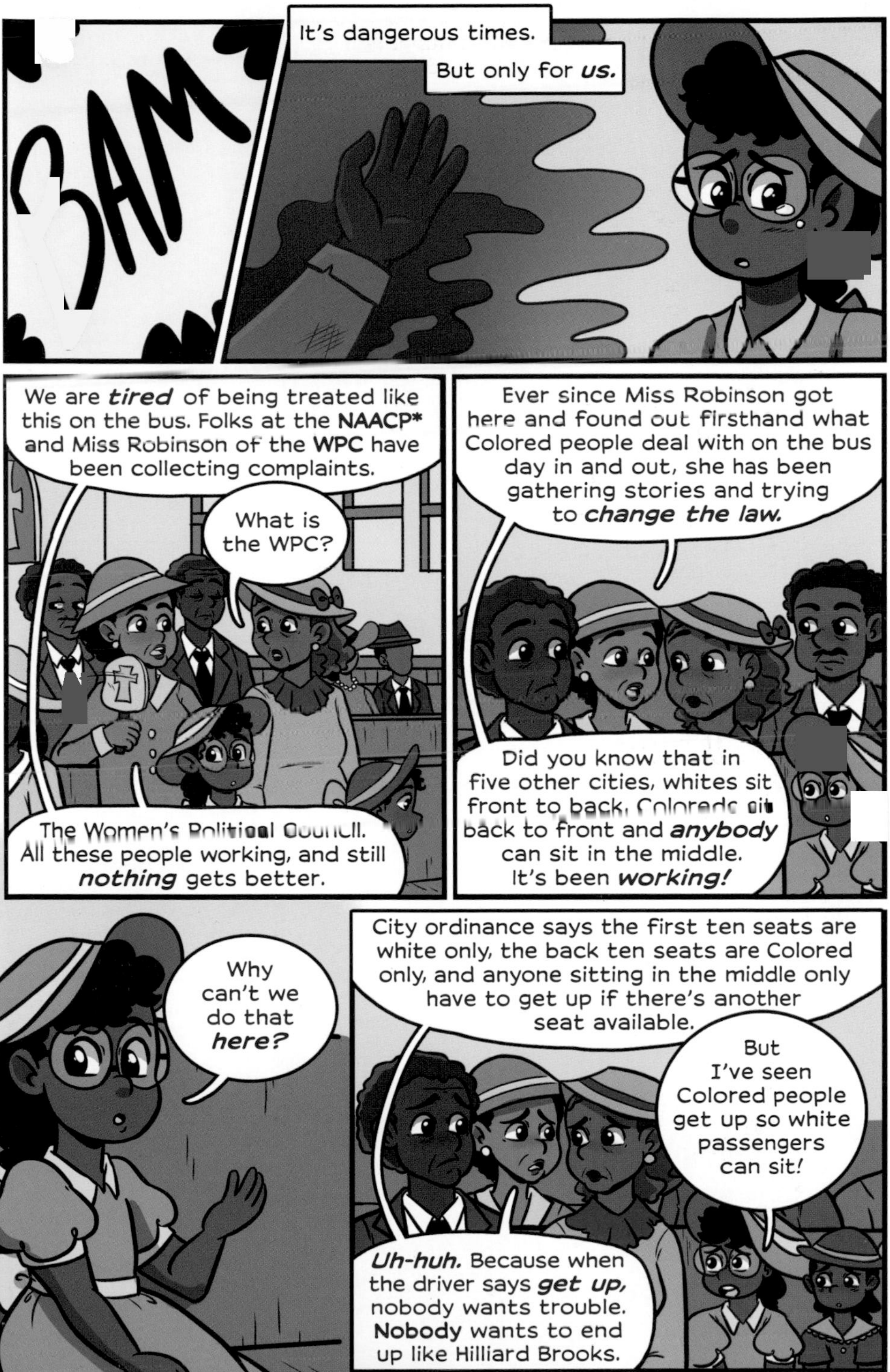
BAM
It's dangerous times.
But only for *us.*
We are *tired* of being treated like this on the bus. Folks at the **NAACP*** and Miss Robinson of the **WPC** have been collecting complaints.
What is the WPC?
The Women's Political Council. All these people working, and still *nothing* gets better.
Ever since Miss Robinson got here and found out firsthand what Colored people deal with on the bus day in and out, she has been gathering stories and trying to *change the law.*
Did you know that in five other cities, whites sit front to back, Coloreds sit back to front and *anybody* can sit in the middle. It's been *working!*
Why can't we do that *here?*
City ordinance says the first ten seats are white only, the back ten seats are Colored only, and anyone sitting in the middle only have to get up if there's another seat available.
But I've seen Colored people get up so white passengers can sit!
Uh-huh. Because when the driver says *get up,* nobody wants trouble. **Nobody** wants to end up like Hilliard Brooks.

*National Association for the Advancement of Colored People

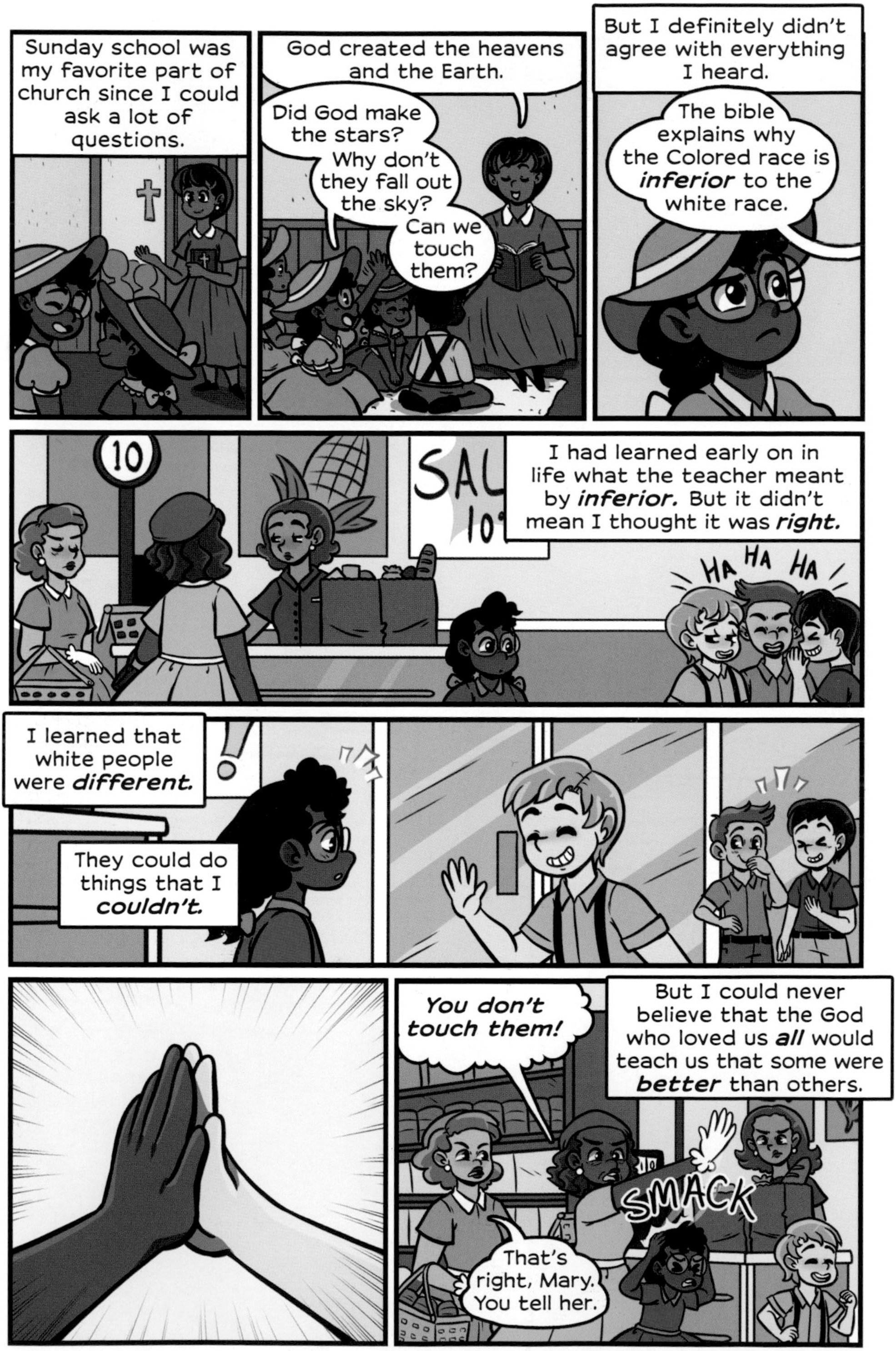

Sunday school was my favorite part of church since I could ask a lot of questions.
God created the heavens and the Earth.
Did God make the stars?
Why don't they fall out the sky?
Can we touch them?
But I definitely didn't agree with everything I heard.
The bible explains why the Colored race is *inferior* to the white race.
10
SAL
10
I had learned early on in life what the teacher meant by *inferior.* But it didn't mean I thought it was *right.*
HA HA HA
I learned that white people were *different.*
They could do things that I *couldn't.*
You don't touch them!
But I could never believe that the God who loved us *all* would teach us that some were *better* than others.
SMACK
That's right, Mary. You tell her.

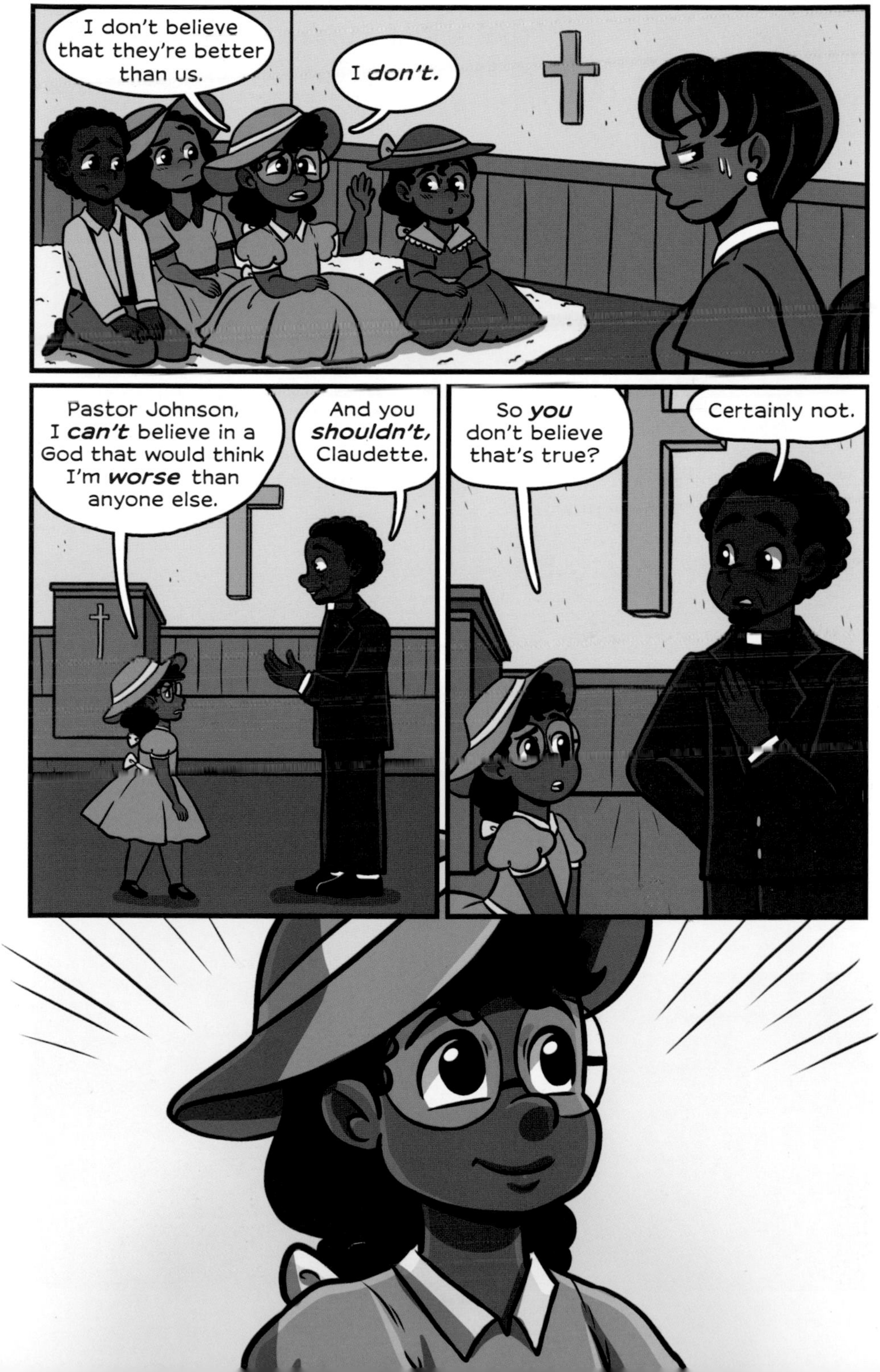
I don't believe that they're better than us.
I *don't.*
Pastor Johnson, I *can't* believe in a God that would think I'm *worse* than anyone else.
And you *shouldn't,* Claudette.
So *you* don't believe that's true?
Certainly not.

But there was *one* incident that made me question God more than anything.

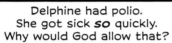

Delphine had polio. She got sick *so* quickly. Why would God allow that?

The *last* time I saw Delphine, she was headed to the hospital.

Delphine passed away on my thirteenth birthday.

I was never quite the same.

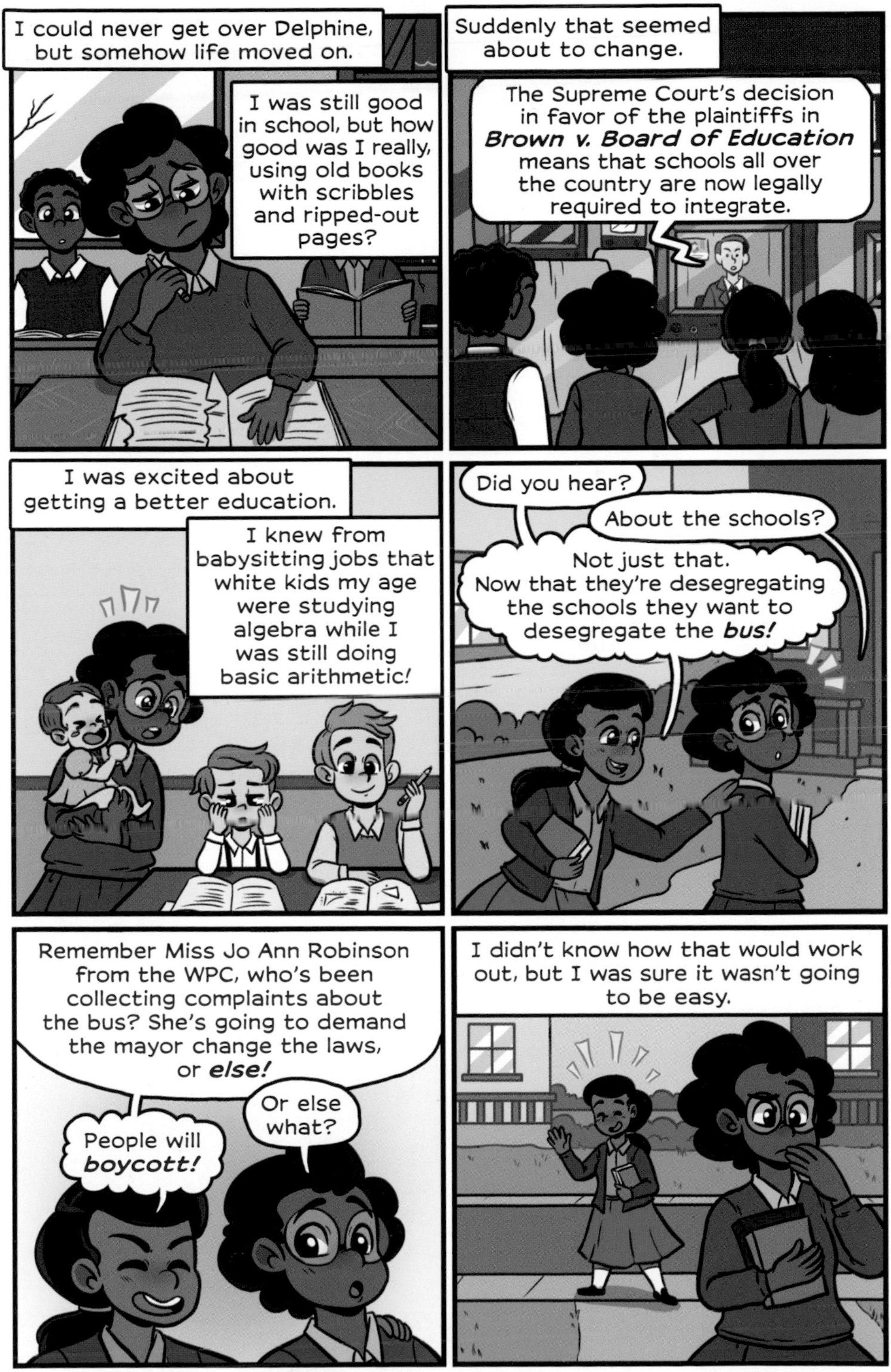

I could never get over Delphine, but somehow life moved on.
I was still good in school, but how good was I really, using old books with scribbles and ripped-out pages?
Suddenly that seemed about to change.
The Supreme Court's decision in favor of the plaintiffs in ***Brown v. Board of Education*** means that schools all over the country are now legally required to integrate.
I was excited about getting a better education.
I knew from babysitting jobs that white kids my age were studying algebra while I was still doing basic arithmetic!
Did you hear?
About the schools?
Not just that. Now that they're desegregating the schools they want to desegregate the ***bus!***
Remember Miss Jo Ann Robinson from the WPC, who's been collecting complaints about the bus? She's going to demand the mayor change the laws, or ***else!***
People will ***boycott!***
Or else what?
I didn't know how that would work out, but I was sure it wasn't going to be easy.

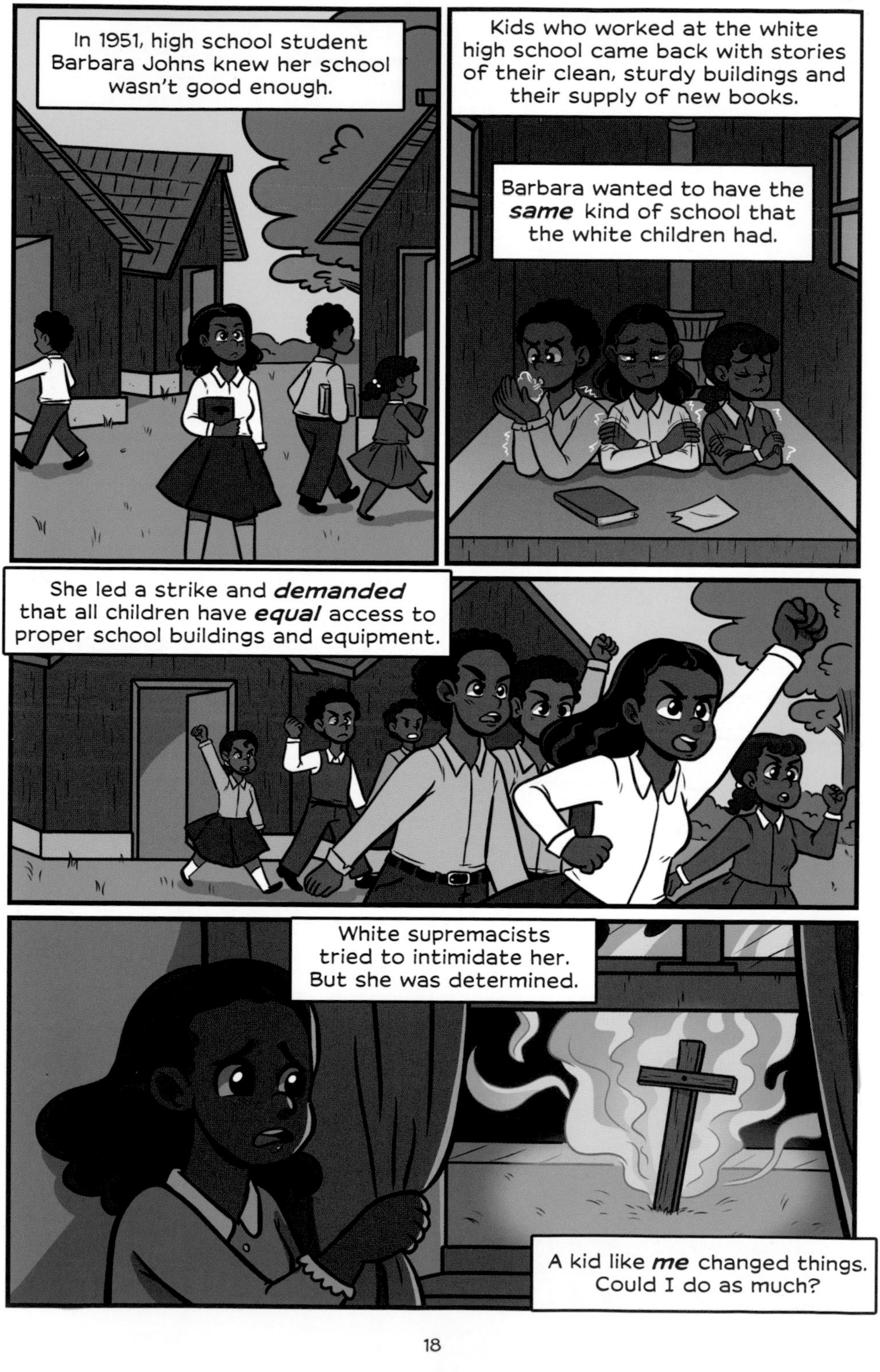
In 1951, high school student Barbara Johns knew her school wasn't good enough.
Kids who worked at the white high school came back with stories of their clean, sturdy buildings and their supply of new books.
Barbara wanted to have the ***same*** kind of school that the white children had.
She led a strike and ***demanded*** that all children have ***equal*** access to proper school buildings and equipment.
White supremacists tried to intimidate her. But she was determined.
A kid like ***me*** changed things. Could I do as much?

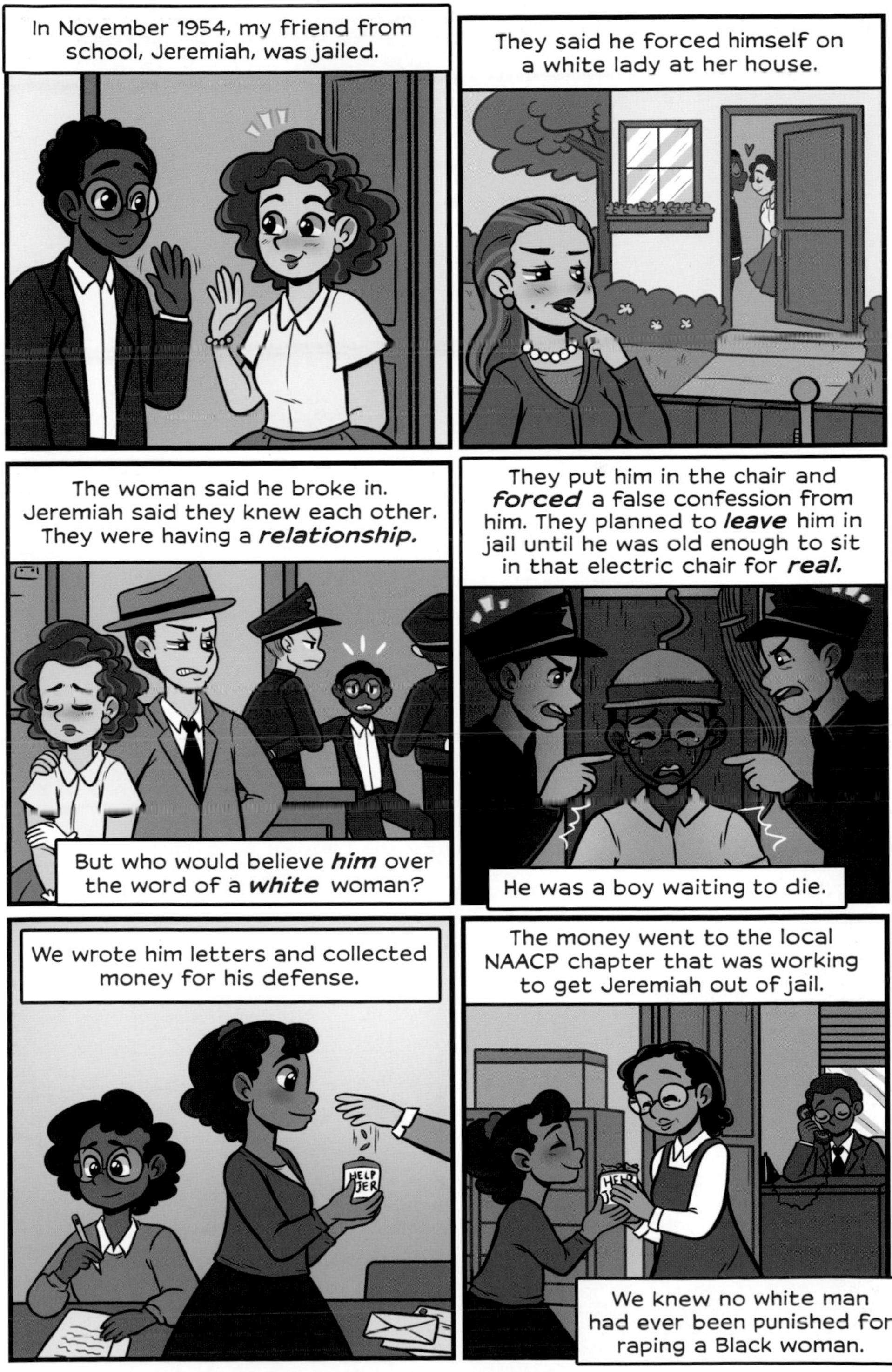

In November 1954, my friend from school, Jeremiah, was jailed.
They said he forced himself on a white lady at her house.
The woman said he broke in. Jeremiah said they knew each other. They were having a ***relationship.***
But who would believe ***him*** over the word of a ***white*** woman?
They put him in the chair and ***forced*** a false confession from him. They planned to ***leave*** him in jail until he was old enough to sit in that electric chair for ***real.***
He was a boy waiting to die.
We wrote him letters and collected money for his defense.
HELP JER
The money went to the local NAACP chapter that was working to get Jeremiah out of jail.
We knew no white man had ever been punished for raping a Black woman.

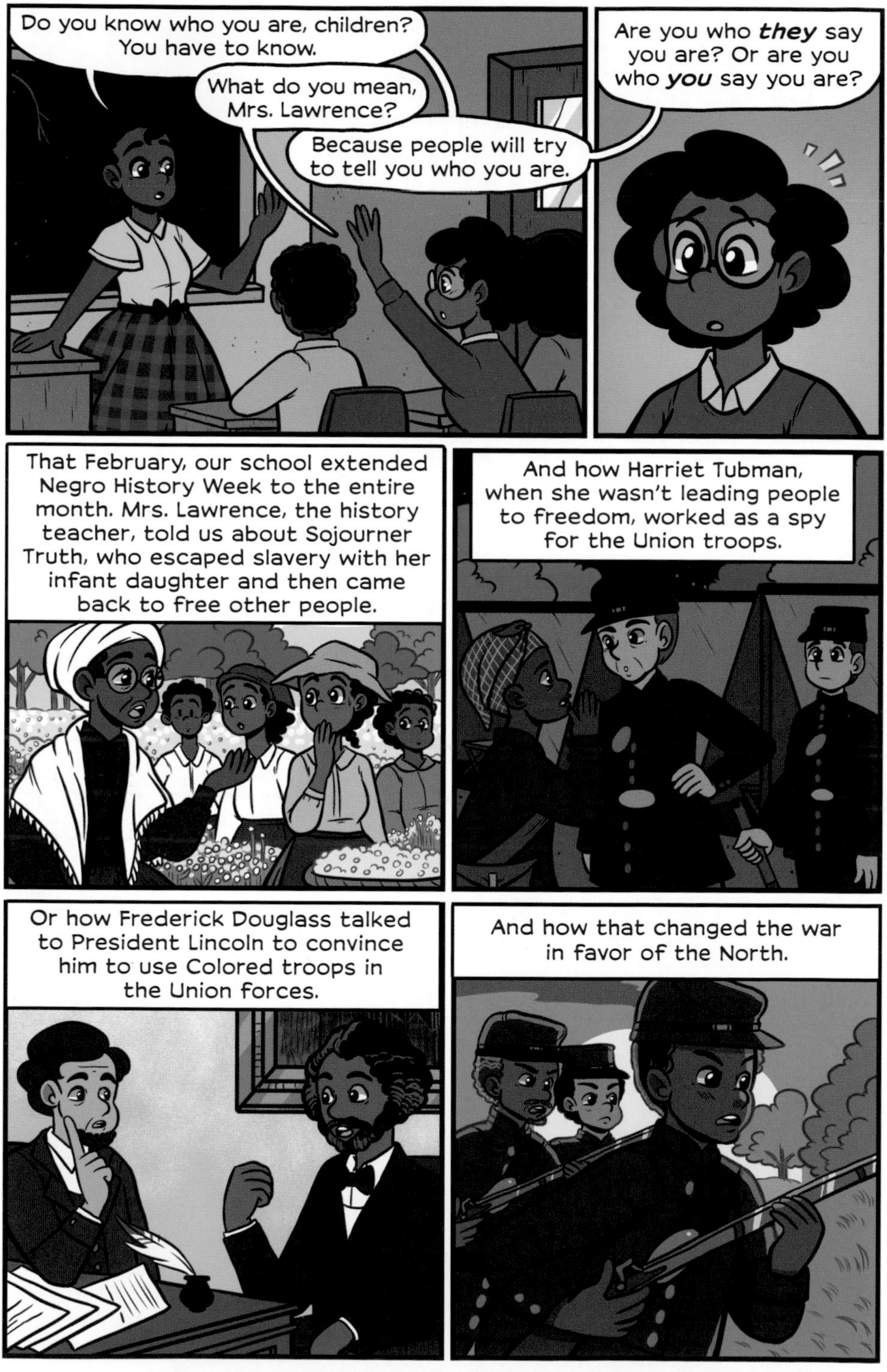
Do you know who you are, children? You have to know.
What do you mean, Mrs. Lawrence?
Because people will try to tell you who you are.
Are you who *they* say you are? Or are you who *you* say you are?
That February, our school extended Negro History Week to the entire month. Mrs. Lawrence, the history teacher, told us about Sojourner Truth, who escaped slavery with her infant daughter and then came back to free other people.
And how Harriet Tubman, when she wasn't leading people to freedom, worked as a spy for the Union troops.
Or how Frederick Douglass talked to President Lincoln to convince him to use Colored troops in the Union forces.
And how that changed the war in favor of the North.

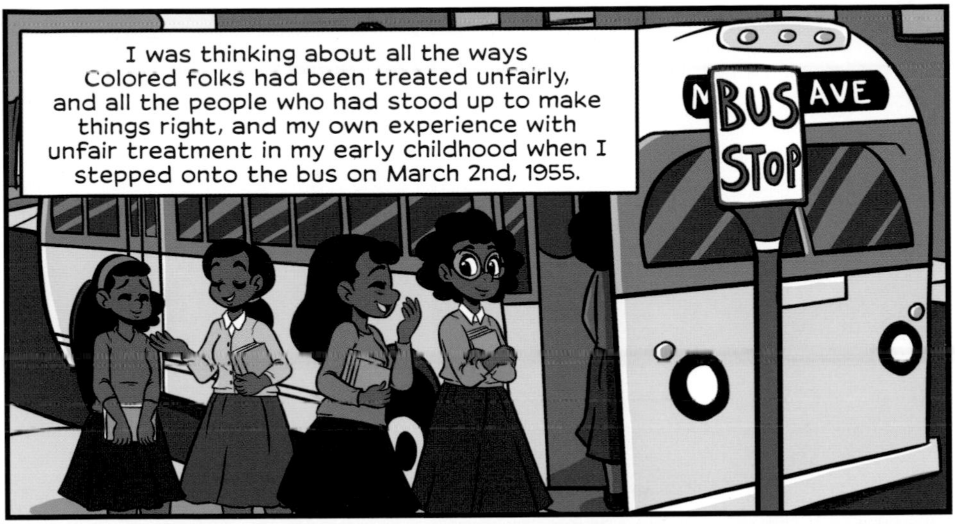
I was thinking about all the ways Colored folks had been treated unfairly, and all the people who had stood up to make things right, and my own experience with unfair treatment in my early childhood when I stepped onto the bus on March 2nd, 1955.
AVE
BUS STOP

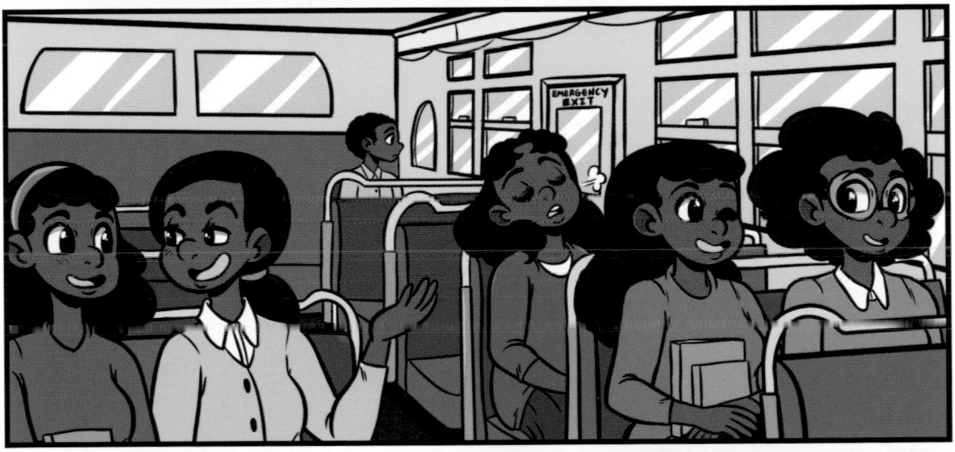
EMERGENCY EXIT

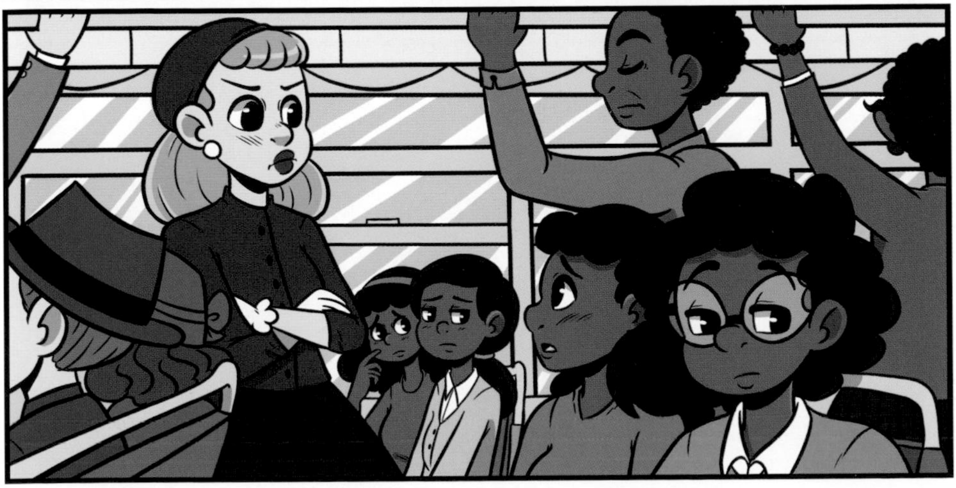

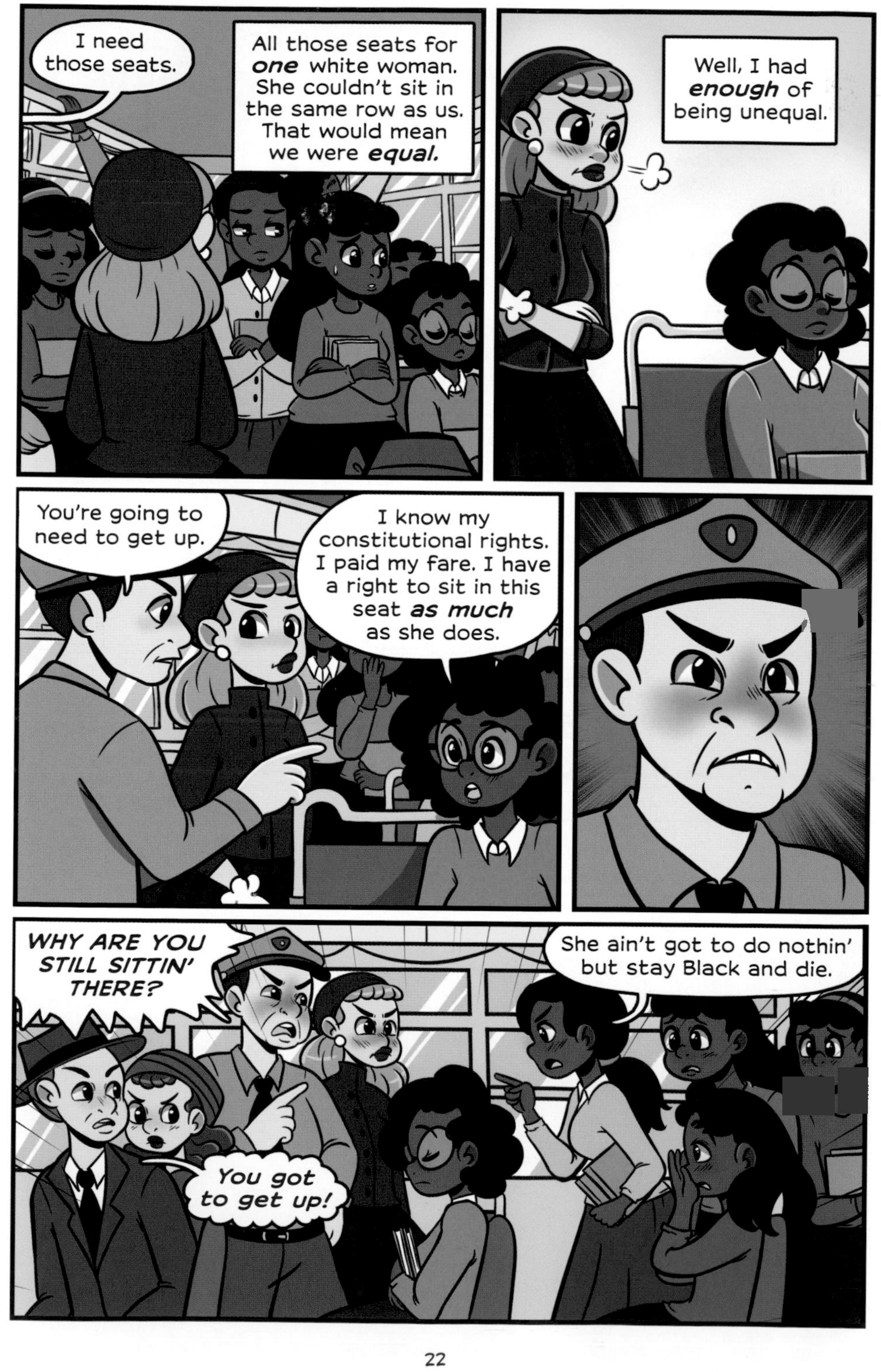
I need those seats.
All those seats for *one* white woman. She couldn't sit in the same row as us. That would mean we were *equal.*
Well, I had *enough* of being unequal.
You're going to need to get up.
I know my constitutional rights. I paid my fare. I have a right to sit in this seat *as much* as she does.
WHY ARE YOU STILL SITTIN' THERE?
You got to get up!
She ain't got to do nothin' but stay Black and die.

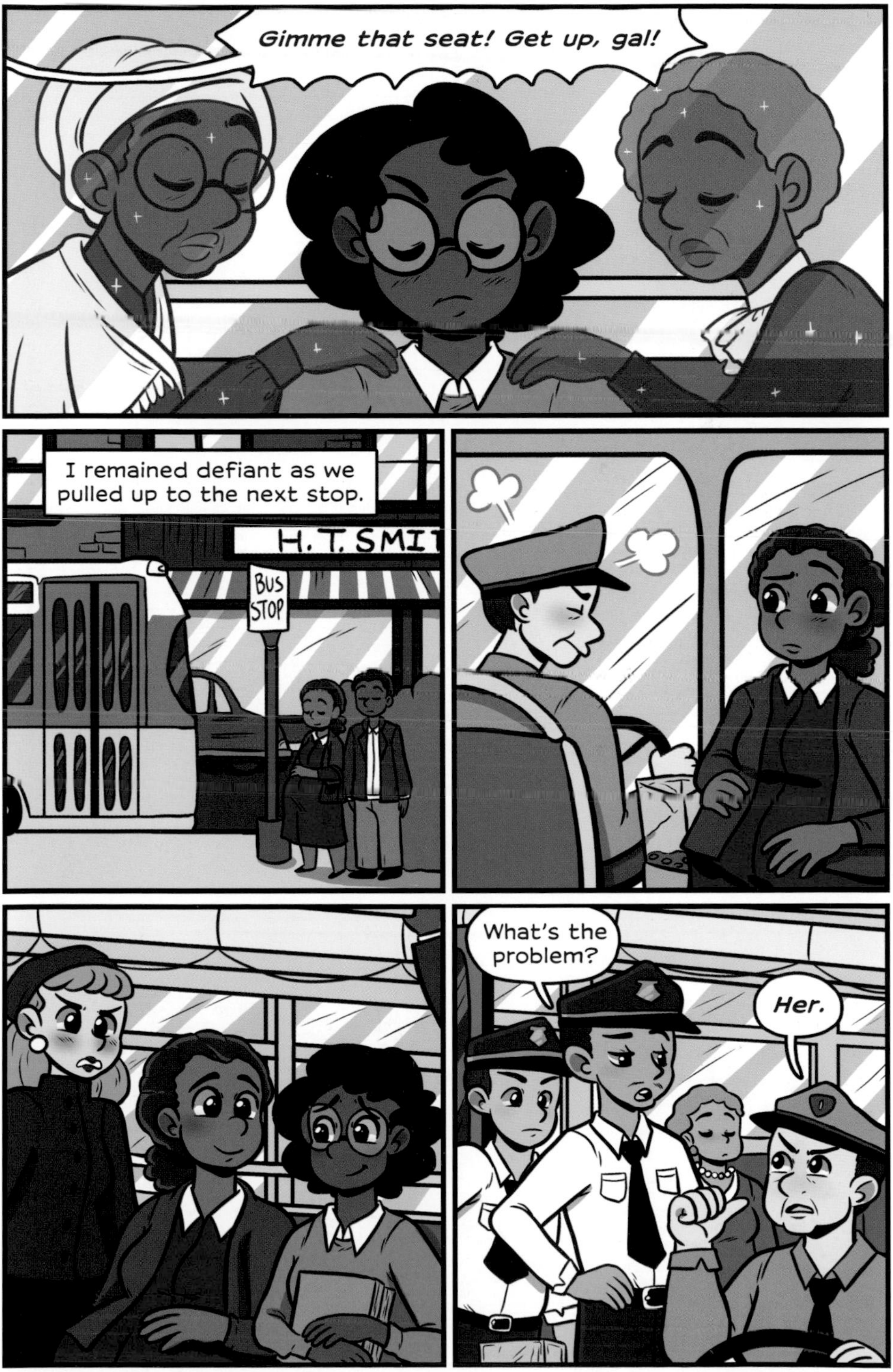

Gimme that seat! Get up, gal!
I remained defiant as we pulled up to the next stop.
H.T. SMI
BUS STOP
What's the problem?
Her.

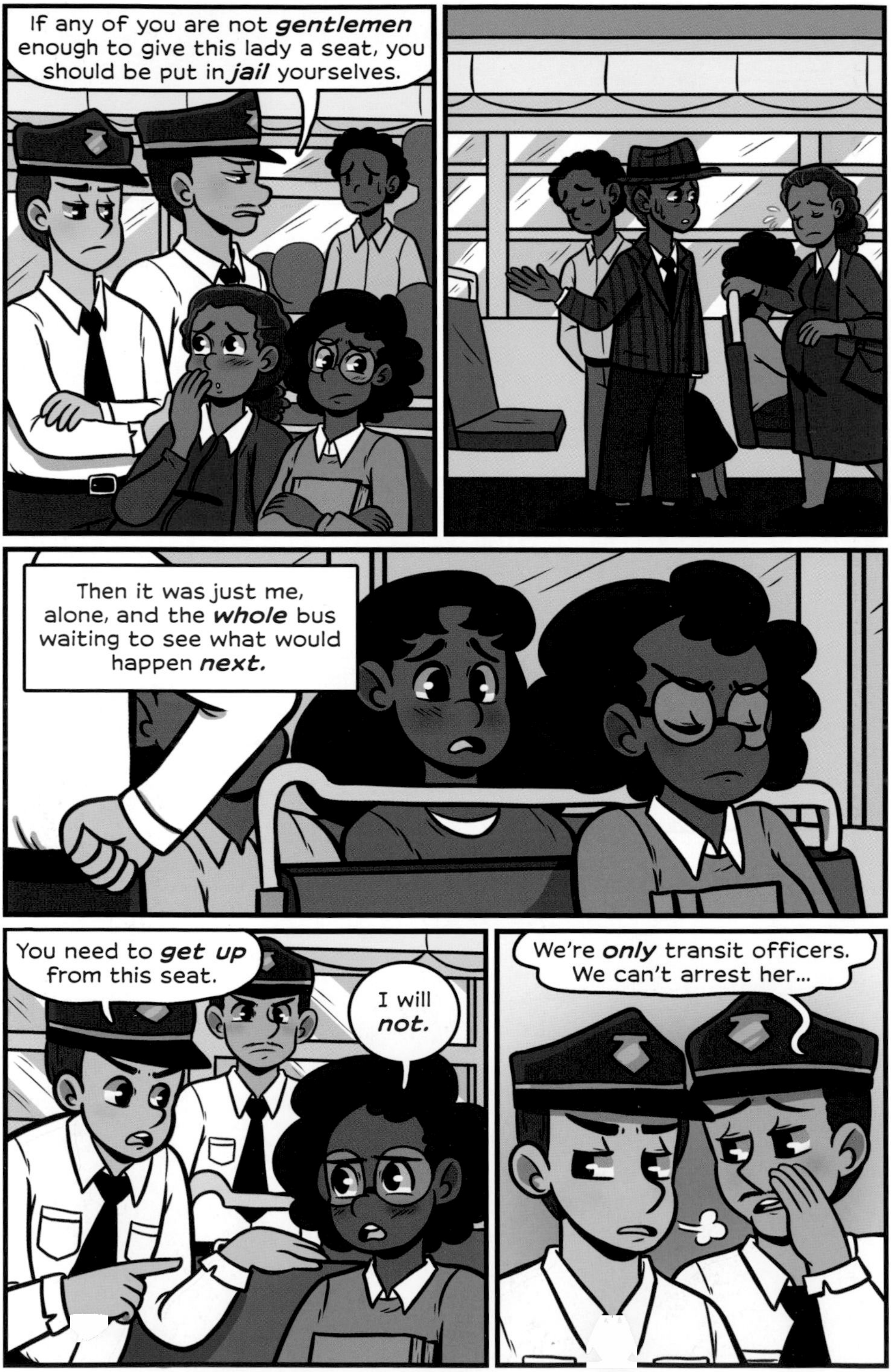
If any of you are not *gentlemen* enough to give this lady a seat, you should be put in *jail* yourselves.
Then it was just me, alone, and the *whole* bus waiting to see what would happen *next.*
You need to *get up* from this seat.
I will *not.*
We're *only* transit officers. We can't arrest her...

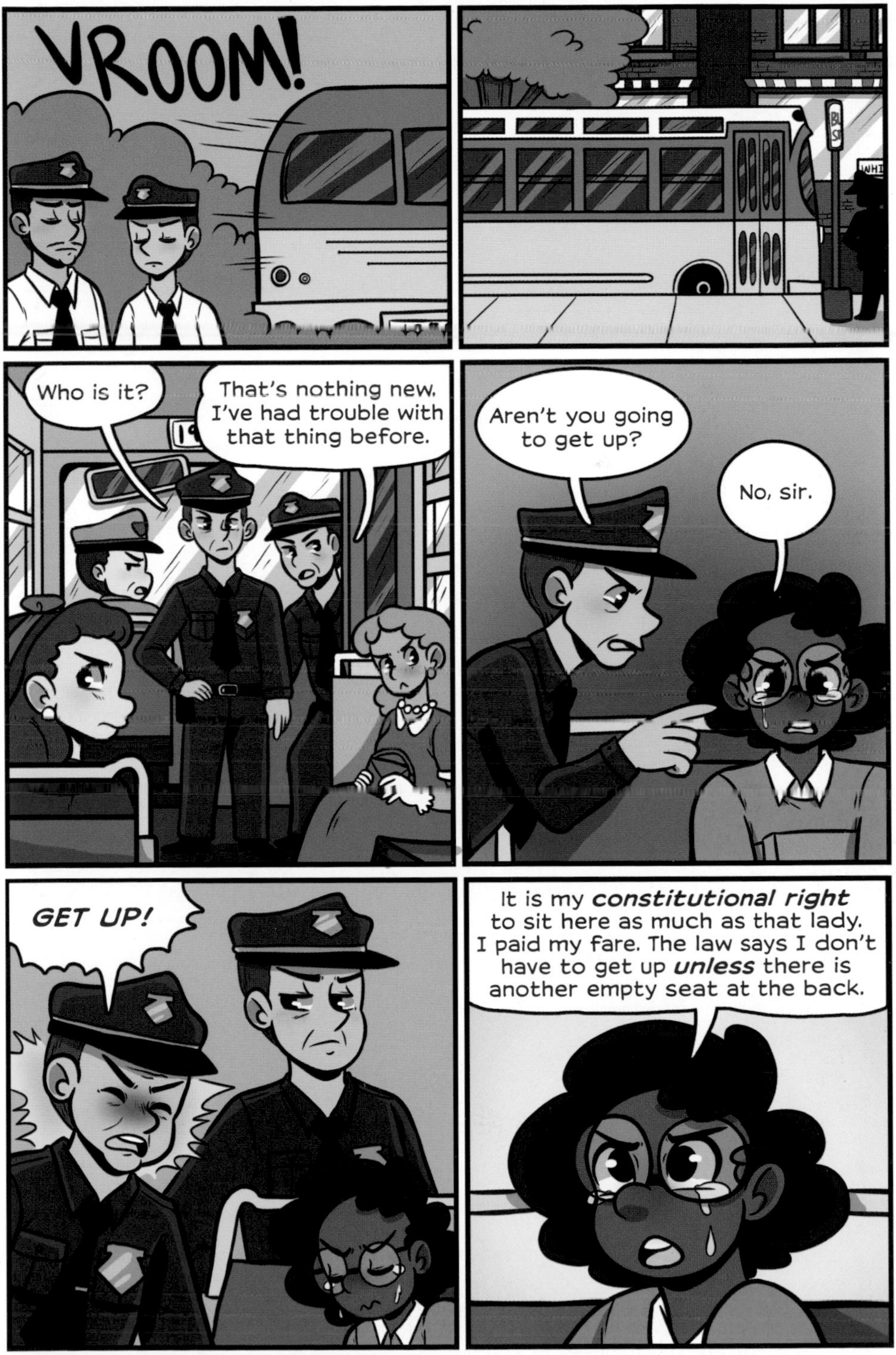
VROOM!
Who is it?
That's nothing new. I've had trouble with that thing before.
Aren't you going to get up?
No, sir.
GET UP!
It is my ***constitutional right*** to sit here as much as that lady. I paid my fare. The law says I don't have to get up ***unless*** there is another empty seat at the back.

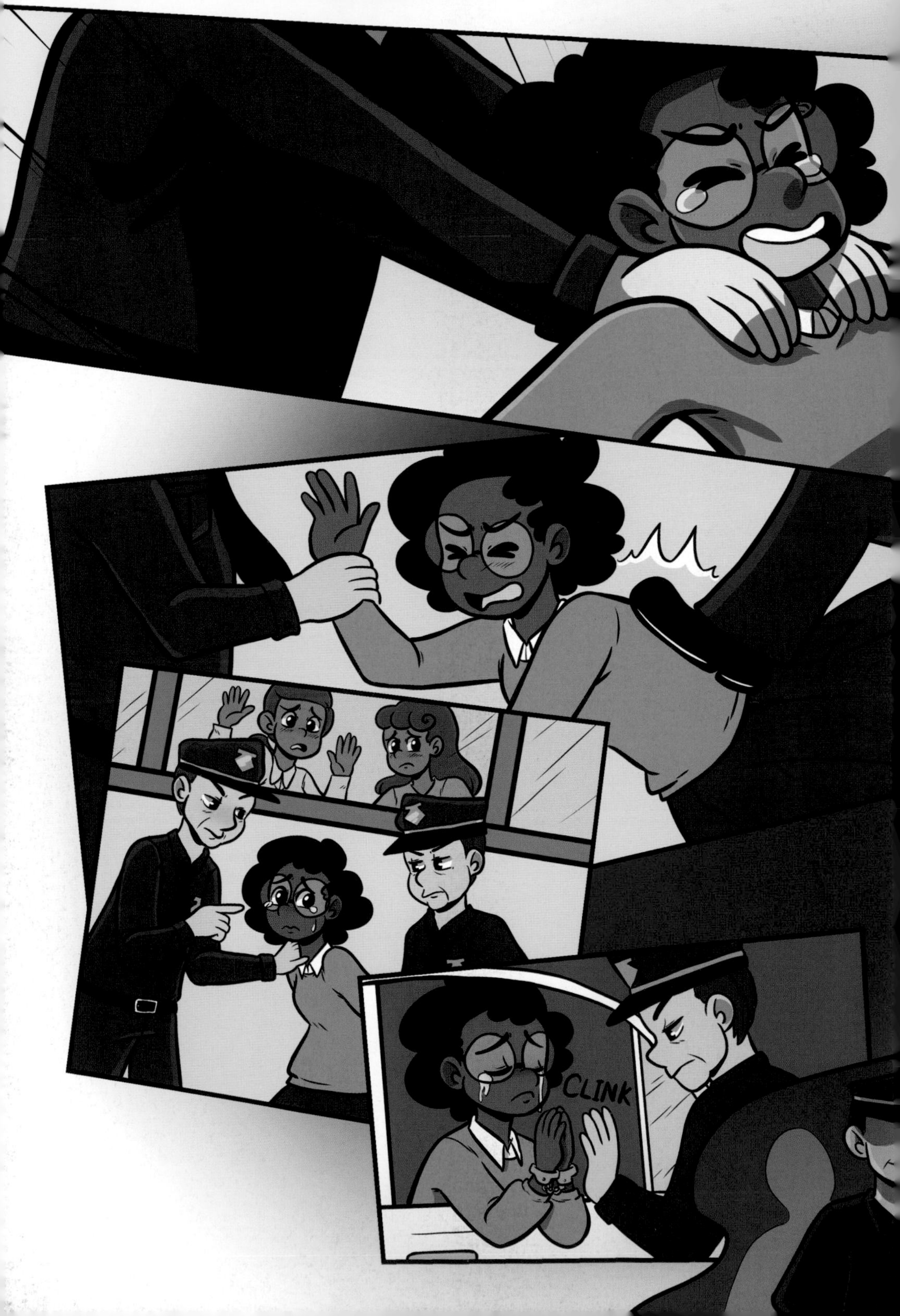
CLINK

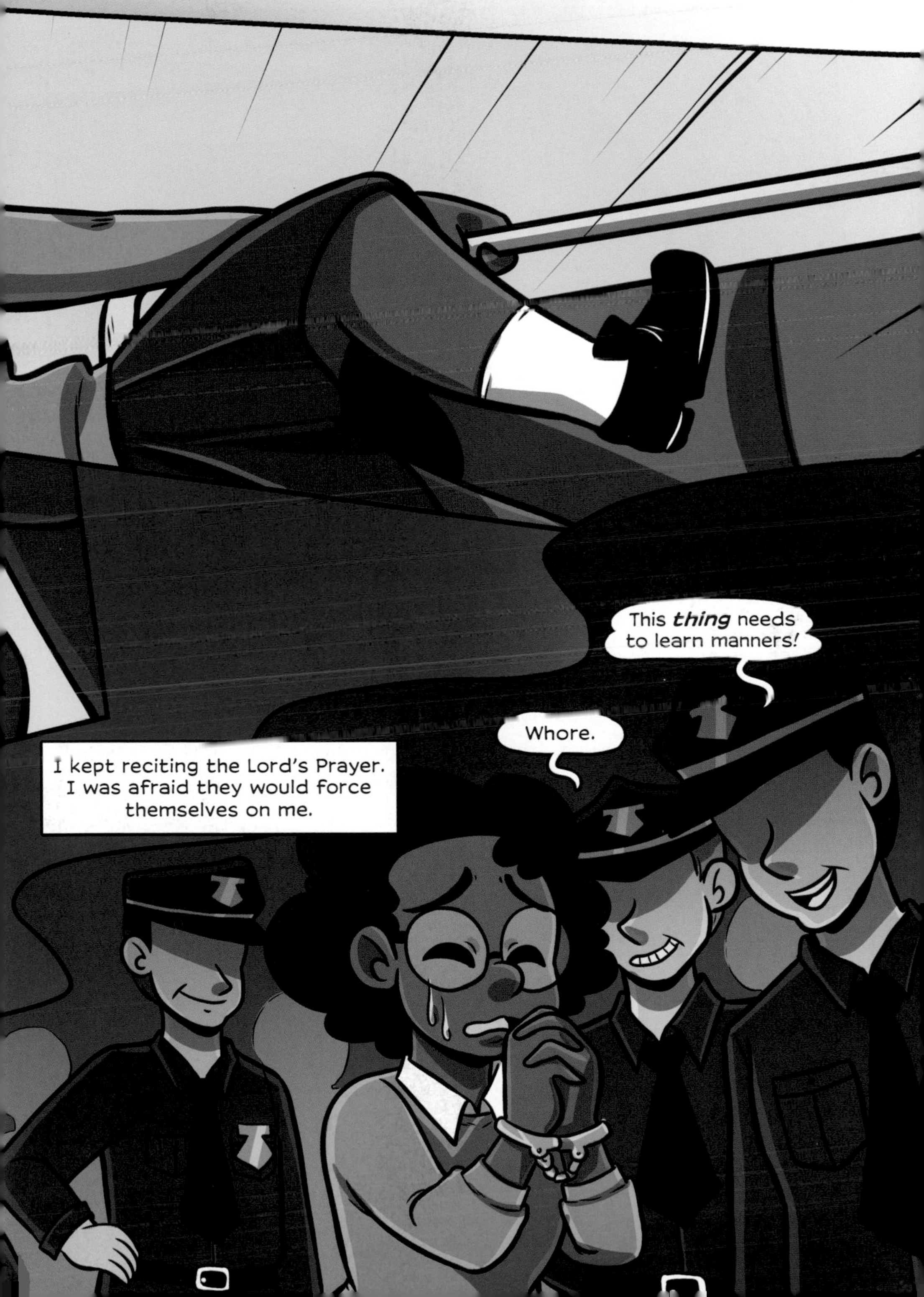
This *thing* needs to learn manners!
Whore.
I kept reciting the Lord's Prayer. I was afraid they would force themselves on me.

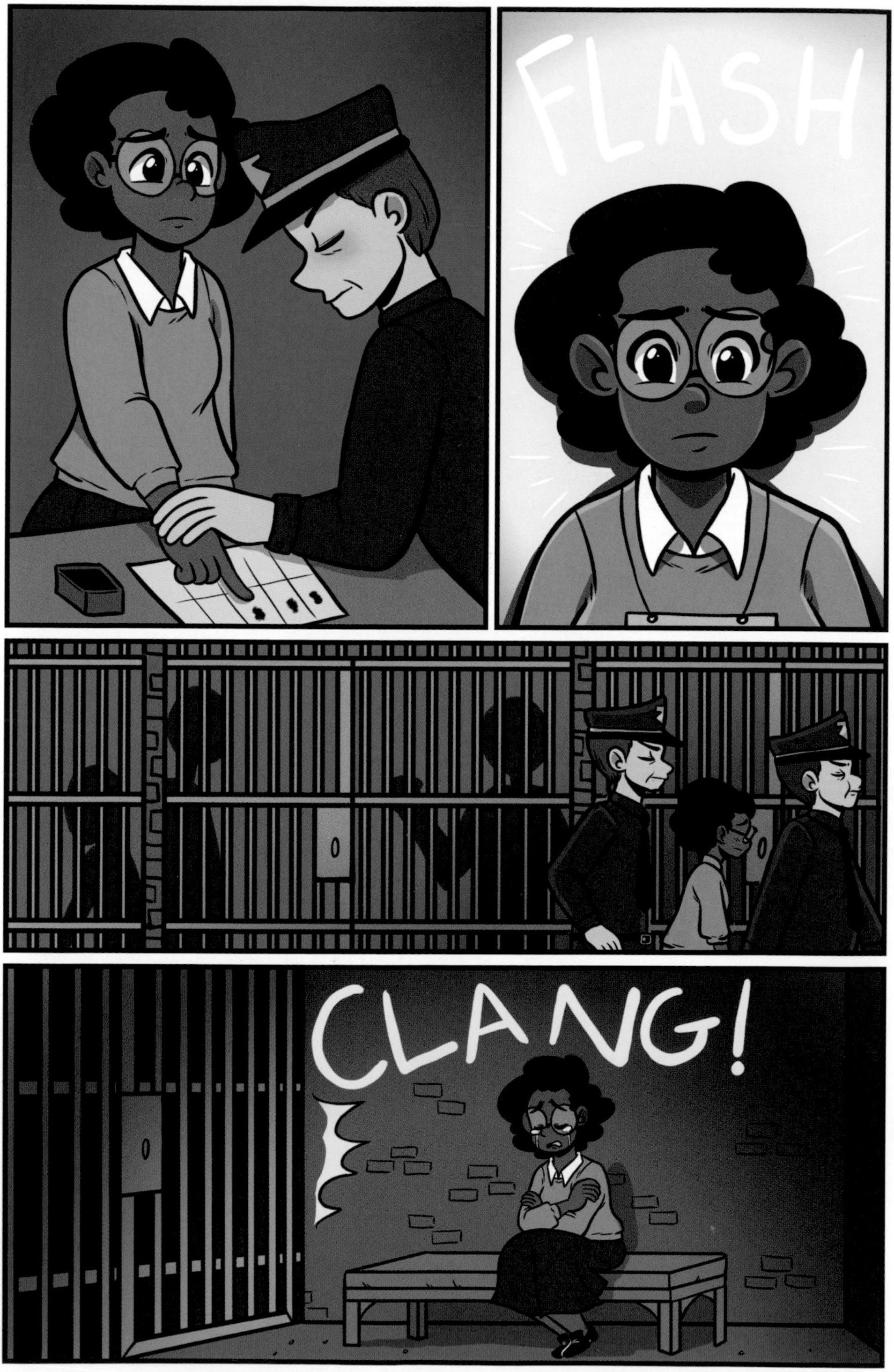
FLASH
CLANG!

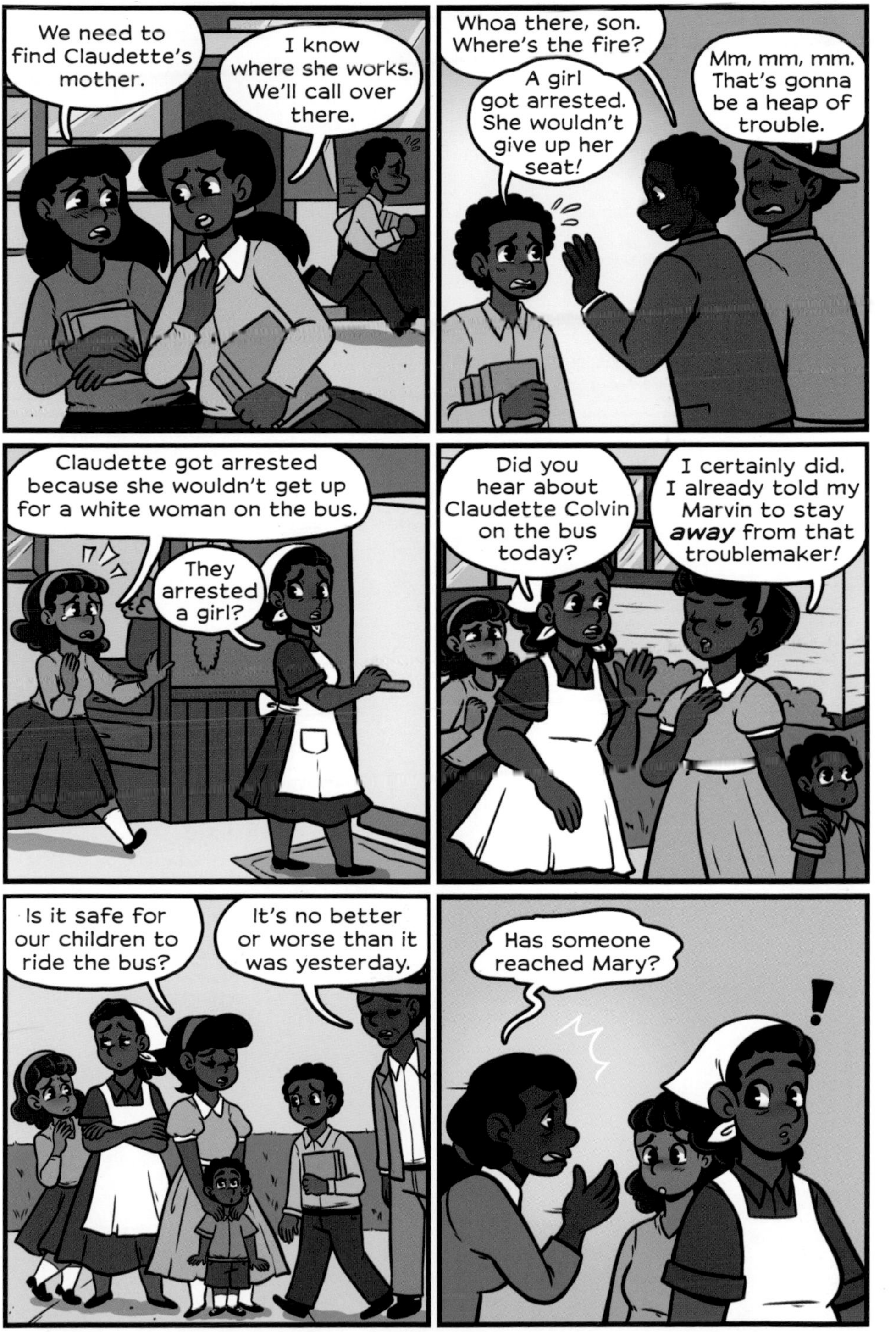
We need to find Claudette's mother.
I know where she works. We'll call over there.
Whoa there, son. Where's the fire?
A girl got arrested. She wouldn't give up her seat!
Mm, mm, mm. That's gonna be a heap of trouble.
Claudette got arrested because she wouldn't get up for a white woman on the bus.
They arrested a girl?
Did you hear about Claudette Colvin on the bus today?
I certainly did. I already told my Marvin to stay ***away*** from that troublemaker!
Is it safe for our children to ride the bus?
It's no better or worse than it was yesterday.
Has someone reached Mary?
!

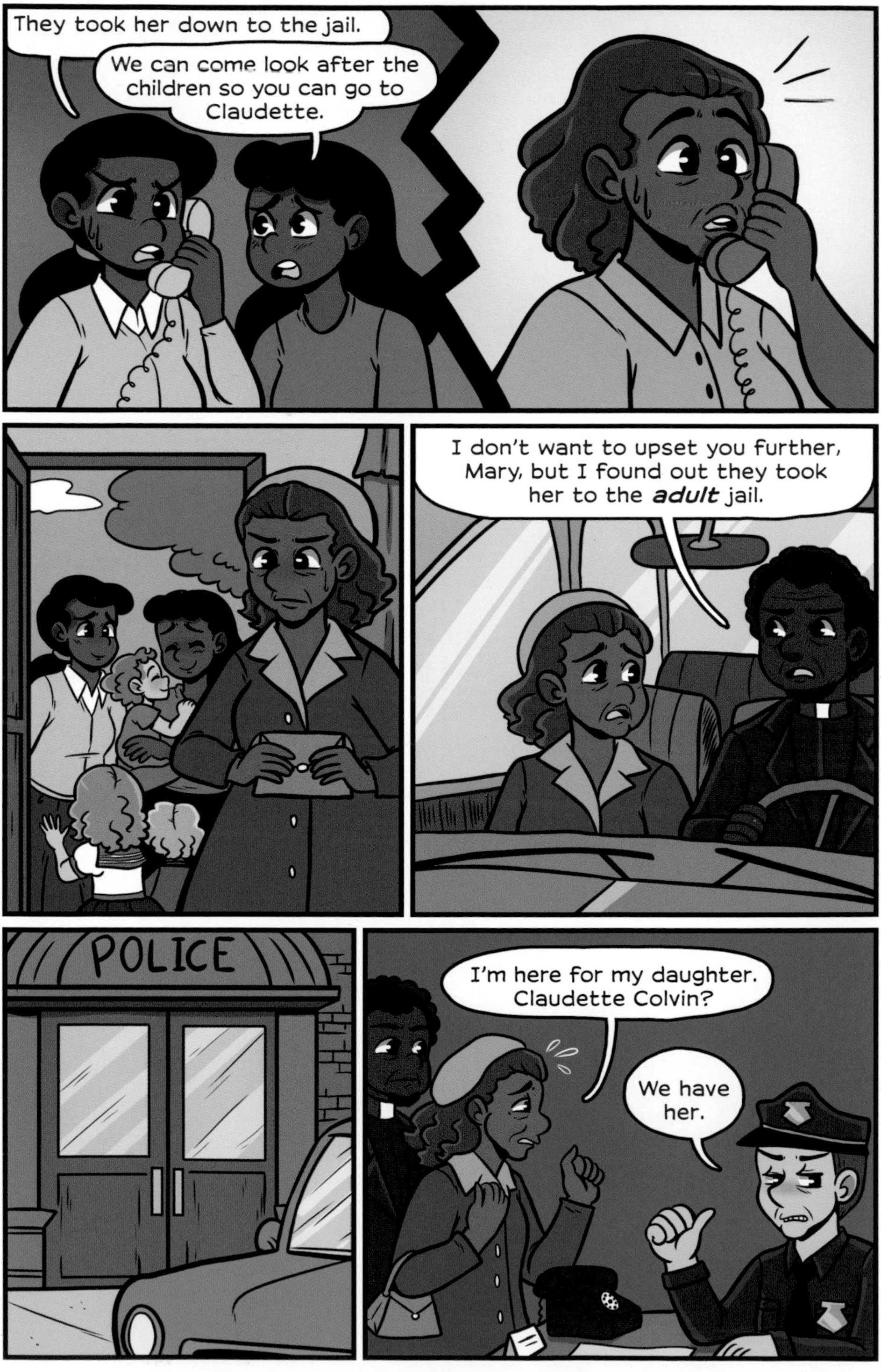
They took her down to the jail.
We can come look after the children so you can go to Claudette.
I don't want to upset you further, Mary, but I found out they took her to the *adult* jail.
POLICE
I'm here for my daughter. Claudette Colvin?
We have her.

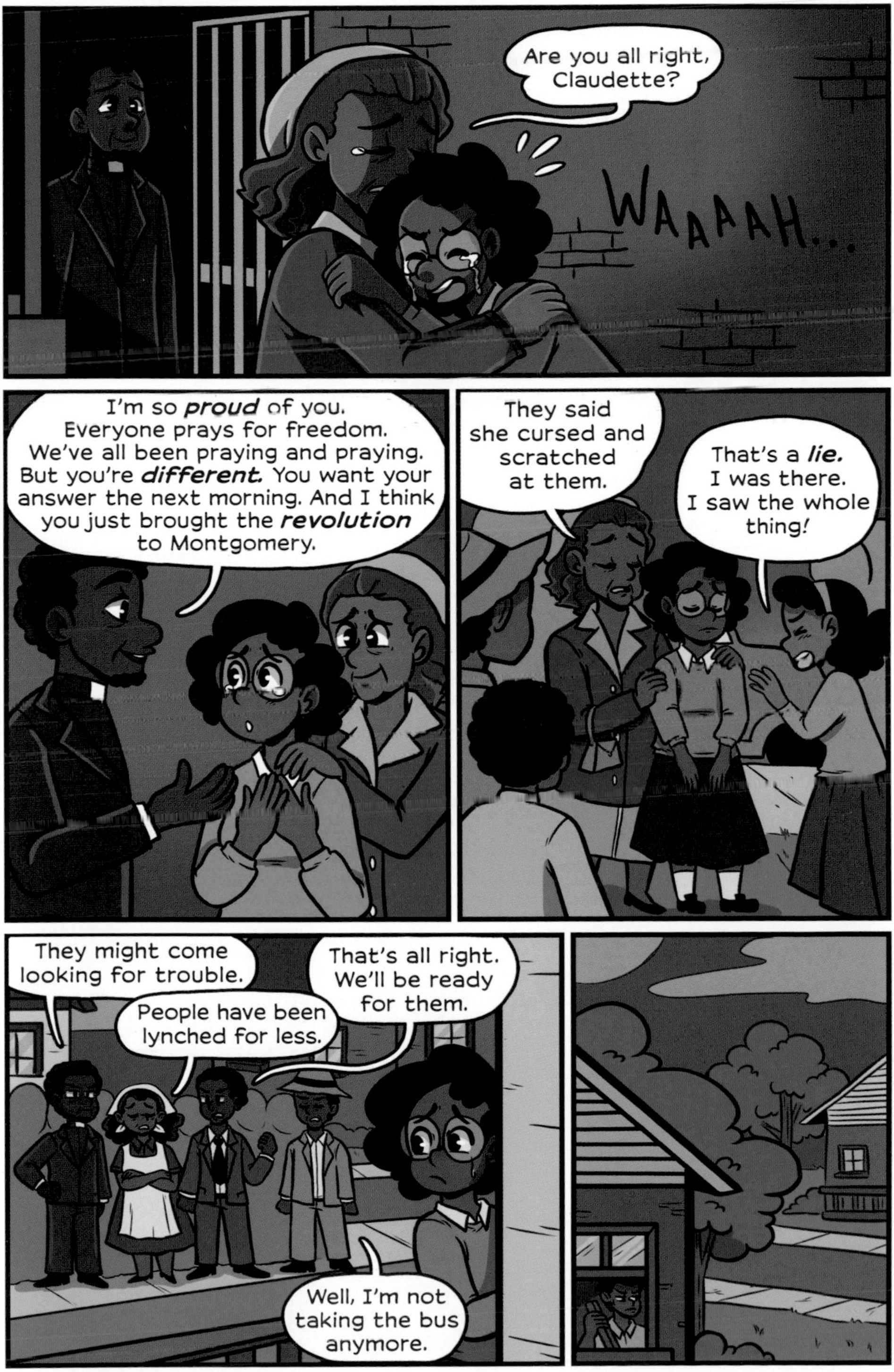
Are you all right, Claudette?
WAAAAH...
I'm so *proud* of you. Everyone prays for freedom. We've all been praying and praying. But you're *different.* You want your answer the next morning. And I think you just brought the *revolution* to Montgomery.
They said she cursed and scratched at them.
That's a *lie.* I was there. I saw the whole thing!
They might come looking for trouble.
People have been lynched for less.
That's all right. We'll be ready for them.
Well, I'm not taking the bus anymore.

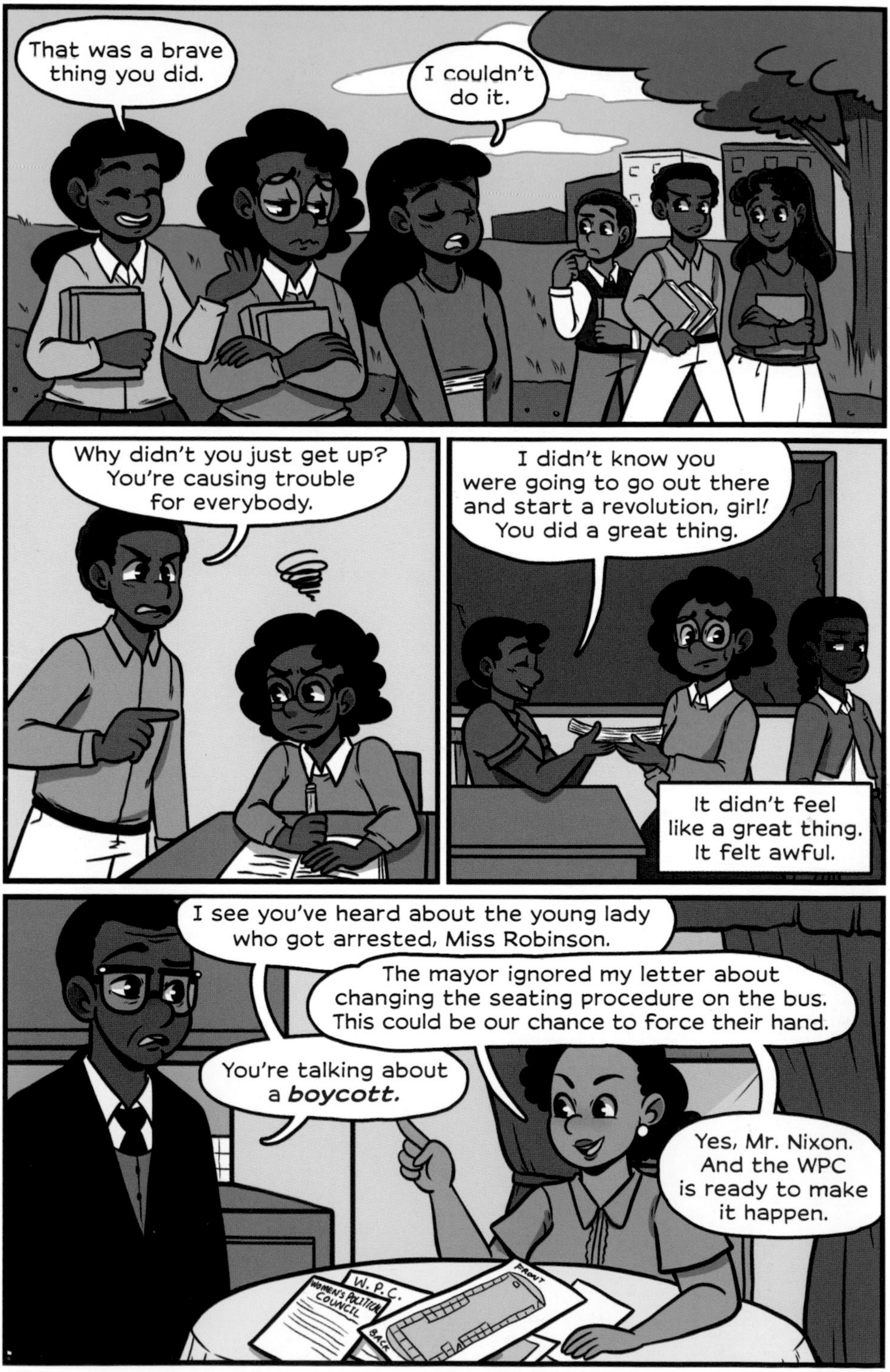
That was a brave thing you did.
I couldn't do it.
Why didn't you just get up? You're causing trouble for everybody.
I didn't know you were going to go out there and start a revolution, girl! You did a great thing.
It didn't feel like a great thing. It felt awful.
I see you've heard about the young lady who got arrested, Miss Robinson.
The mayor ignored my letter about changing the seating procedure on the bus. This could be our chance to force their hand.
You're talking about a ***boycott.***
Yes, Mr. Nixon. And the WPC is ready to make it happen.
W. P. C.
WOMEN'S POLITICAL COUNCIL
FRONT
BACK

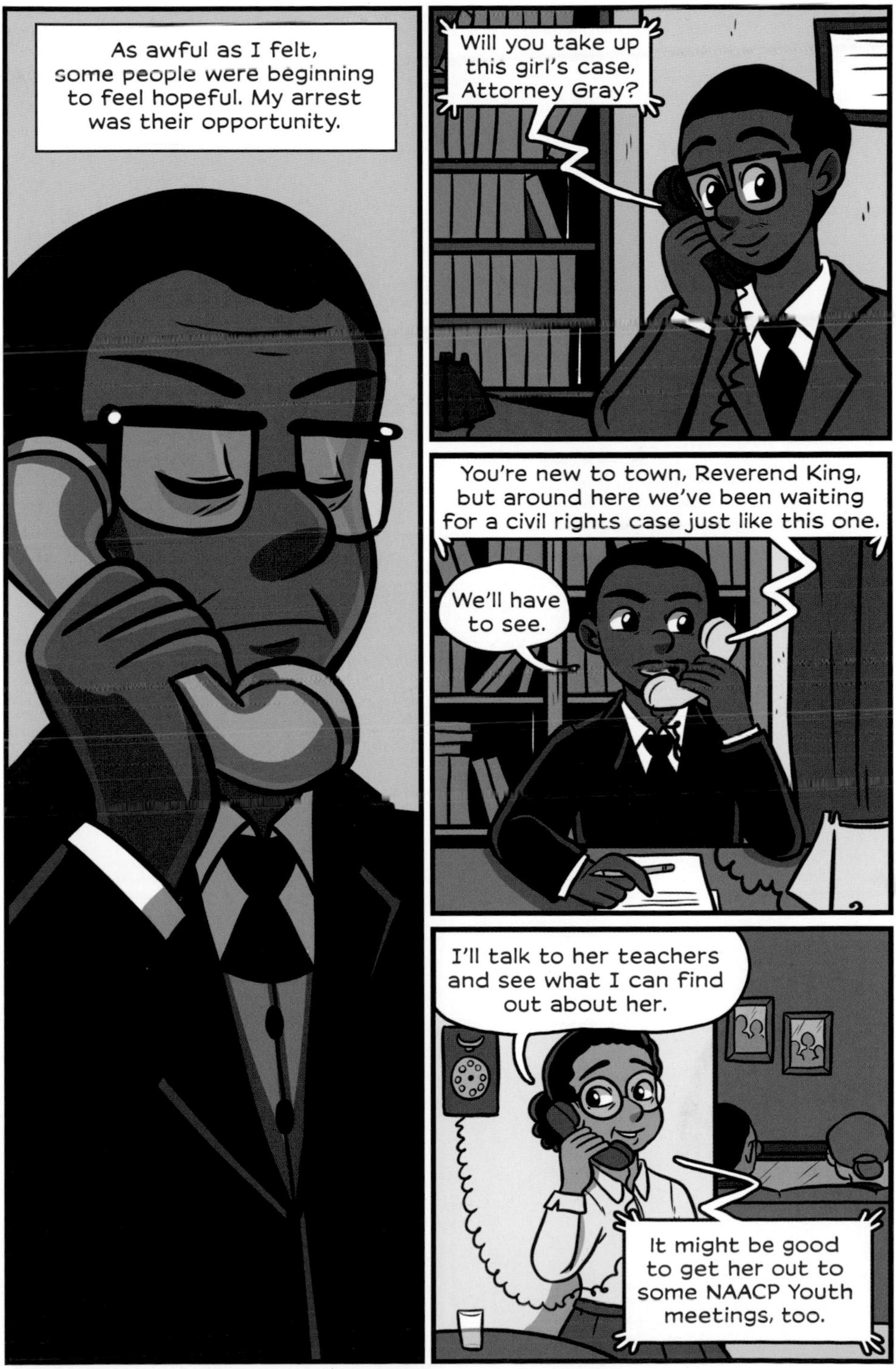
As awful as I felt, some people were beginning to feel hopeful. My arrest was their opportunity.
Will you take up this girl's case, Attorney Gray?
You're new to town, Reverend King, but around here we've been waiting for a civil rights case just like this one.
We'll have to see.
I'll talk to her teachers and see what I can find out about her.
It might be good to get her out to some NAACP Youth meetings, too.

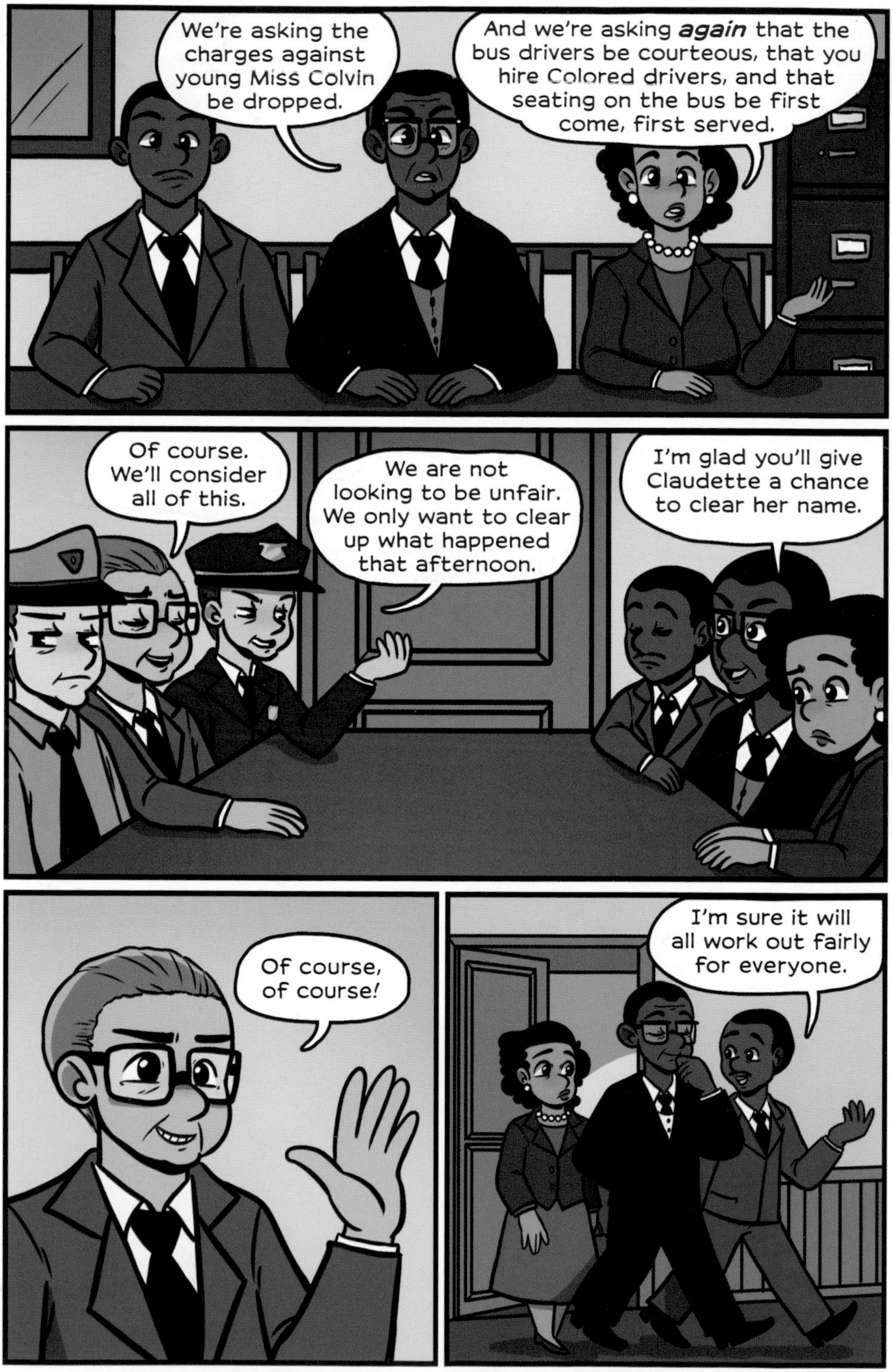
We're asking the charges against young Miss Colvin be dropped.
And we're asking ***again*** that the bus drivers be courteous, that you hire Colored drivers, and that seating on the bus be first come, first served.
Of course. We'll consider all of this.
We are not looking to be unfair. We only want to clear up what happened that afternoon.
I'm glad you'll give Claudette a chance to clear her name.
Of course, of course!
I'm sure it will all work out fairly for everyone.

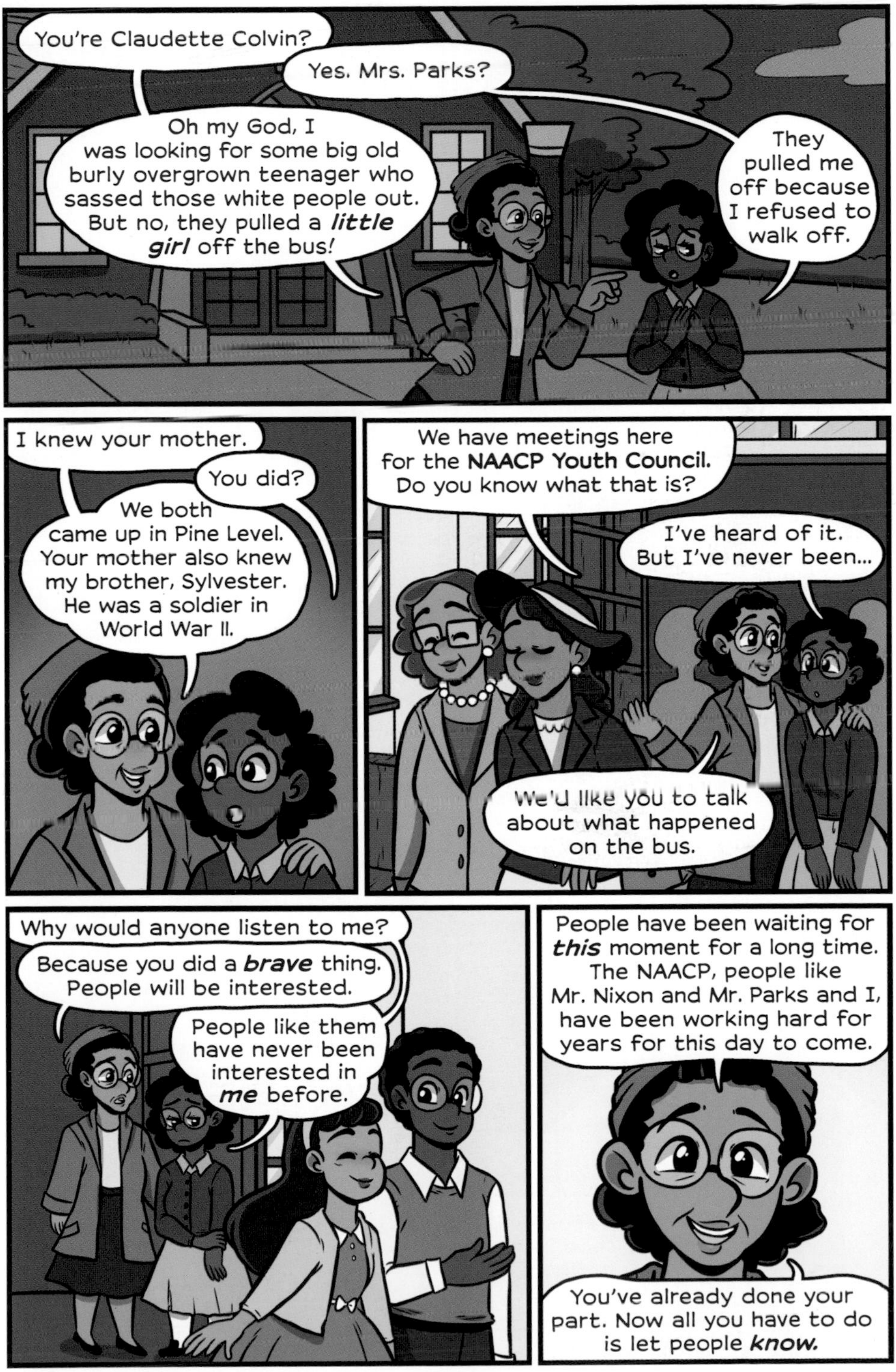
You're Claudette Colvin?
Yes. Mrs. Parks?
Oh my God, I was looking for some big old burly overgrown teenager who sassed those white people out. But no, they pulled a *little girl* off the bus!
They pulled me off because I refused to walk off.
I knew your mother.
You did?
We both came up in Pine Level. Your mother also knew my brother, Sylvester. He was a soldier in World War II.
We have meetings here for the **NAACP Youth Council.** Do you know what that is?
I've heard of it. But I've never been...
We'd like you to talk about what happened on the bus.
Why would anyone listen to me?
Because you did a *brave* thing. People will be interested.
People like them have never been interested in *me* before.
People have been waiting for *this* moment for a long time. The NAACP, people like Mr. Nixon and Mr. Parks and I, have been working hard for years for this day to come.
You've already done your part. Now all you have to do is let people *know.*

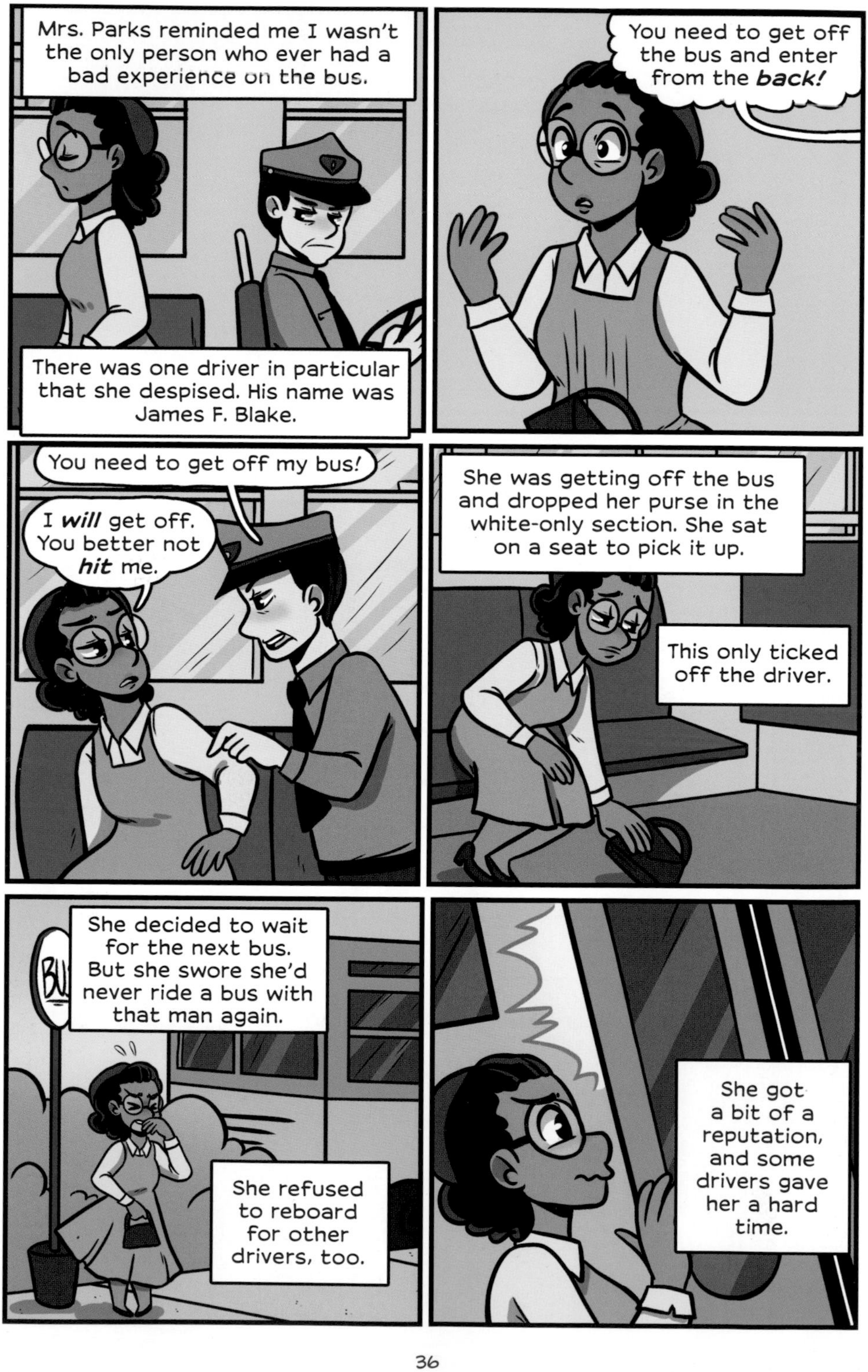
Mrs. Parks reminded me I wasn't the only person who ever had a bad experience on the bus.
There was one driver in particular that she despised. His name was James F. Blake.
You need to get off the bus and enter from the **back!**
You need to get off my bus!
I **will** get off. You better not **hit** me.
She was getting off the bus and dropped her purse in the white-only section. She sat on a seat to pick it up.
This only ticked off the driver.
She decided to wait for the next bus. But she swore she'd never ride a bus with that man again.
She refused to reboard for other drivers, too.
She got a bit of a reputation, and some drivers gave her a hard time.

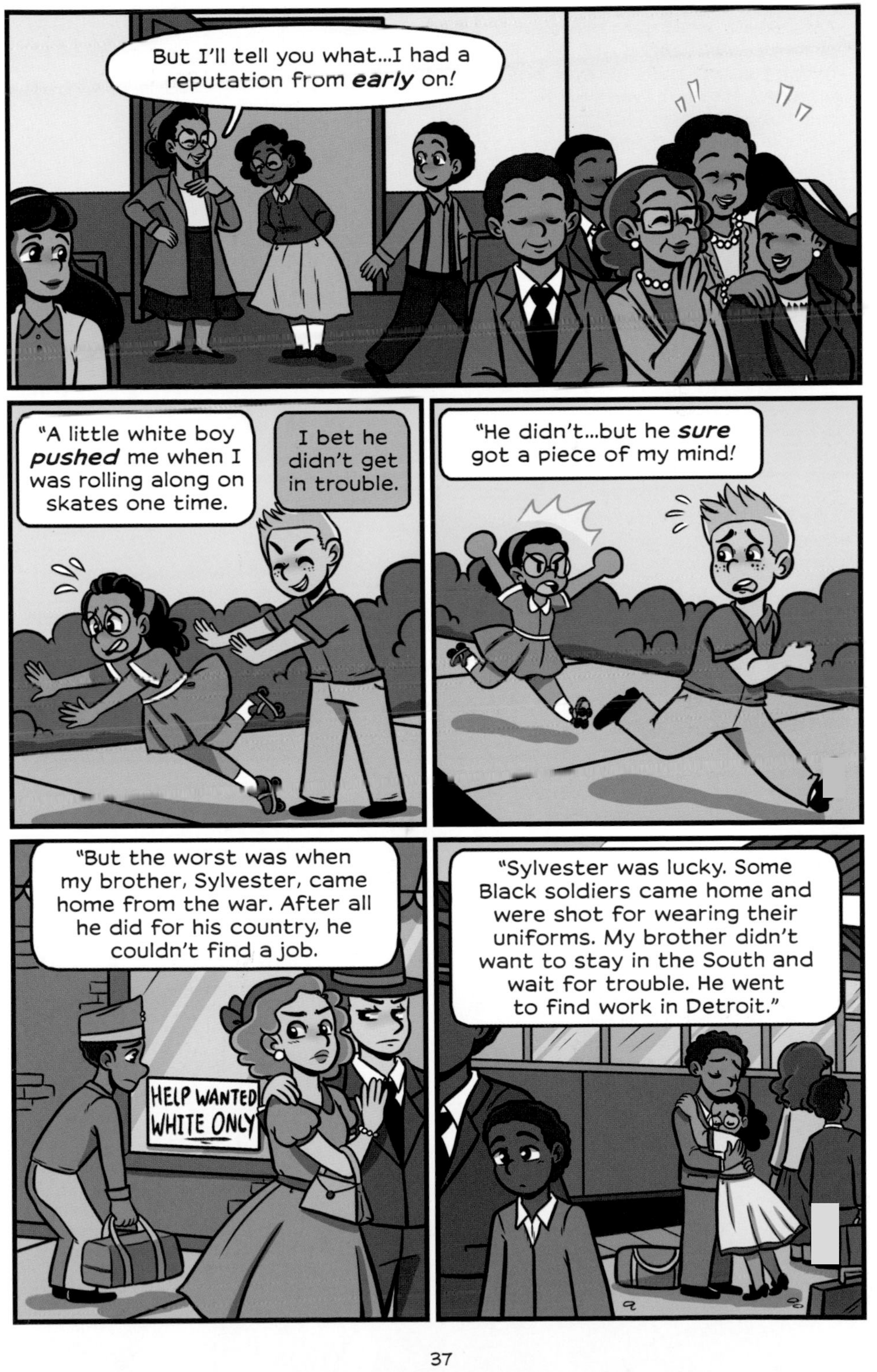

But I'll tell you what...I had a reputation from *early* on!
"A little white boy *pushed* me when I was rolling along on skates one time.
I bet he didn't get in trouble.
"He didn't...but he *sure* got a piece of my mind!
"But the worst was when my brother, Sylvester, came home from the war. After all he did for his country, he couldn't find a job.
HELP WANTED WHITE ONLY
"Sylvester was lucky. Some Black soldiers came home and were shot for wearing their uniforms. My brother didn't want to stay in the South and wait for trouble. He went to find work in Detroit."

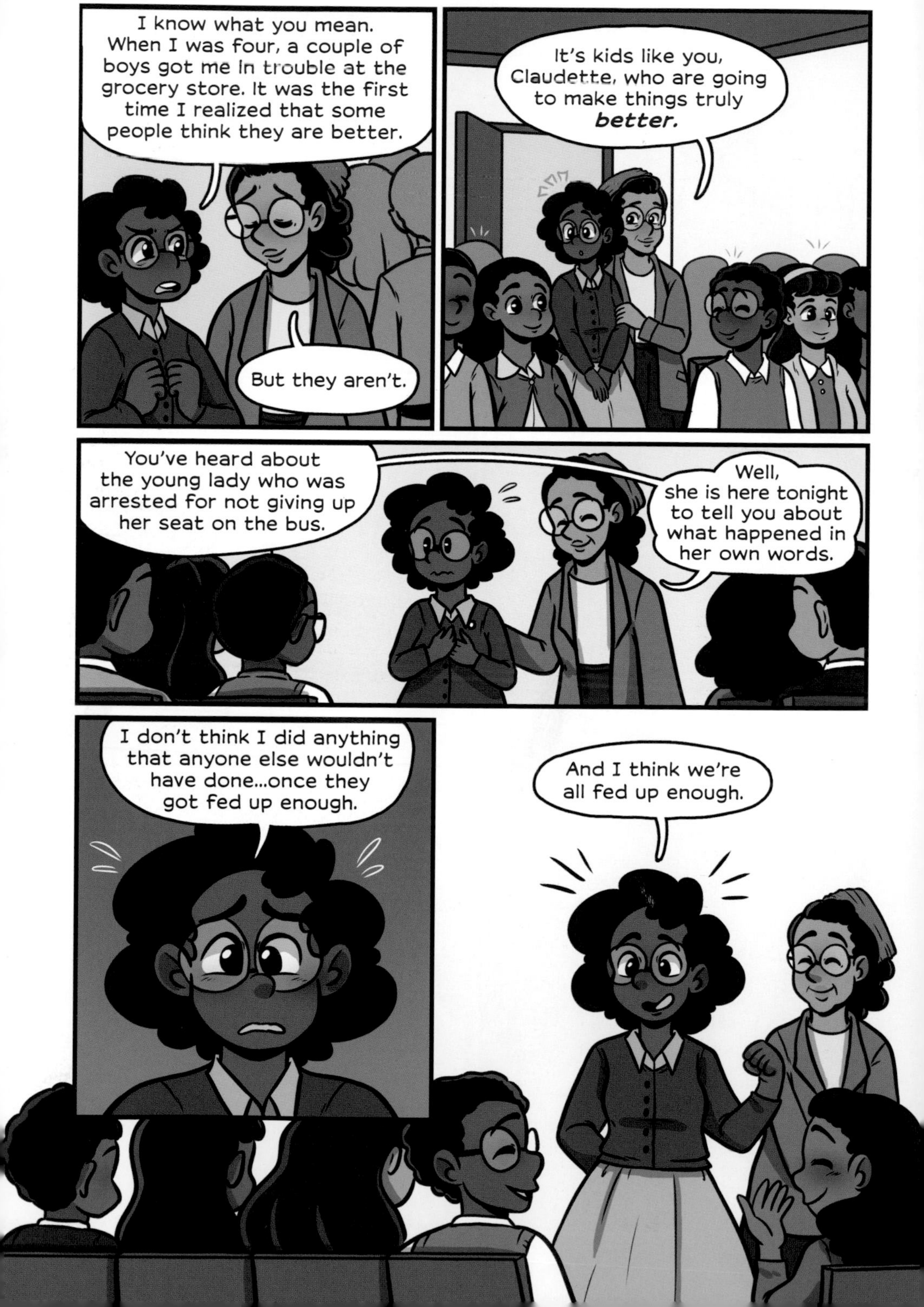
I know what you mean. When I was four, a couple of boys got me in trouble at the grocery store. It was the first time I realized that some people think they are better.
But they aren't.
It's kids like you, Claudette, who are going to make things truly ***better.***
You've heard about the young lady who was arrested for not giving up her seat on the bus.
Well, she is here tonight to tell you about what happened in her own words.
I don't think I did anything that anyone else wouldn't have done...once they got fed up enough.
And I think we're all fed up enough.

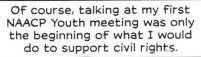
Of course, talking at my first NAACP Youth meeting was only the beginning of what I would do to support civil rights.

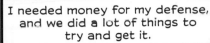
I needed money for my defense, and we did a lot of things to try and get it.

CLAUDETTE LEGAL FUND

Everyone tried to help.

This brave young lady is one of our own. And today the second collection will be for her defense fund.

I even entered a beauty pageant for the winnings.

Even though I didn't win the pageant, all the money went to my defense fund anyway.

WINNER

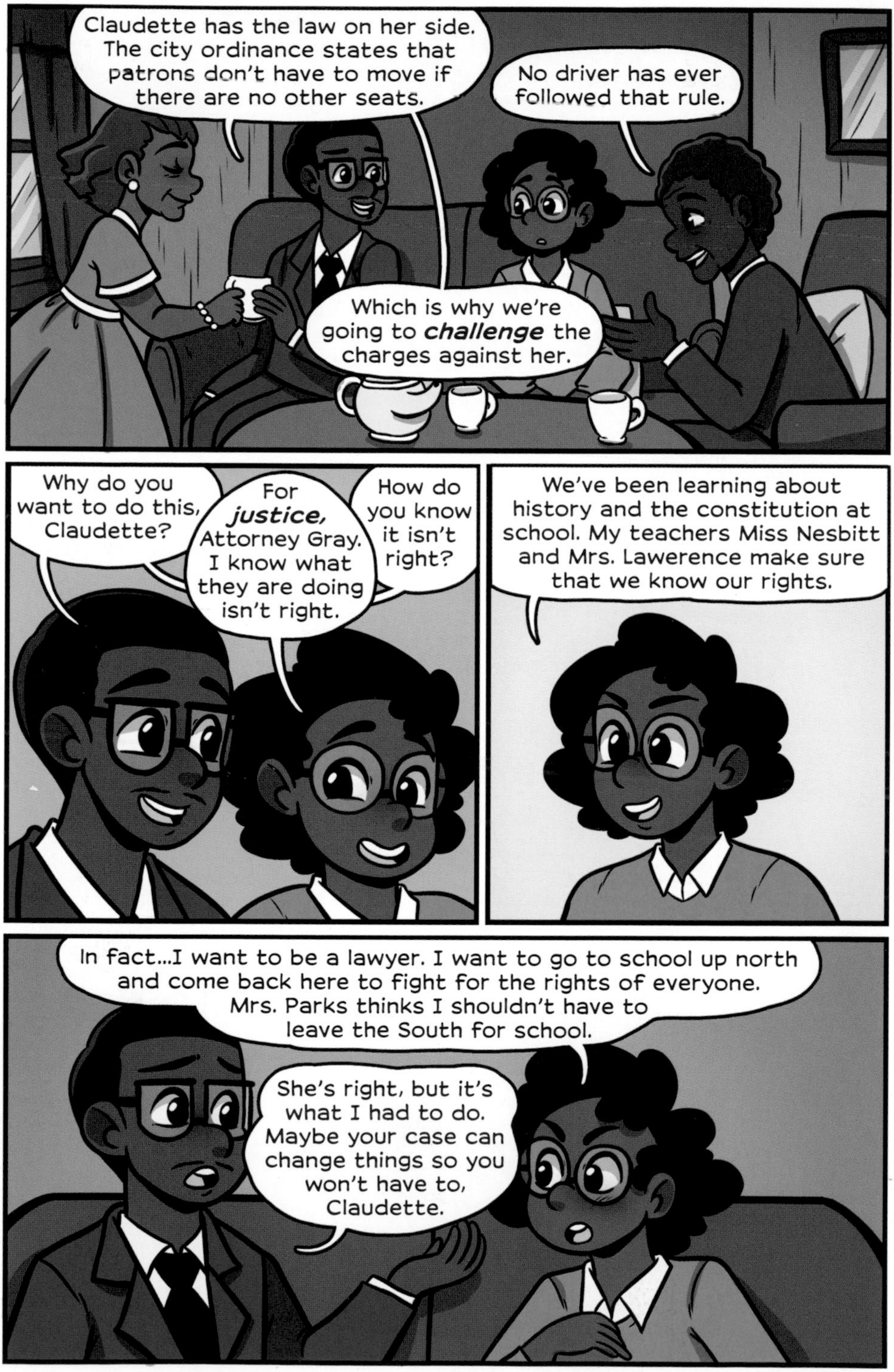
Claudette has the law on her side. The city ordinance states that patrons don't have to move if there are no other seats.
No driver has ever followed that rule.
Which is why we're going to *challenge* the charges against her.
Why do you want to do this, Claudette?
For *justice,* Attorney Gray. I know what they are doing isn't right.
How do you know it isn't right?
We've been learning about history and the constitution at school. My teachers Miss Nesbitt and Mrs. Lawerence make sure that we know our rights.
In fact...I want to be a lawyer. I want to go to school up north and come back here to fight for the rights of everyone. Mrs. Parks thinks I shouldn't have to leave the South for school.
She's right, but it's what I had to do. Maybe your case can change things so you won't have to, Claudette.

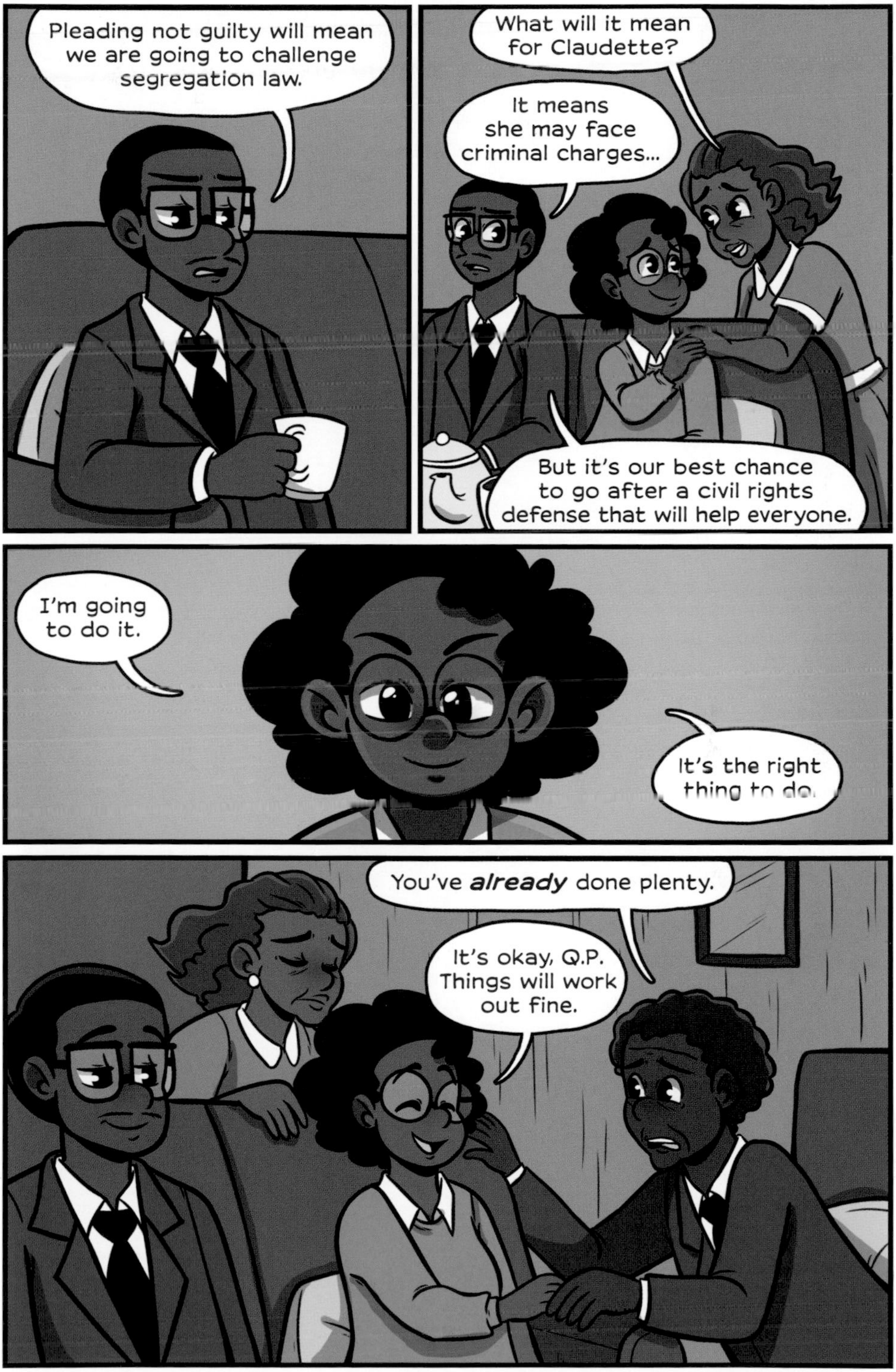
Pleading not guilty will mean we are going to challenge segregation law.
What will it mean for Claudette?
It means she may face criminal charges...
But it's our best chance to go after a civil rights defense that will help everyone.
I'm going to do it.
It's the right thing to do.
You've *already* done plenty.
It's okay, Q.P. Things will work out fine.

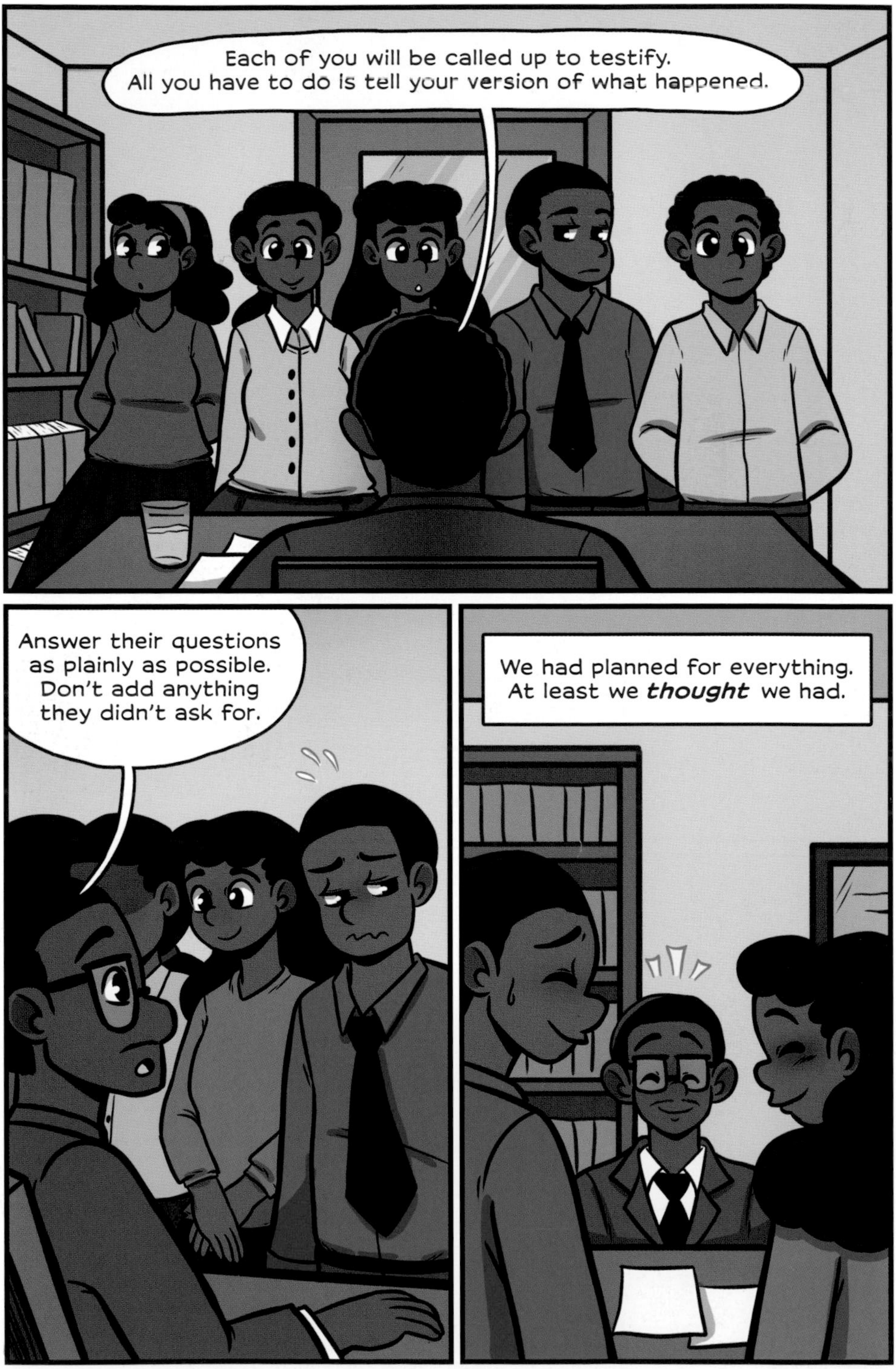
Each of you will be called up to testify.
All you have to do is tell your version of what happened.
Answer their questions as plainly as possible. Don't add anything they didn't ask for.
We had planned for everything. At least we *thought* we had.

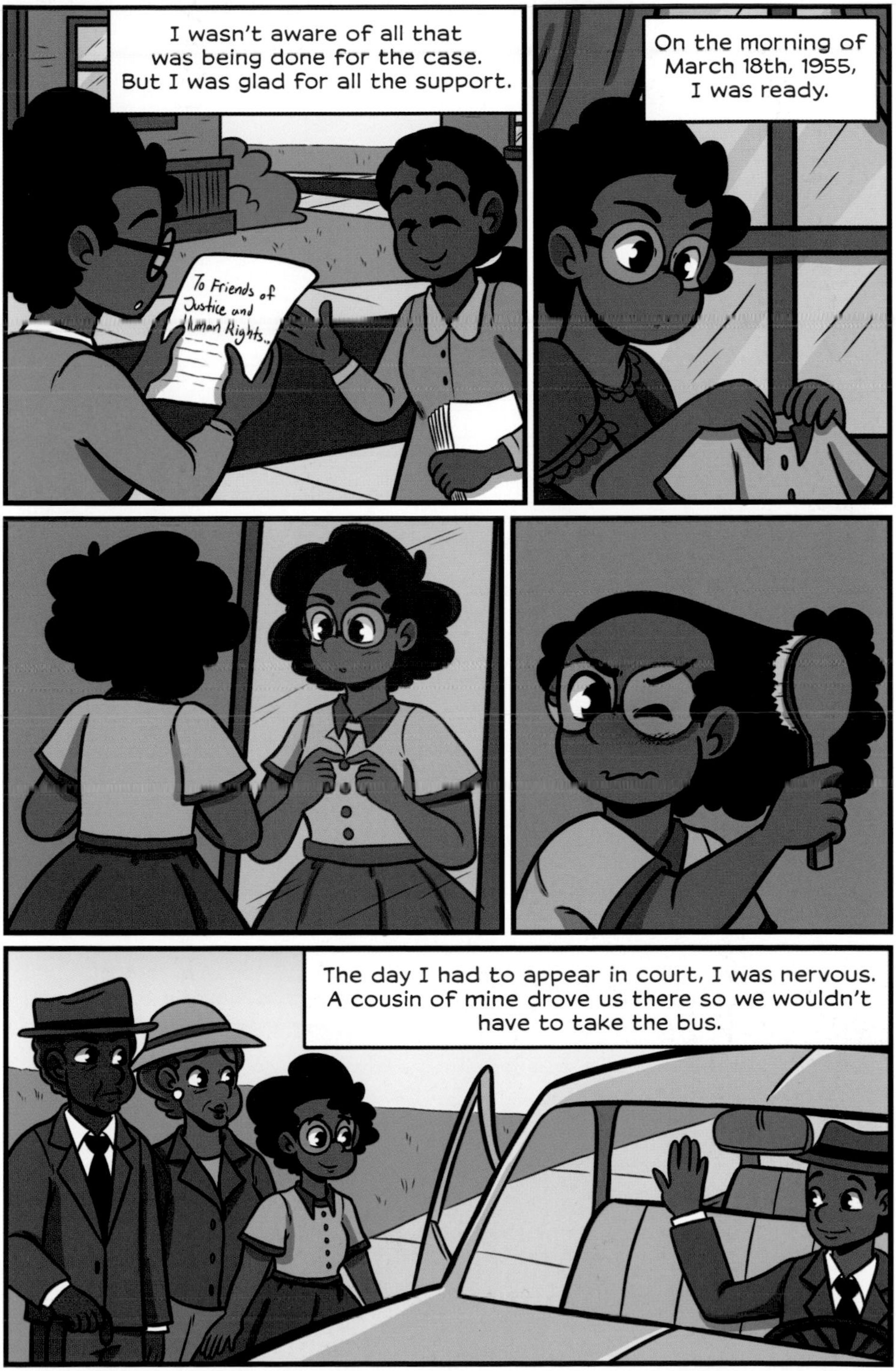
I wasn't aware of all that was being done for the case. But I was glad for all the support.
To Friends of Justice and Human Rights...
On the morning of March 18th, 1955, I was ready.
The day I had to appear in court, I was nervous. A cousin of mine drove us there so we wouldn't have to take the bus.

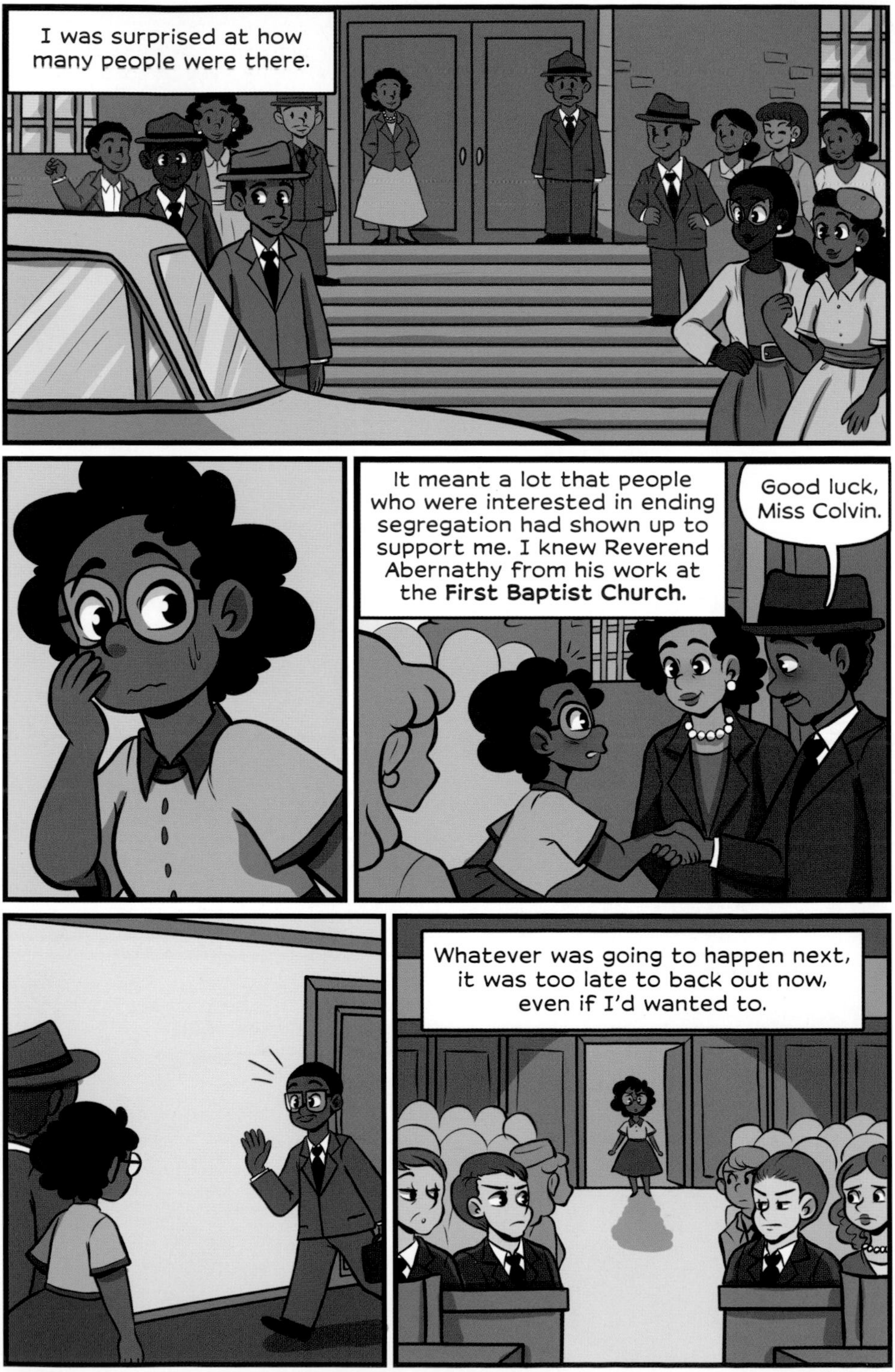
I was surprised at how many people were there.
It meant a lot that people who were interested in ending segregation had shown up to support me. I knew Reverend Abernathy from his work at the **First Baptist Church.**
Good luck, Miss Colvin.
Whatever was going to happen next, it was too late to back out now, even if I'd wanted to.

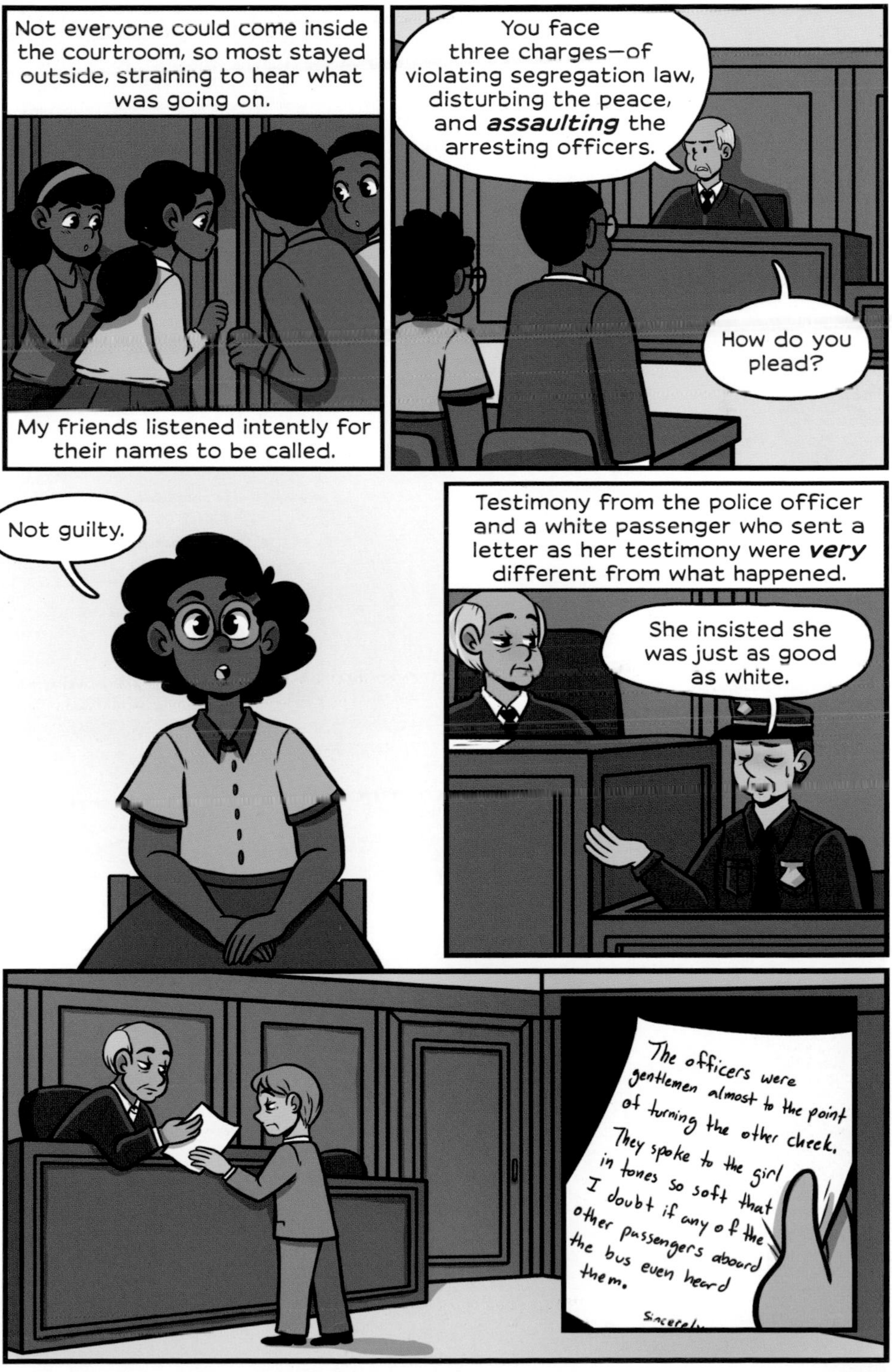

Not everyone could come inside the courtroom, so most stayed outside, straining to hear what was going on.
My friends listened intently for their names to be called.
You face three charges—of violating segregation law, disturbing the peace, and ***assaulting*** the arresting officers.
How do you plead?
Not guilty.
Testimony from the police officer and a white passenger who sent a letter as her testimony were ***very*** different from what happened.
She insisted she was just as good as white.
The officers were gentlemen almost to the point of turning the other cheek. They spoke to the girl in tones so soft that I doubt if any of the other passengers aboard the bus even heard them.

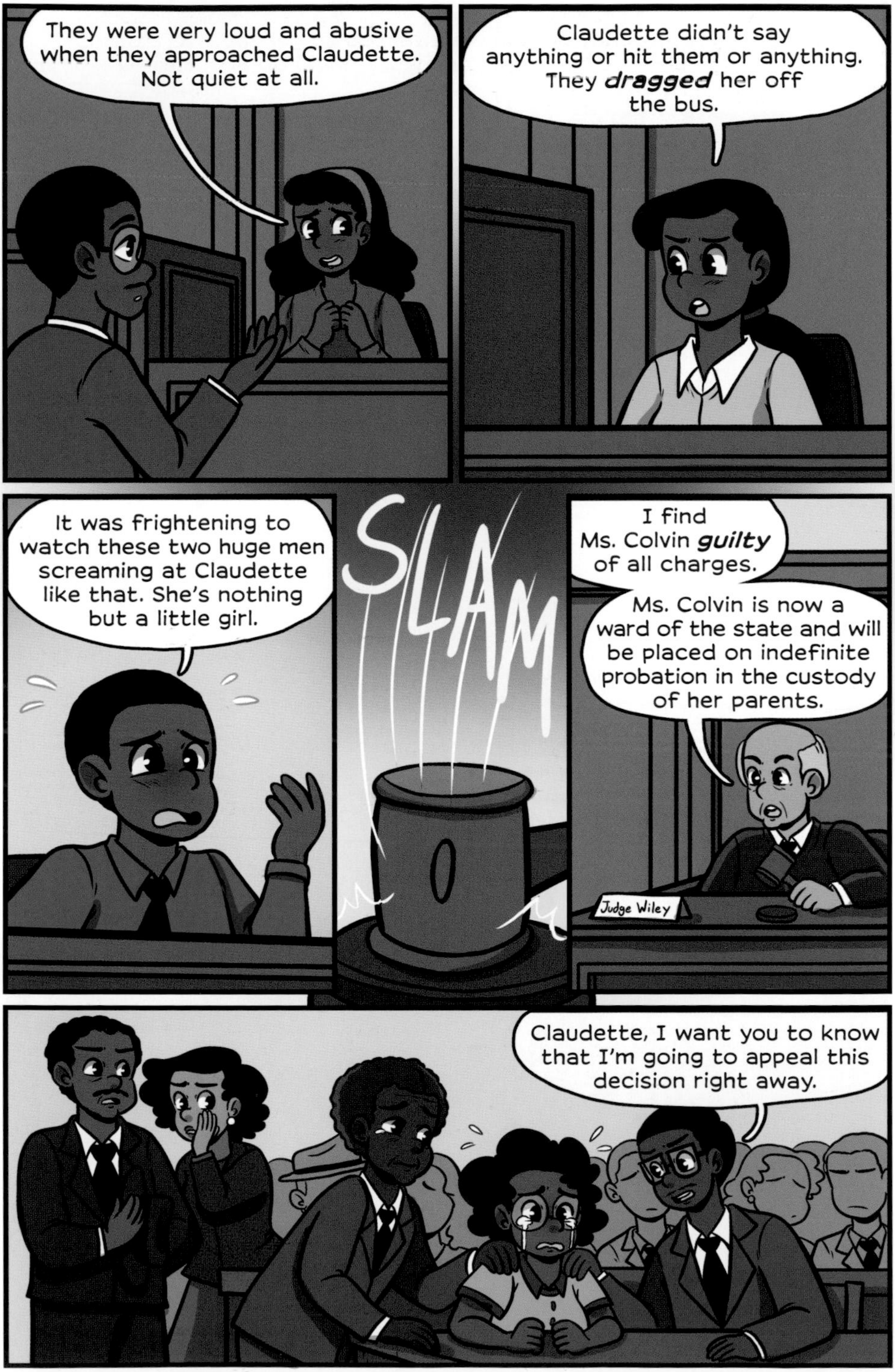
They were very loud and abusive when they approached Claudette. Not quiet at all.
Claudette didn't say anything or hit them or anything. They *dragged* her off the bus.
It was frightening to watch these two huge men screaming at Claudette like that. She's nothing but a little girl.
SLAM
I find Ms. Colvin *guilty* of all charges.
Ms. Colvin is now a ward of the state and will be placed on indefinite probation in the custody of her parents.
Judge Wiley
Claudette, I want you to know that I'm going to appeal this decision right away.

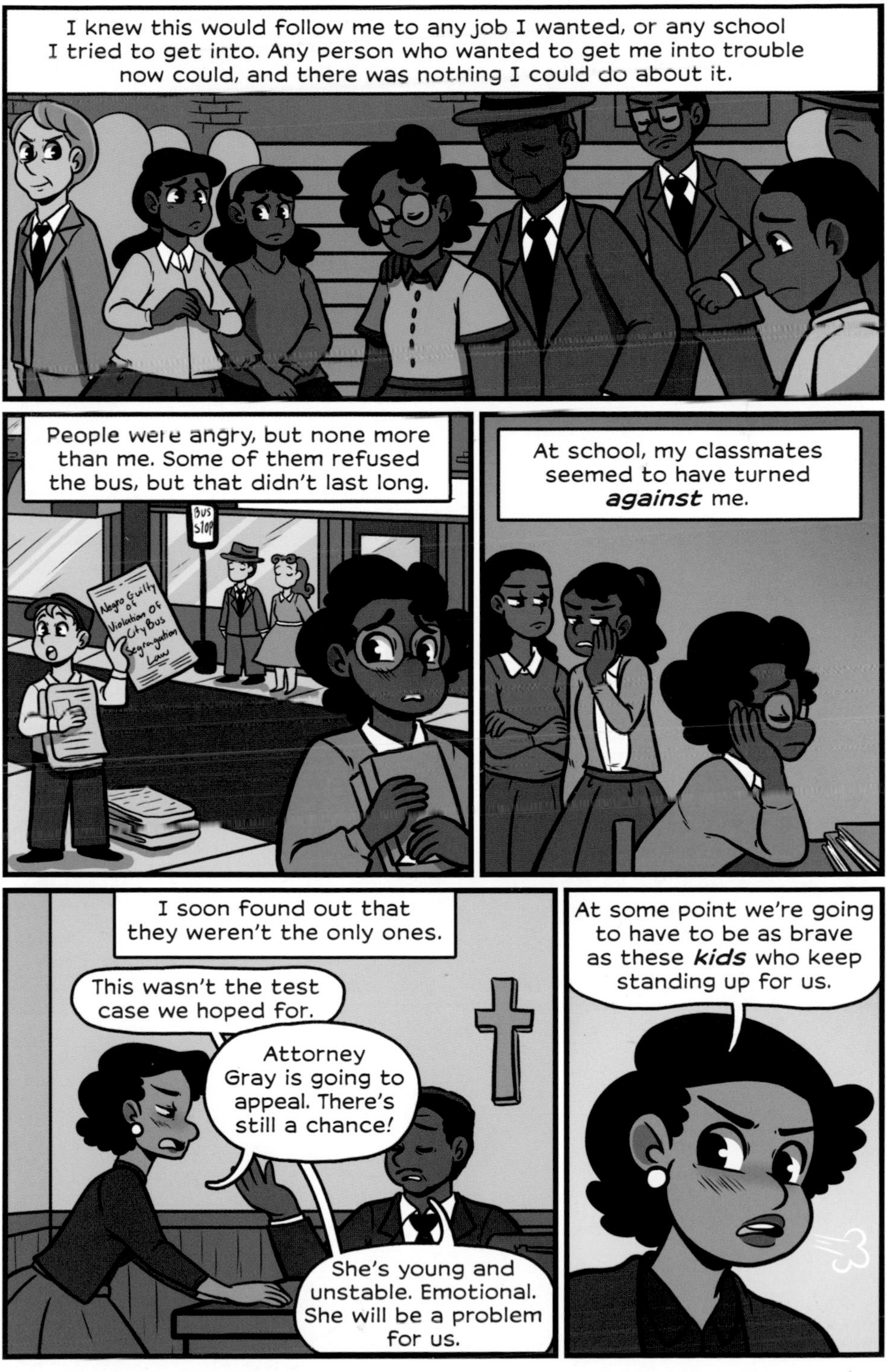
I knew this would follow me to any job I wanted, or any school I tried to get into. Any person who wanted to get me into trouble now could, and there was nothing I could do about it.
People were angry, but none more than me. Some of them refused the bus, but that didn't last long.
BUS STOP
Negro Guilty of Violation Of City Bus Segregation Law
At school, my classmates seemed to have turned ***against*** me.
I soon found out that they weren't the only ones.
This wasn't the test case we hoped for.
Attorney Gray is going to appeal. There's still a chance!
She's young and unstable. Emotional. She will be a problem for us.
At some point we're going to have to be as brave as these ***kids*** who keep standing up for us.

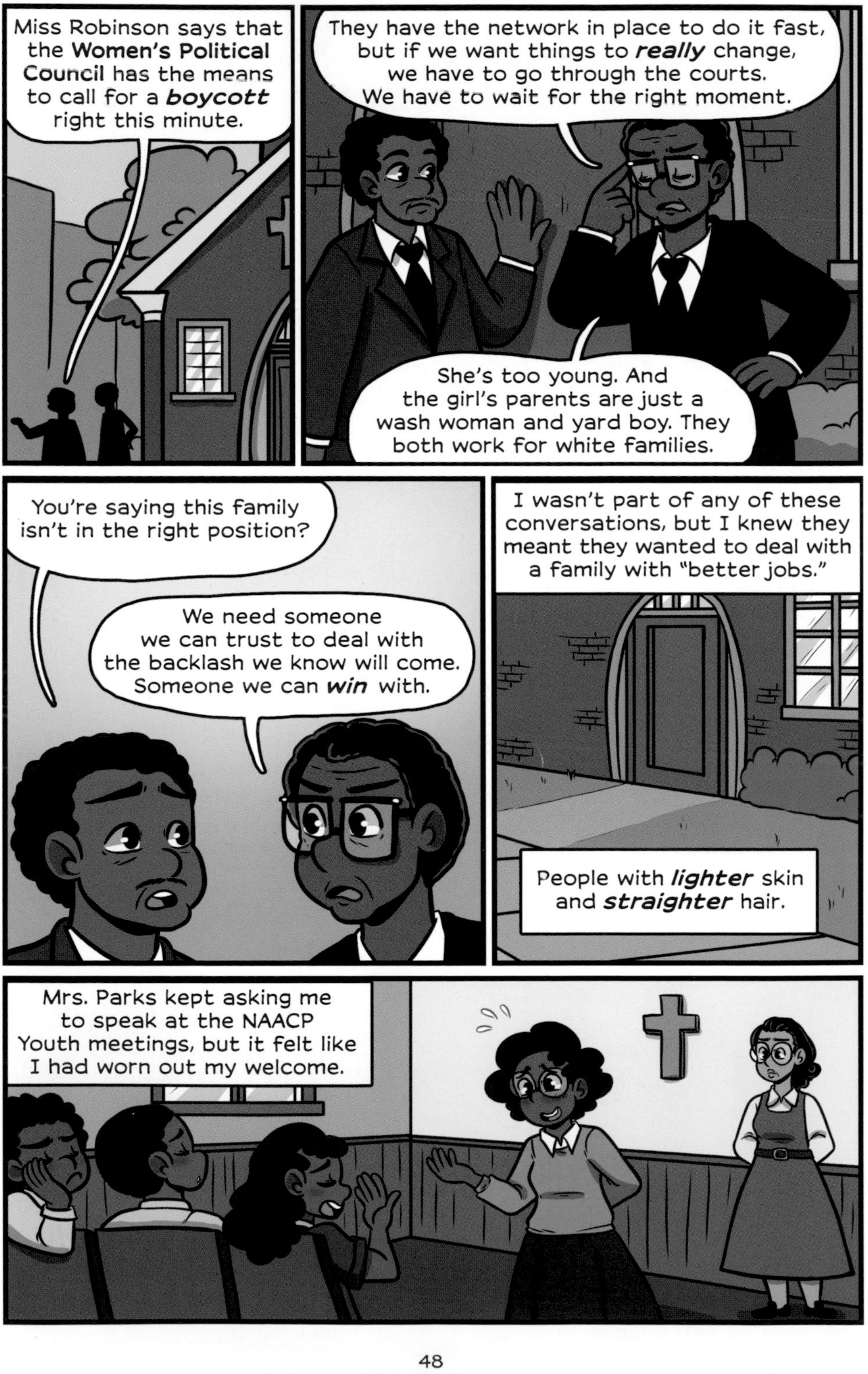

Miss Robinson says that the **Women's Political Council** has the means to call for a ***boycott*** right this minute.
They have the network in place to do it fast, but if we want things to ***really*** change, we have to go through the courts. We have to wait for the right moment.
She's too young. And the girl's parents are just a wash woman and yard boy. They both work for white families.
You're saying this family isn't in the right position?
We need someone we can trust to deal with the backlash we know will come. Someone we can ***win*** with.
I wasn't part of any of these conversations, but I knew they meant they wanted to deal with a family with "better jobs."
People with ***lighter*** skin and ***straighter*** hair.
Mrs. Parks kept asking me to speak at the NAACP Youth meetings, but it felt like I had worn out my welcome.

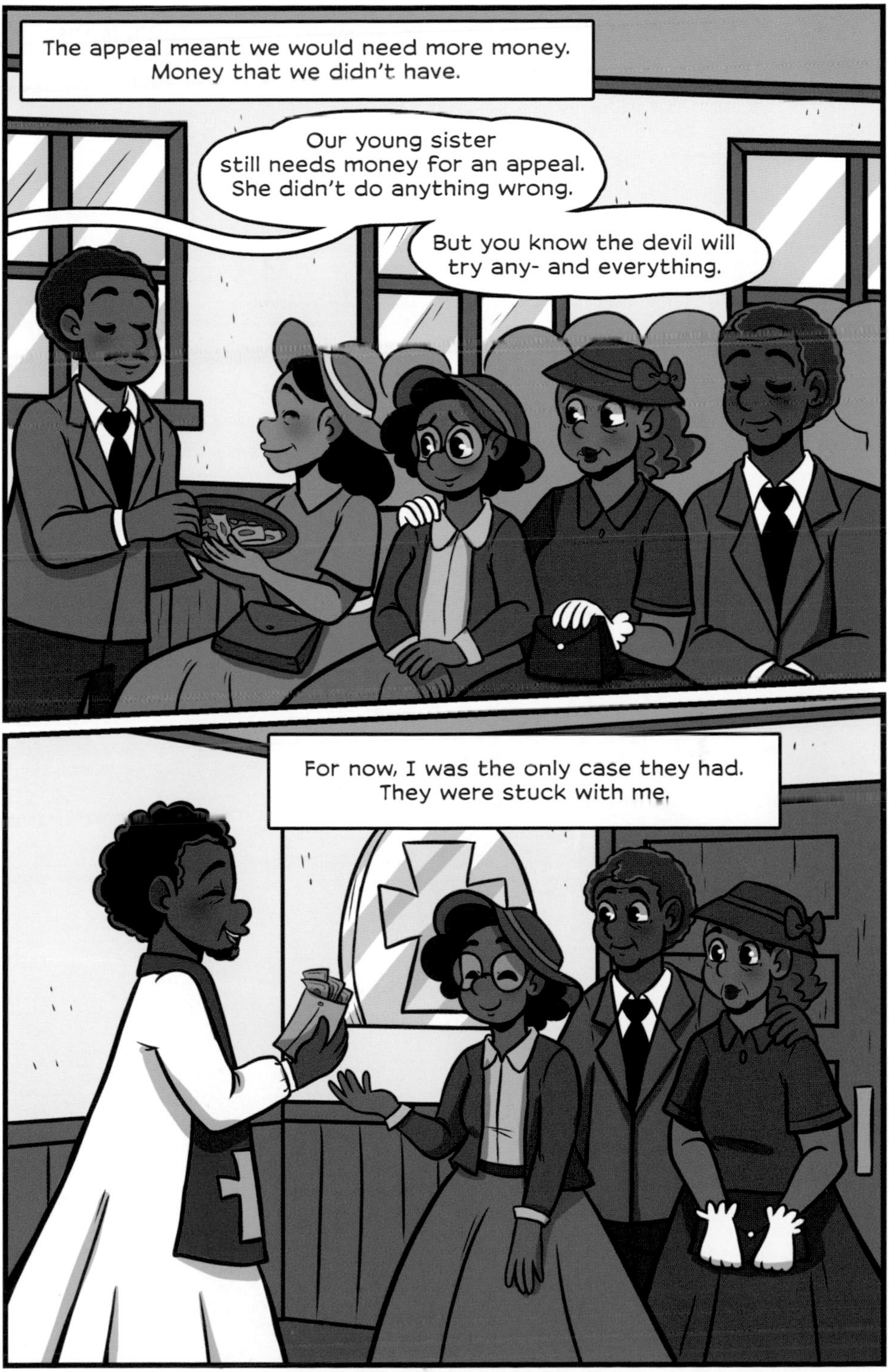
The appeal meant we would need more money. Money that we didn't have.
Our young sister still needs money for an appeal. She didn't do anything wrong.
But you know the devil will try any- and everything.
For now, I was the only case they had. They were stuck with me.

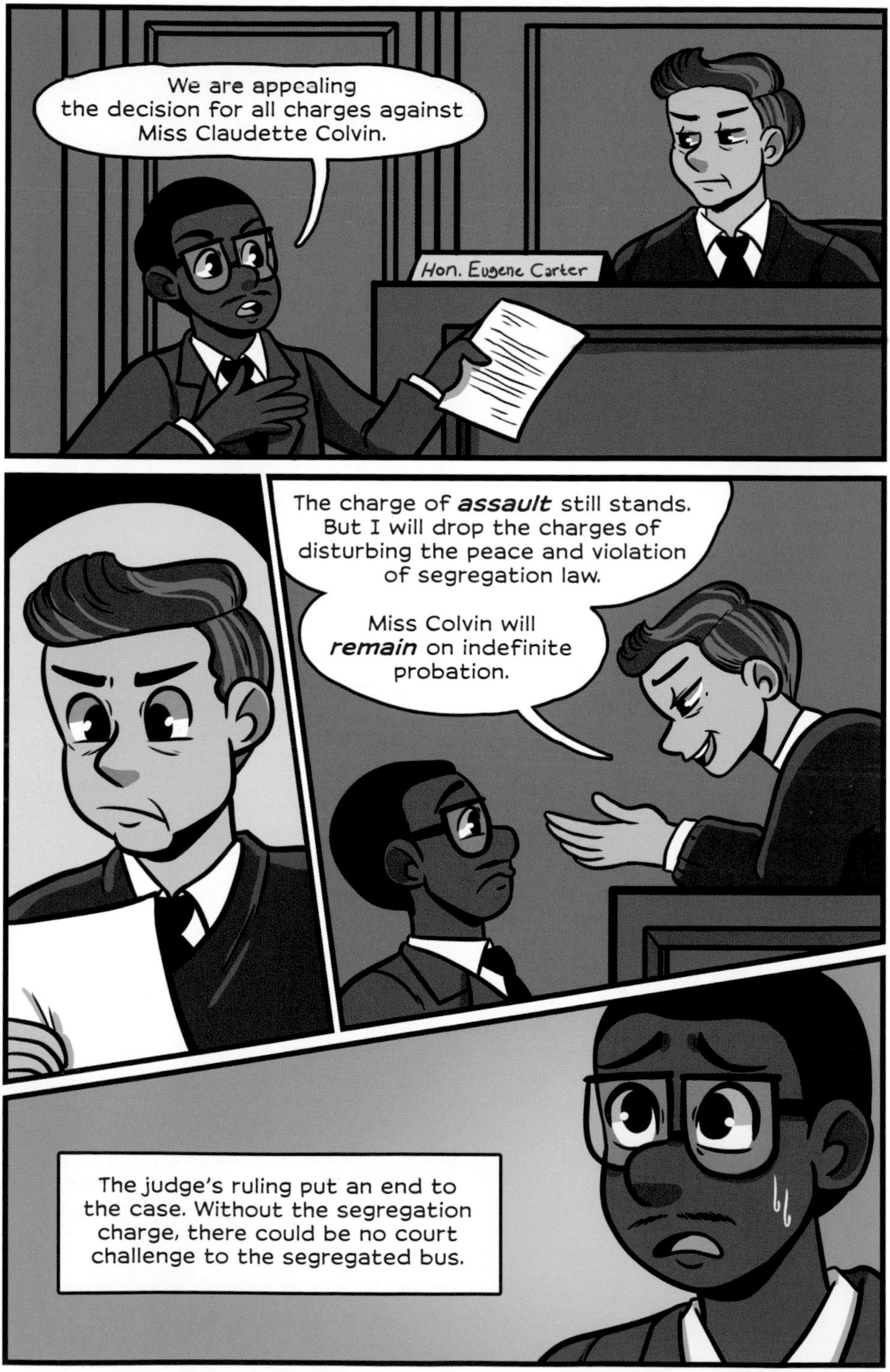
We are appealing the decision for all charges against Miss Claudette Colvin.
Hon. Eugene Carter
The charge of ***assault*** still stands. But I will drop the charges of disturbing the peace and violation of segregation law.
Miss Colvin will ***remain*** on indefinite probation.
The judge's ruling put an end to the case. Without the segregation charge, there could be no court challenge to the segregated bus.

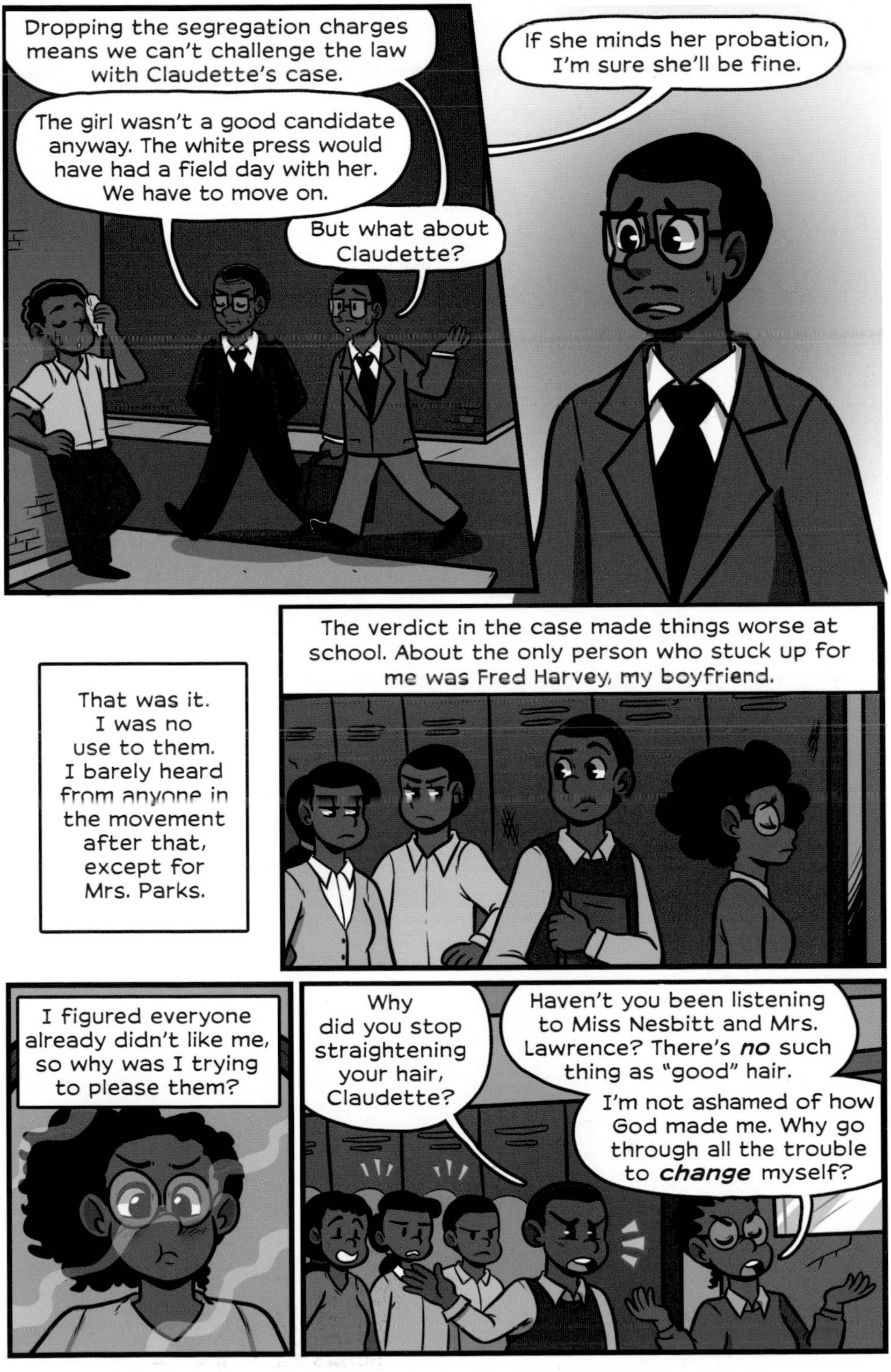
Dropping the segregation charges means we can't challenge the law with Claudette's case.
The girl wasn't a good candidate anyway. The white press would have had a field day with her. We have to move on.
But what about Claudette?
If she minds her probation, I'm sure she'll be fine.
That was it. I was no use to them. I barely heard from anyone in the movement after that, except for Mrs. Parks.
The verdict in the case made things worse at school. About the only person who stuck up for me was Fred Harvey, my boyfriend.
I figured everyone already didn't like me, so why was I trying to please them?
Why did you stop straightening your hair, Claudette?
Haven't you been listening to Miss Nesbitt and Mrs. Lawrence? There's ***no*** such thing as "good" hair.
I'm not ashamed of how God made me. Why go through all the trouble to ***change*** myself?

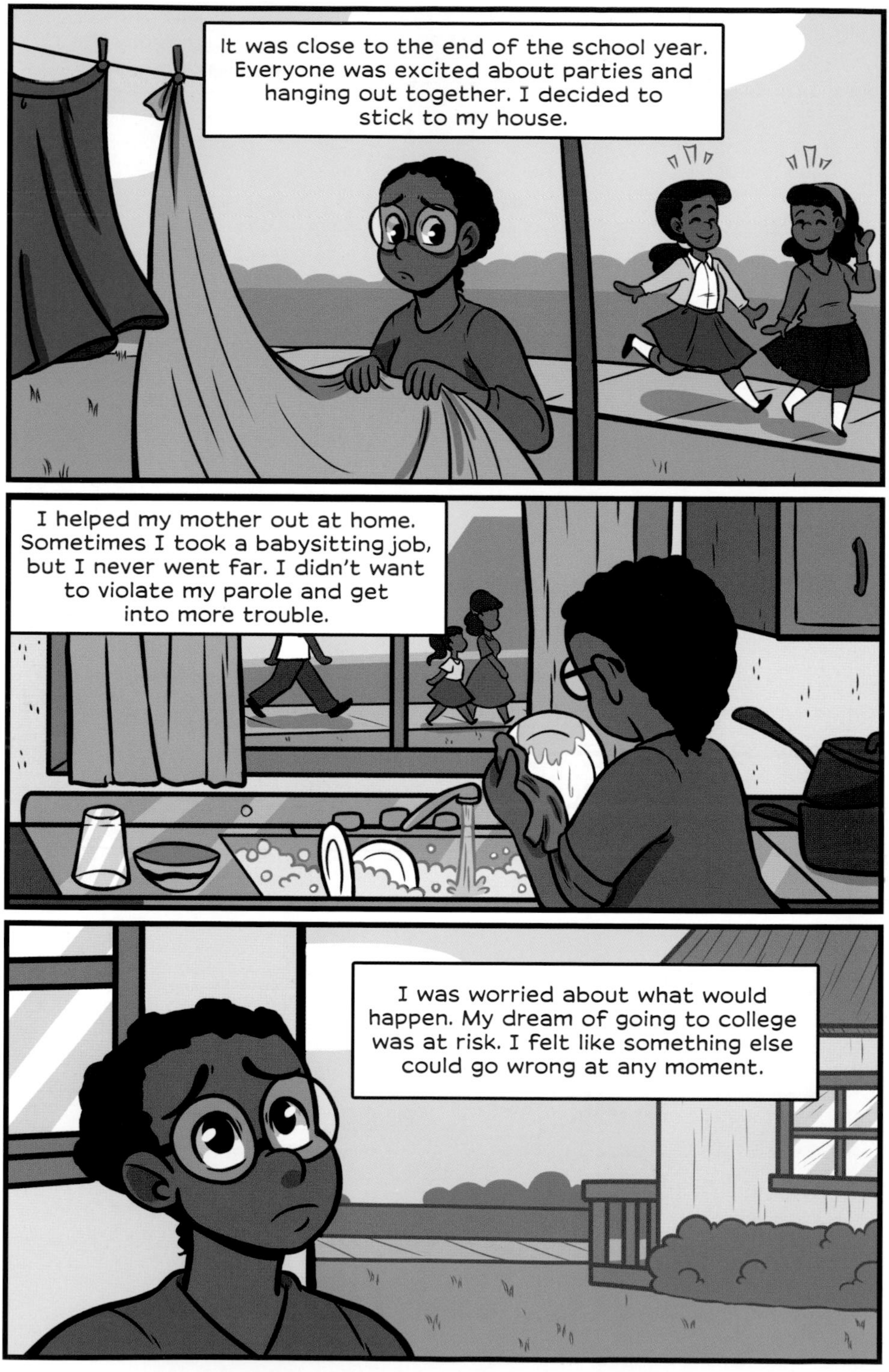
It was close to the end of the school year. Everyone was excited about parties and hanging out together. I decided to stick to my house.
I helped my mother out at home. Sometimes I took a babysitting job, but I never went far. I didn't want to violate my parole and get into more trouble.
I was worried about what would happen. My dream of going to college was at risk. I felt like something else could go wrong at any moment.

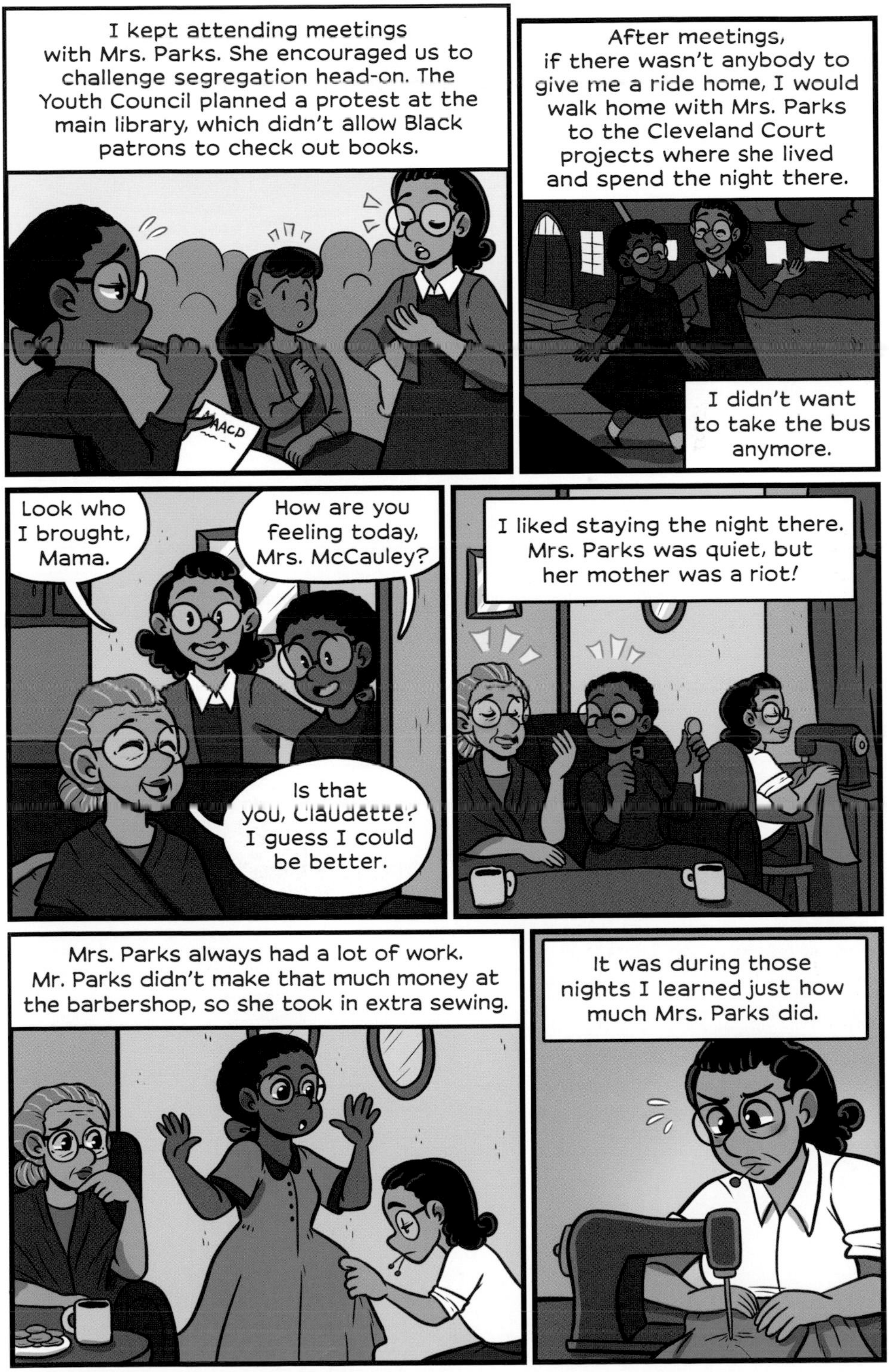
I kept attending meetings with Mrs. Parks. She encouraged us to challenge segregation head-on. The Youth Council planned a protest at the main library, which didn't allow Black patrons to check out books.
After meetings, if there wasn't anybody to give me a ride home, I would walk home with Mrs. Parks to the Cleveland Court projects where she lived and spend the night there.
I didn't want to take the bus anymore.
Look who I brought, Mama.
How are you feeling today, Mrs. McCauley?
Is that you, Claudette? I guess I could be better.
I liked staying the night there. Mrs. Parks was quiet, but her mother was a riot!
Mrs. Parks always had a lot of work. Mr. Parks didn't make that much money at the barbershop, so she took in extra sewing.
It was during those nights I learned just how much Mrs. Parks did.

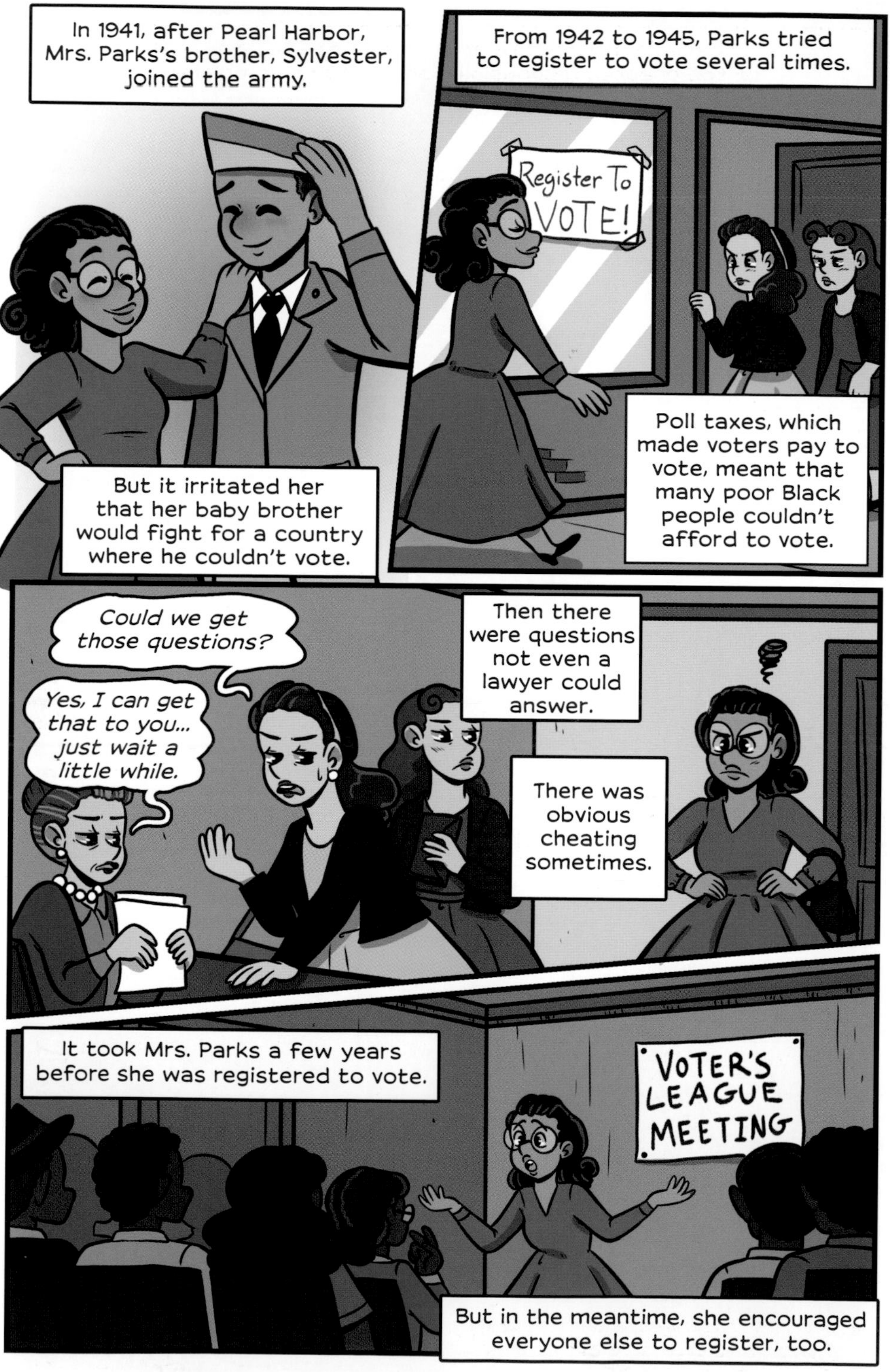
In 1941, after Pearl Harbor, Mrs. Parks's brother, Sylvester, joined the army.
But it irritated her that her baby brother would fight for a country where he couldn't vote.
From 1942 to 1945, Parks tried to register to vote several times.
Register To VOTE!
Poll taxes, which made voters pay to vote, meant that many poor Black people couldn't afford to vote.
Could we get those questions?
Yes, I can get that to you... just wait a little while.
Then there were questions not even a lawyer could answer.
There was obvious cheating sometimes.
It took Mrs. Parks a few years before she was registered to vote.
VOTER'S LEAGUE MEETING
But in the meantime, she encouraged everyone else to register, too.

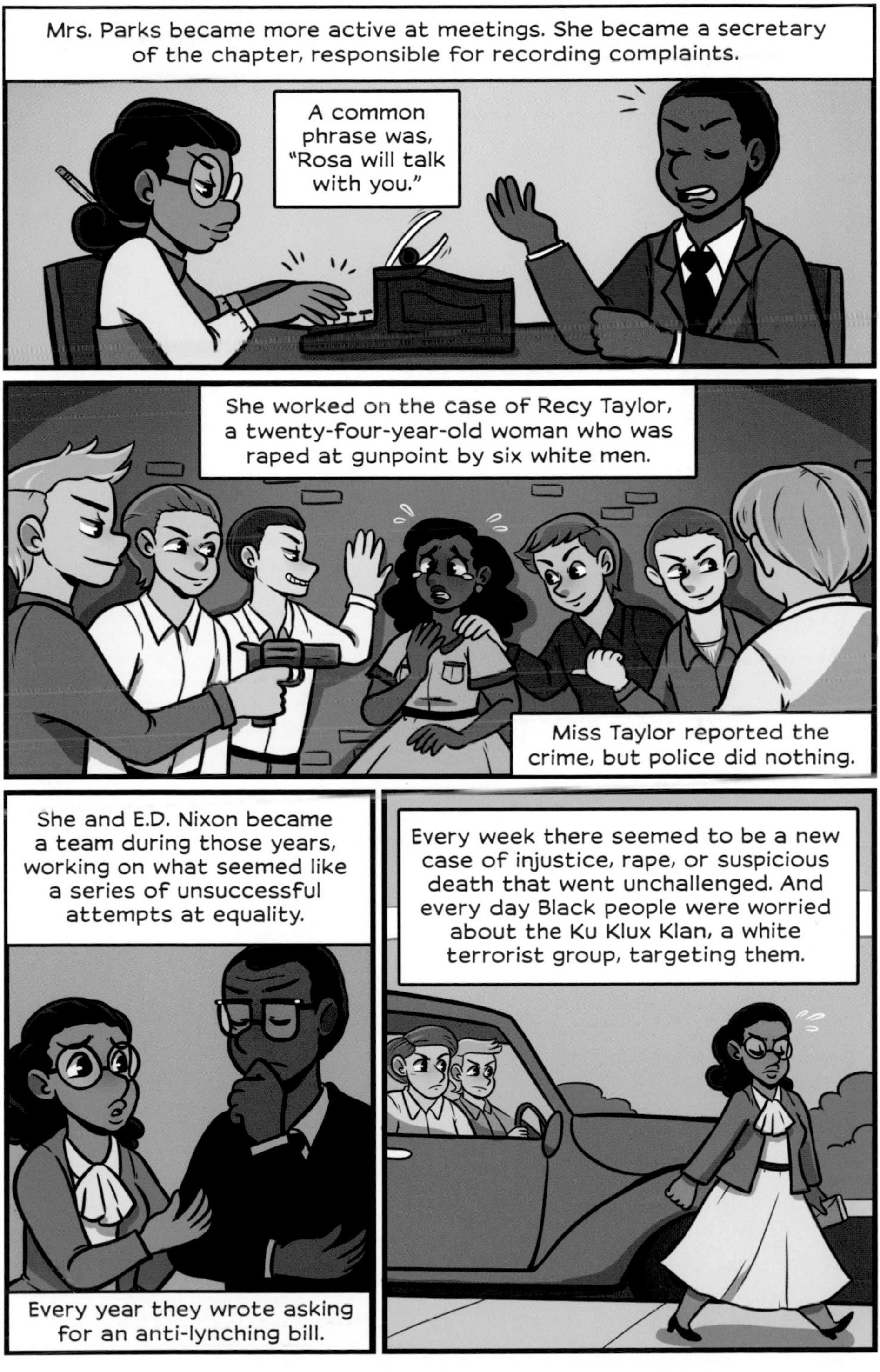
Mrs. Parks became more active at meetings. She became a secretary of the chapter, responsible for recording complaints.
A common phrase was, "Rosa will talk with you."
She worked on the case of Recy Taylor, a twenty-four-year-old woman who was raped at gunpoint by six white men.
Miss Taylor reported the crime, but police did nothing.
She and E.D. Nixon became a team during those years, working on what seemed like a series of unsuccessful attempts at equality.
Every year they wrote asking for an anti-lynching bill.
Every week there seemed to be a new case of injustice, rape, or suspicious death that went unchallenged. And every day Black people were worried about the Ku Klux Klan, a white terrorist group, targeting them.

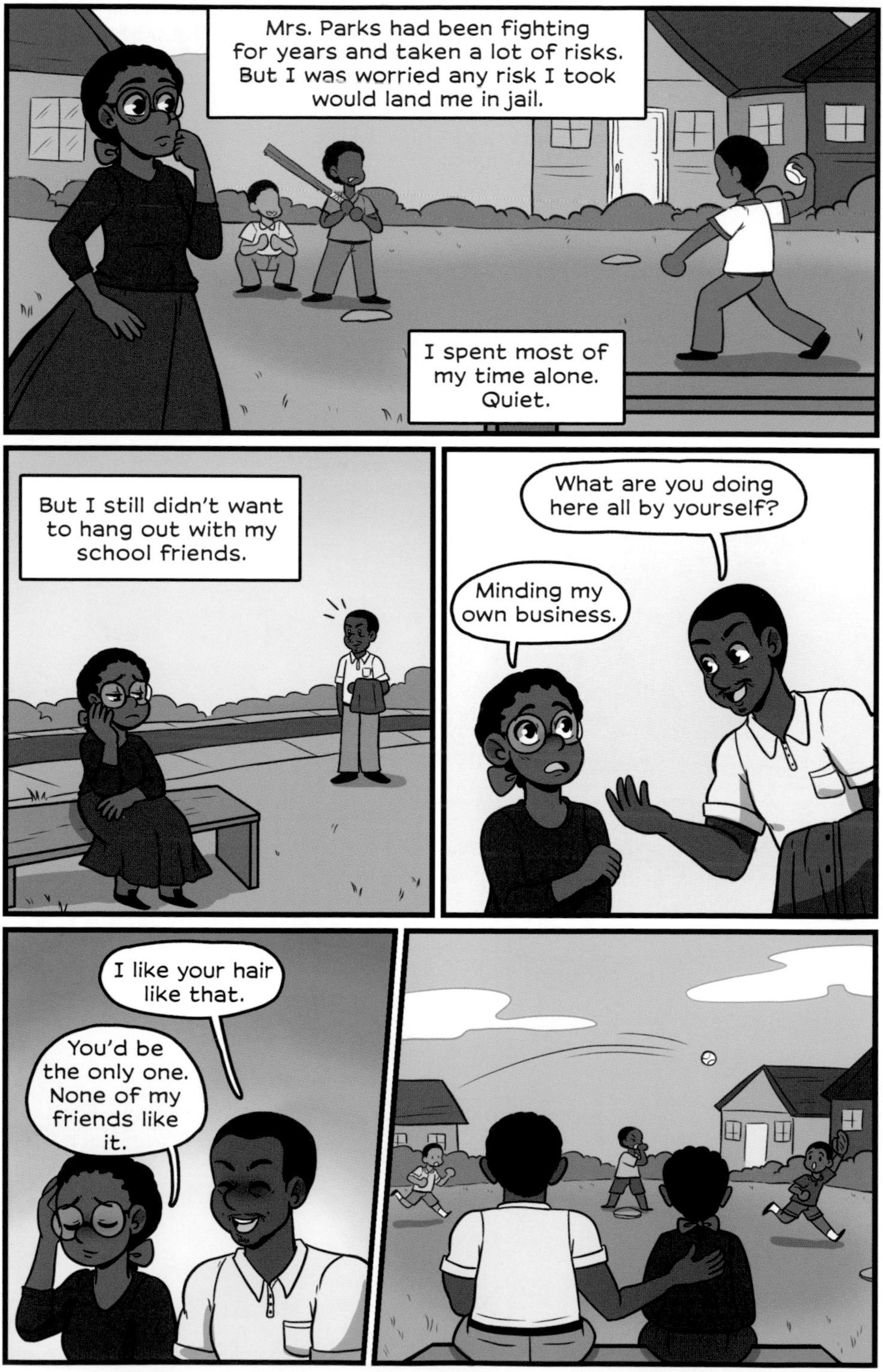
Mrs. Parks had been fighting for years and taken a lot of risks. But I was worried any risk I took would land me in jail.
I spent most of my time alone. Quiet.
But I still didn't want to hang out with my school friends.
What are you doing here all by yourself?
Minding my own business.
I like your hair like that.
You'd be the only one. None of my friends like it.

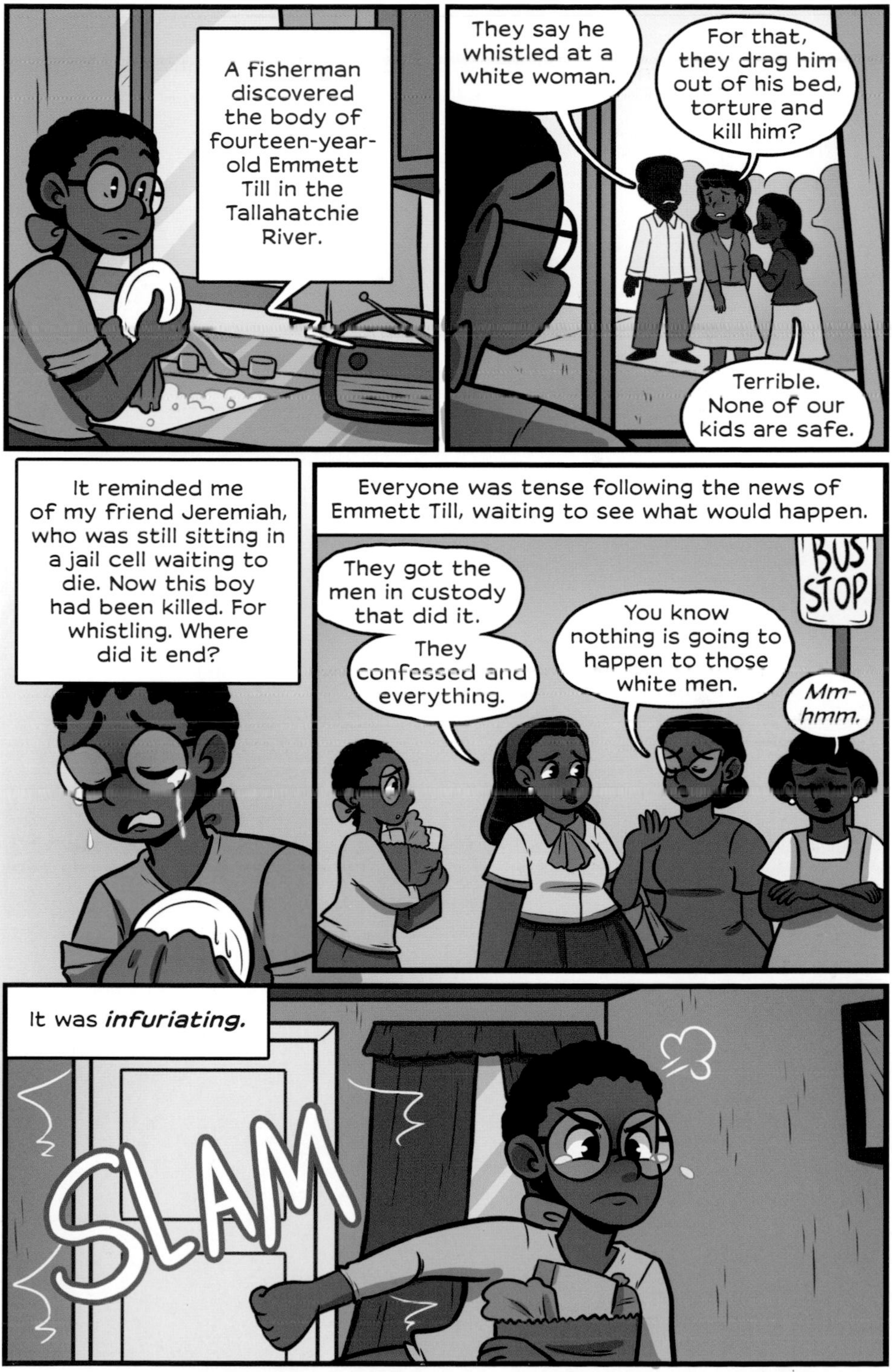
A fisherman discovered the body of fourteen-year-old Emmett Till in the Tallahatchie River.
They say he whistled at a white woman.
For that, they drag him out of his bed, torture and kill him?
Terrible. None of our kids are safe.
It reminded me of my friend Jeremiah, who was still sitting in a jail cell waiting to die. Now this boy had been killed. For whistling. Where did it end?
Everyone was tense following the news of Emmett Till, waiting to see what would happen.
BUS STOP
They got the men in custody that did it.
They confessed and everything.
You know nothing is going to happen to those white men.
Mm-hmm.
It was infuriating.
SLAM

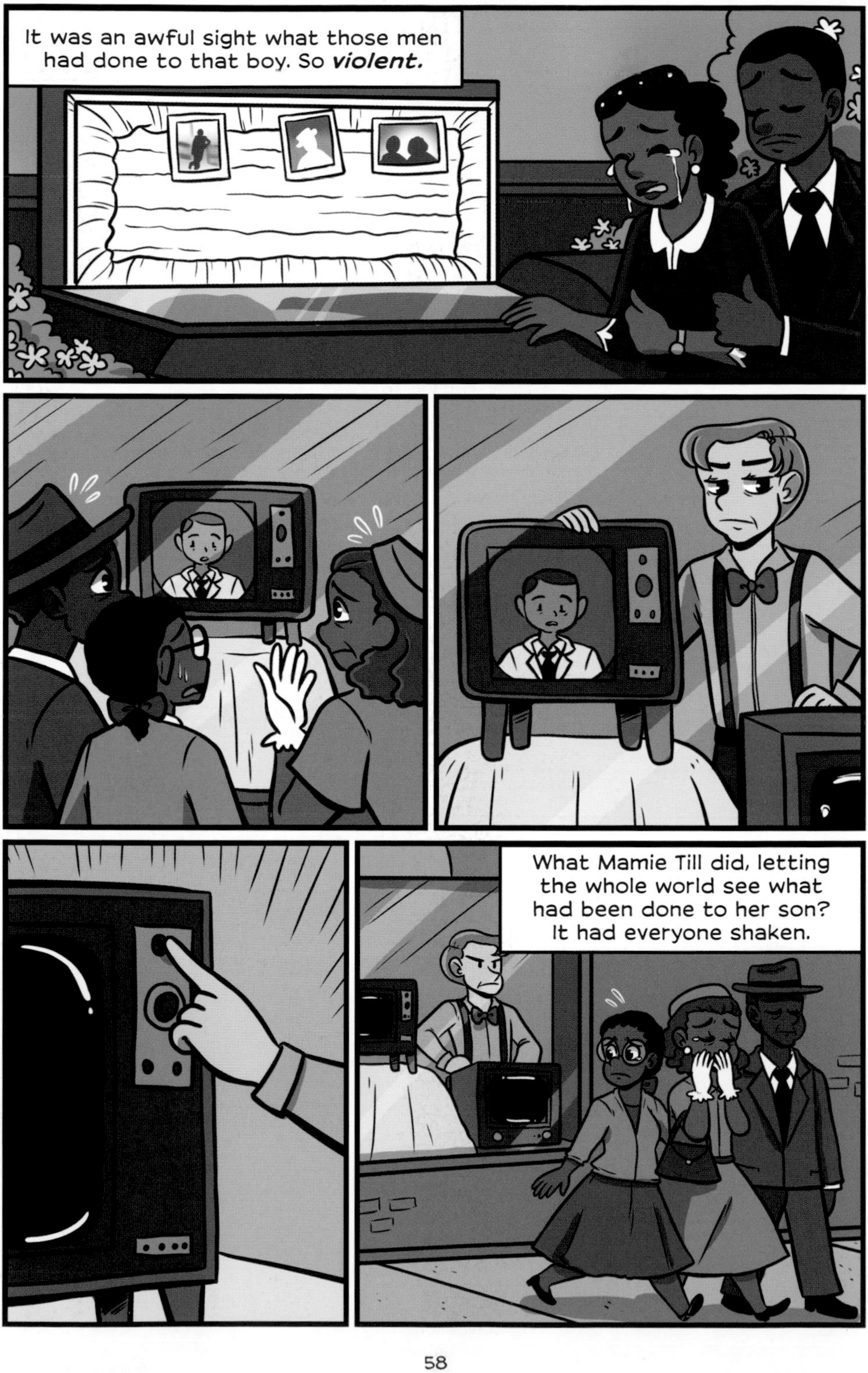
It was an awful sight what those men had done to that boy. So *violent.*
What Mamie Till did, letting the whole world see what had been done to her son? It had everyone shaken.

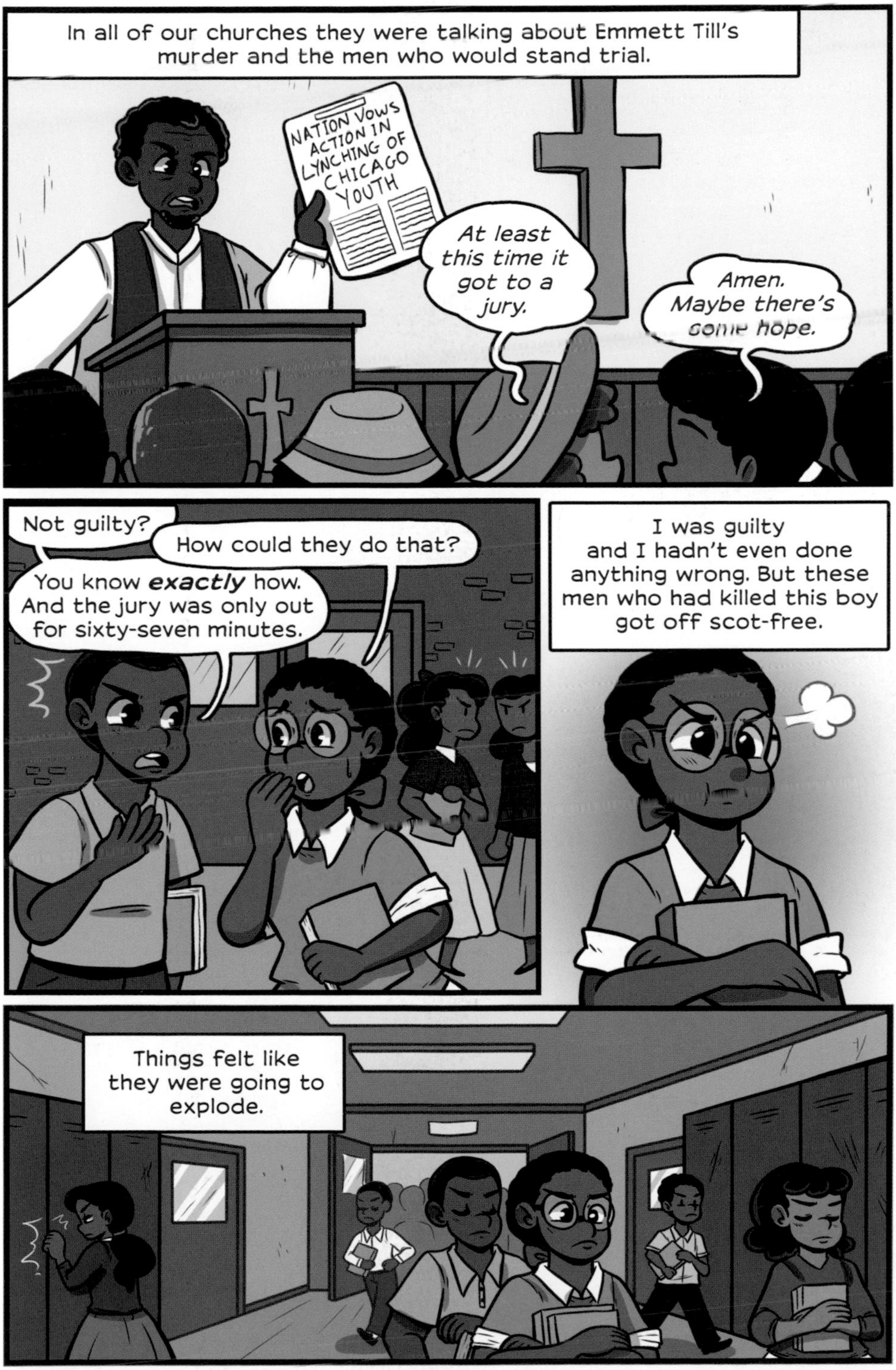

In all of our churches they were talking about Emmett Till's murder and the men who would stand trial.
NATION VOWS ACTION IN LYNCHING OF CHICAGO YOUTH
At least this time it got to a jury.
Amen. Maybe there's some hope.
Not guilty?
How could they do that?
You know **exactly** how. And the jury was only out for sixty-seven minutes.
I was guilty and I hadn't even done anything wrong. But these men who had killed this boy got off scot-free.
Things felt like they were going to explode.

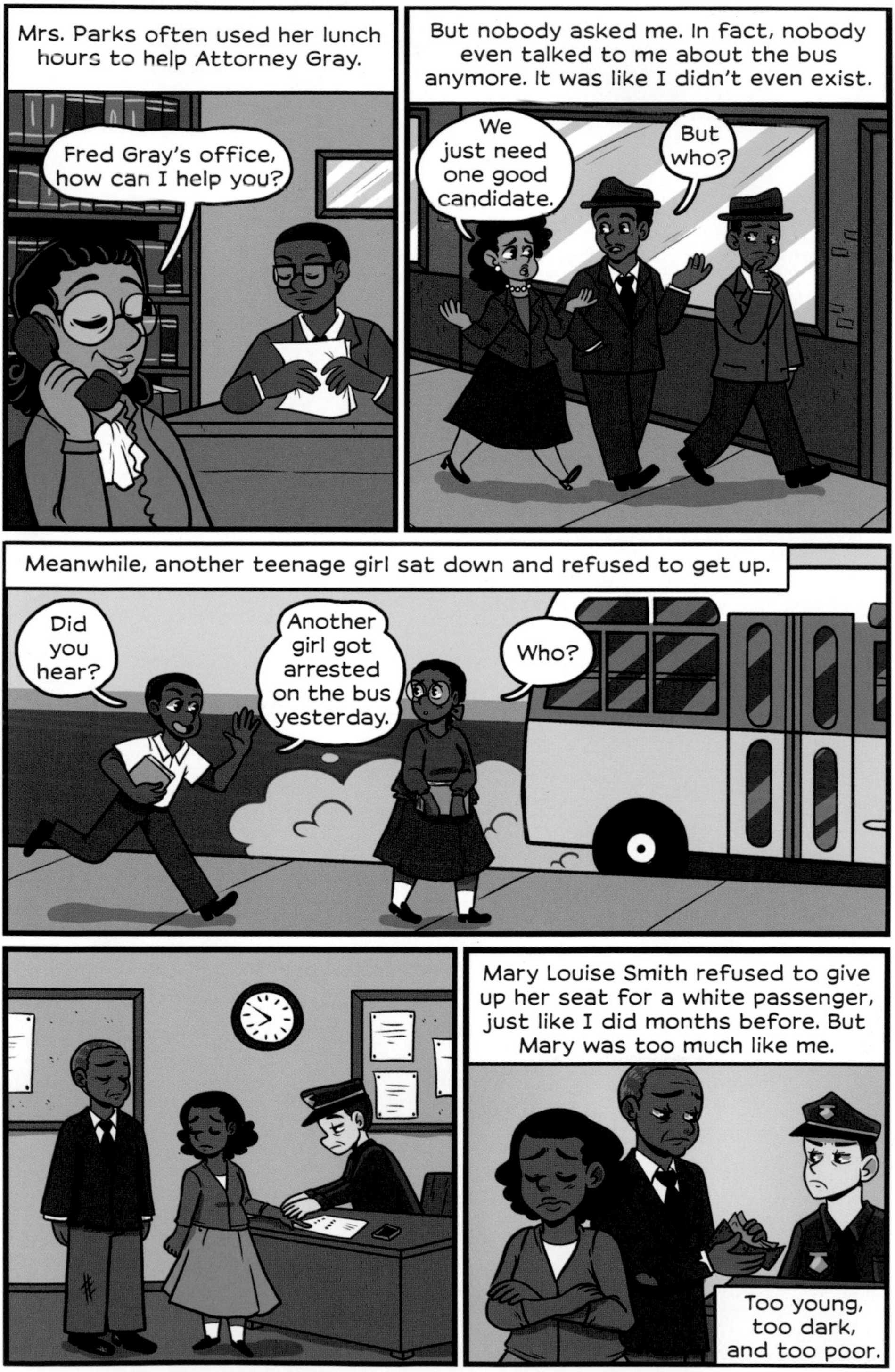
Mrs. Parks often used her lunch hours to help Attorney Gray.
Fred Gray's office, how can I help you?
But nobody asked me. In fact, nobody even talked to me about the bus anymore. It was like I didn't even exist.
We just need one good candidate.
But who?
Meanwhile, another teenage girl sat down and refused to get up.
Did you hear?
Another girl got arrested on the bus yesterday.
Who?
Mary Louise Smith refused to give up her seat for a white passenger, just like I did months before. But Mary was too much like me.
Too young, too dark, and too poor.

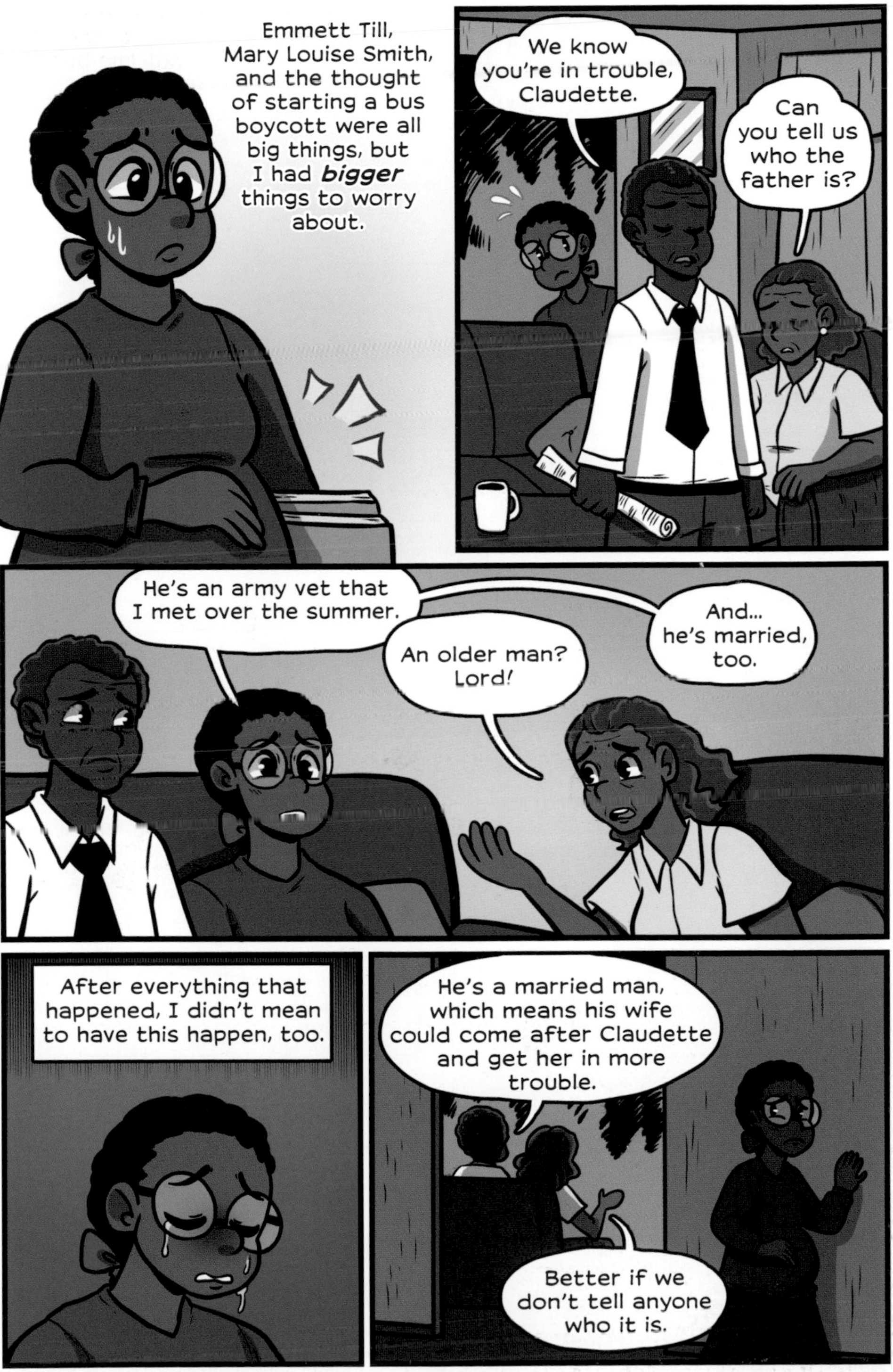
Emmett Till, Mary Louise Smith, and the thought of starting a bus boycott were all big things, but I had **bigger** things to worry about.
We know you're in trouble, Claudette.
Can you tell us who the father is?
He's an army vet that I met over the summer.
An older man? Lord!
And... he's married, too.
After everything that happened, I didn't mean to have this happen, too.
He's a married man, which means his wife could come after Claudette and get her in more trouble.
Better if we don't tell anyone who it is.

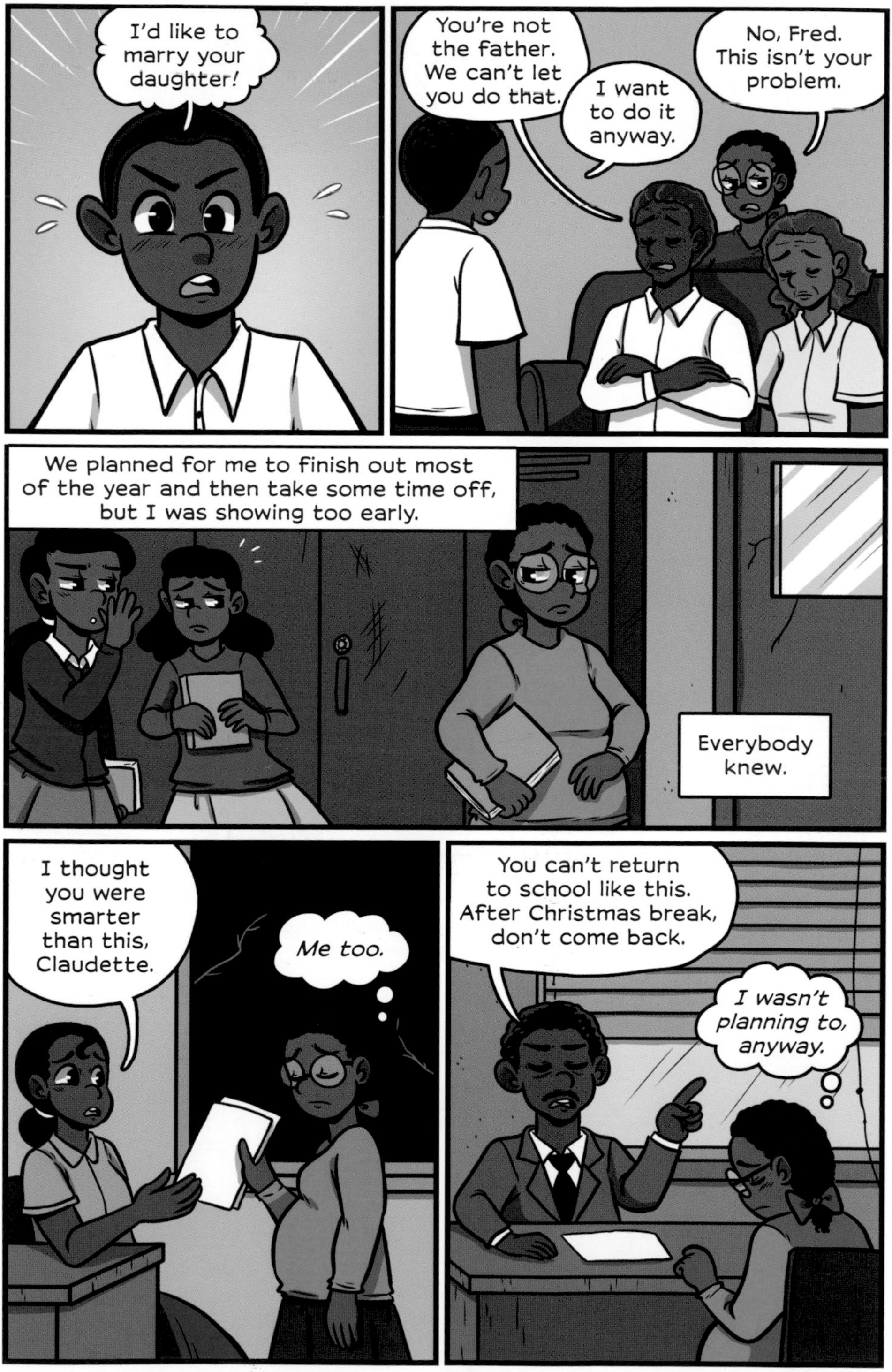
I'd like to marry your daughter!
You're not the father. We can't let you do that.
I want to do it anyway.
No, Fred. This isn't your problem.
We planned for me to finish out most of the year and then take some time off, but I was showing too early.
Everybody knew.
I thought you were smarter than this, Claudette.
Me too.
You can't return to school like this. After Christmas break, don't come back.
I wasn't planning to, anyway.

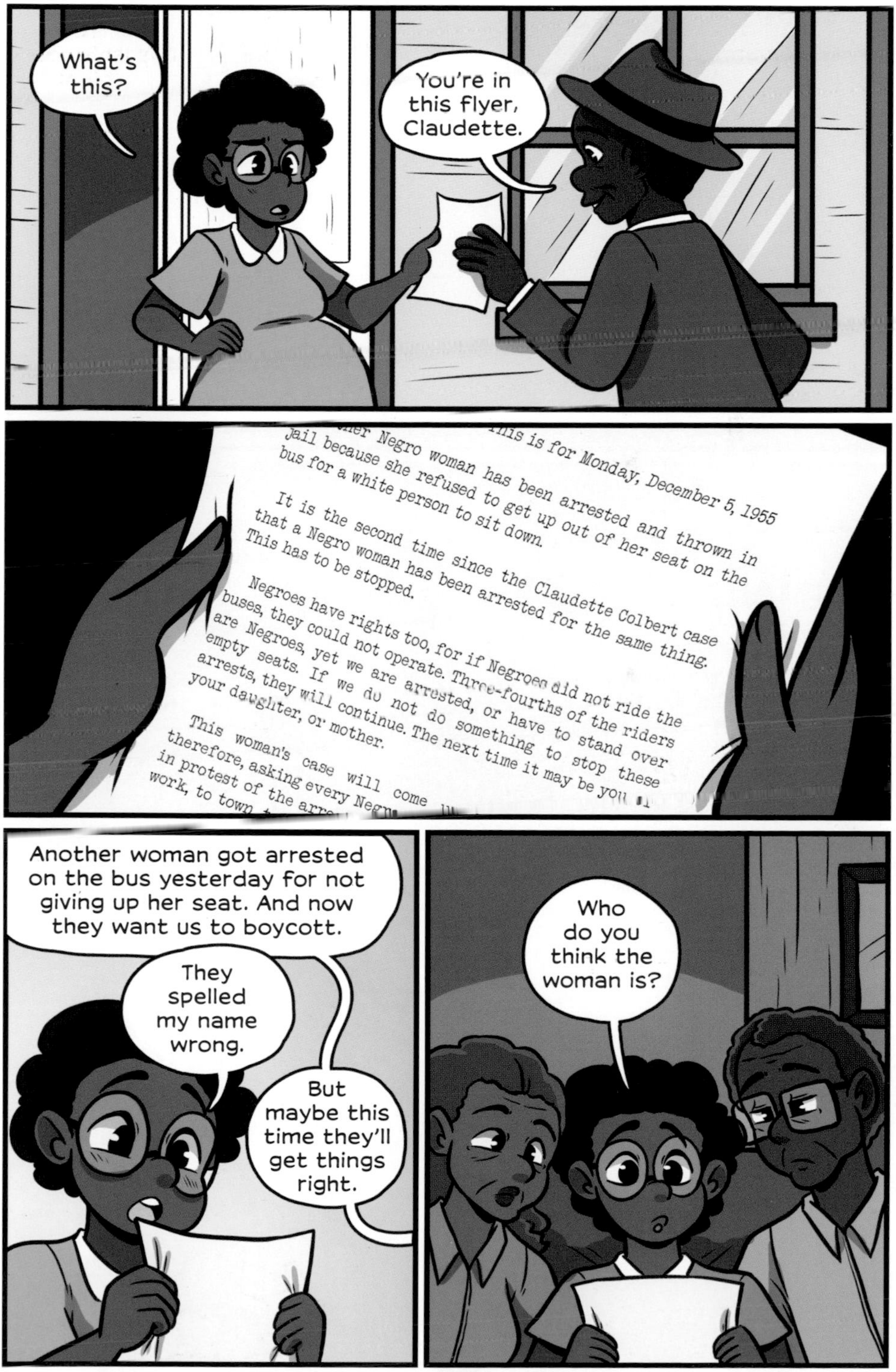
What's this?
You're in this flyer, Claudette.
This is for Monday, December 5, 1955
Negro woman has been arrested and thrown in jail because she refused to get up out of her seat on the bus for a white person to sit down.
It is the second time since the Claudette Colbert case that a Negro woman has been arrested for the same thing. This has to be stopped.
Negroes have rights too, for if Negroes did not ride the buses, they could not operate. Three-fourths of the riders are Negroes, yet we are arrested, or have to stand over empty seats. If we do not do something to stop these arrests, they will continue. The next time it may be you, or your daughter, or mother.
This woman's case will come
therefore, asking every Negro
in protest of the arrest
work, to town
Another woman got arrested on the bus yesterday for not giving up her seat. And now they want us to boycott.
They spelled my name wrong.
But maybe this time they'll get things right.
Who do you think the woman is?

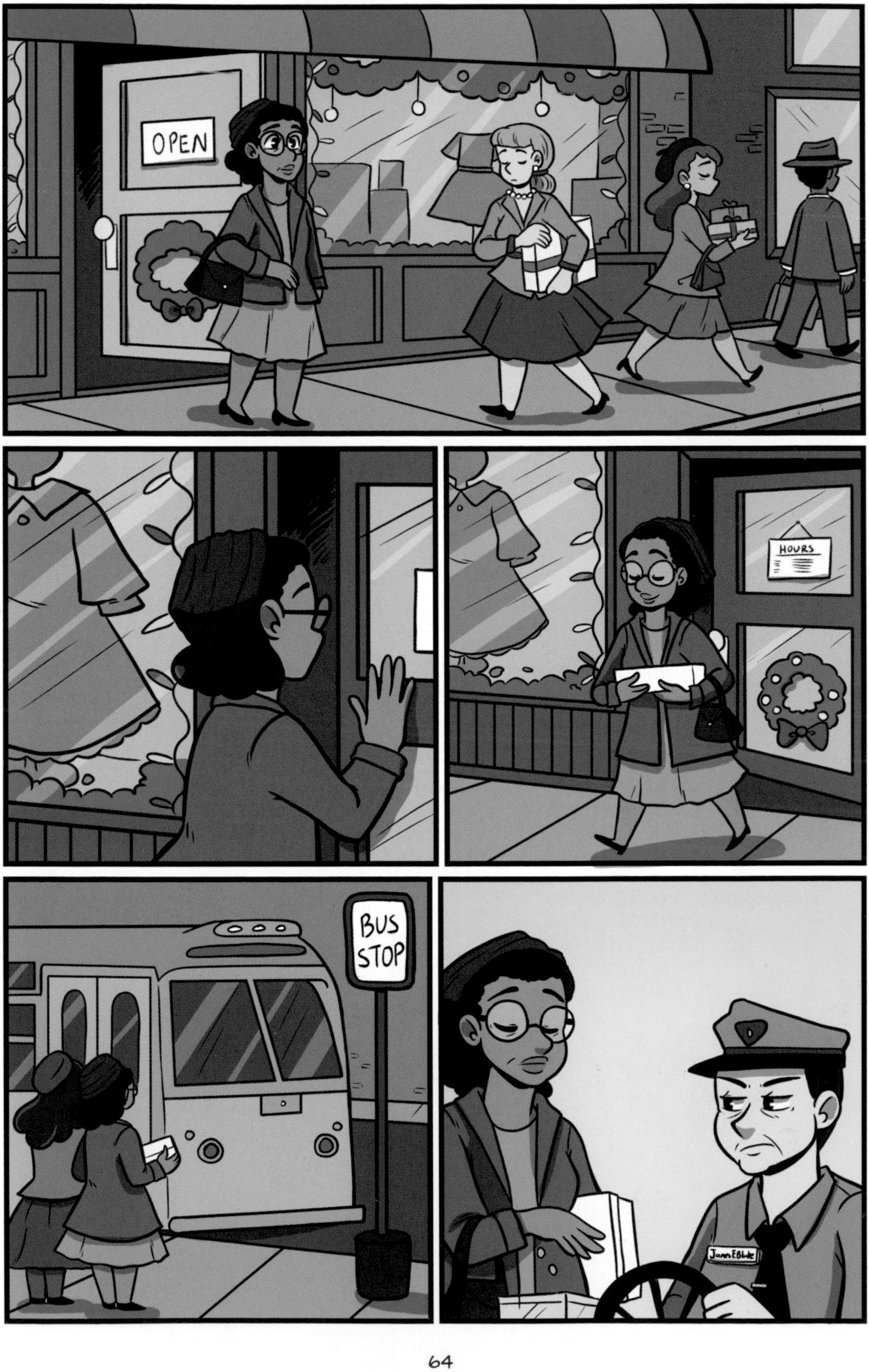

OPEN
HOURS
BUS STOP
James F Blake

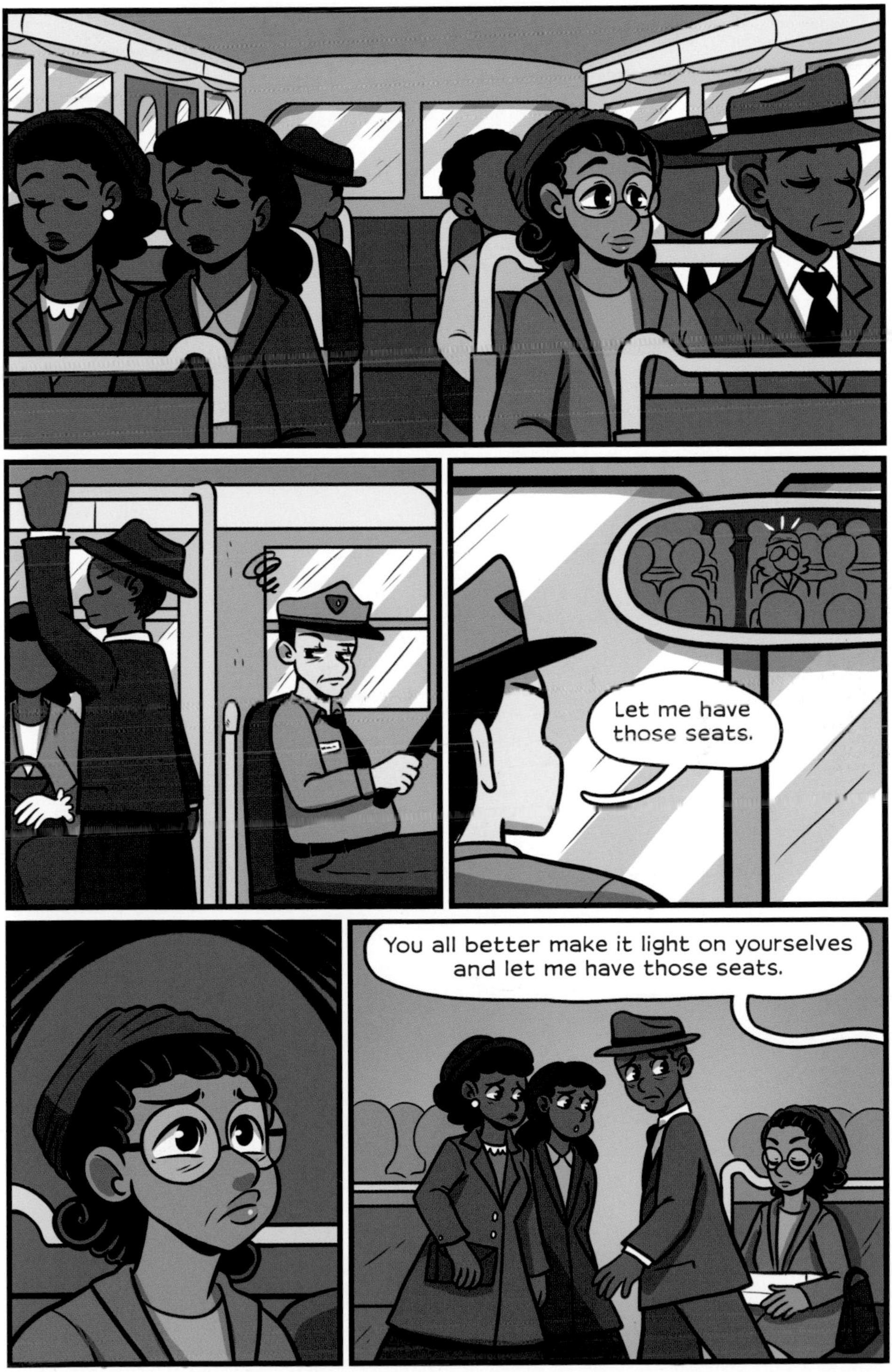
Let me have those seats.
You all better make it light on yourselves and let me have those seats.

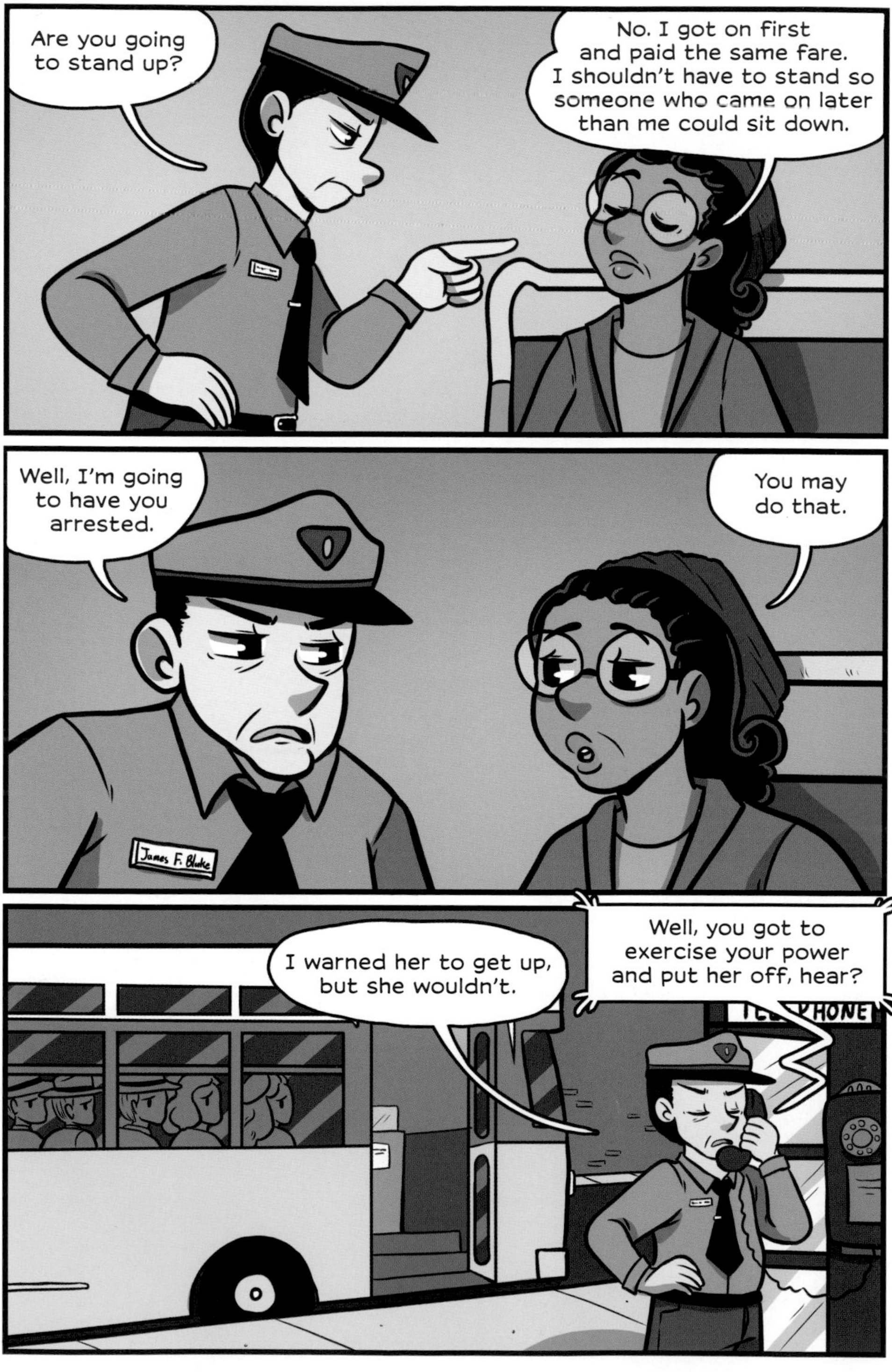
Are you going to stand up?
No. I got on first and paid the same fare. I shouldn't have to stand so someone who came on later than me could sit down.
Well, I'm going to have you arrested.
You may do that.
James F. Blake
I warned her to get up, but she wouldn't.
Well, you got to exercise your power and put her off, hear?

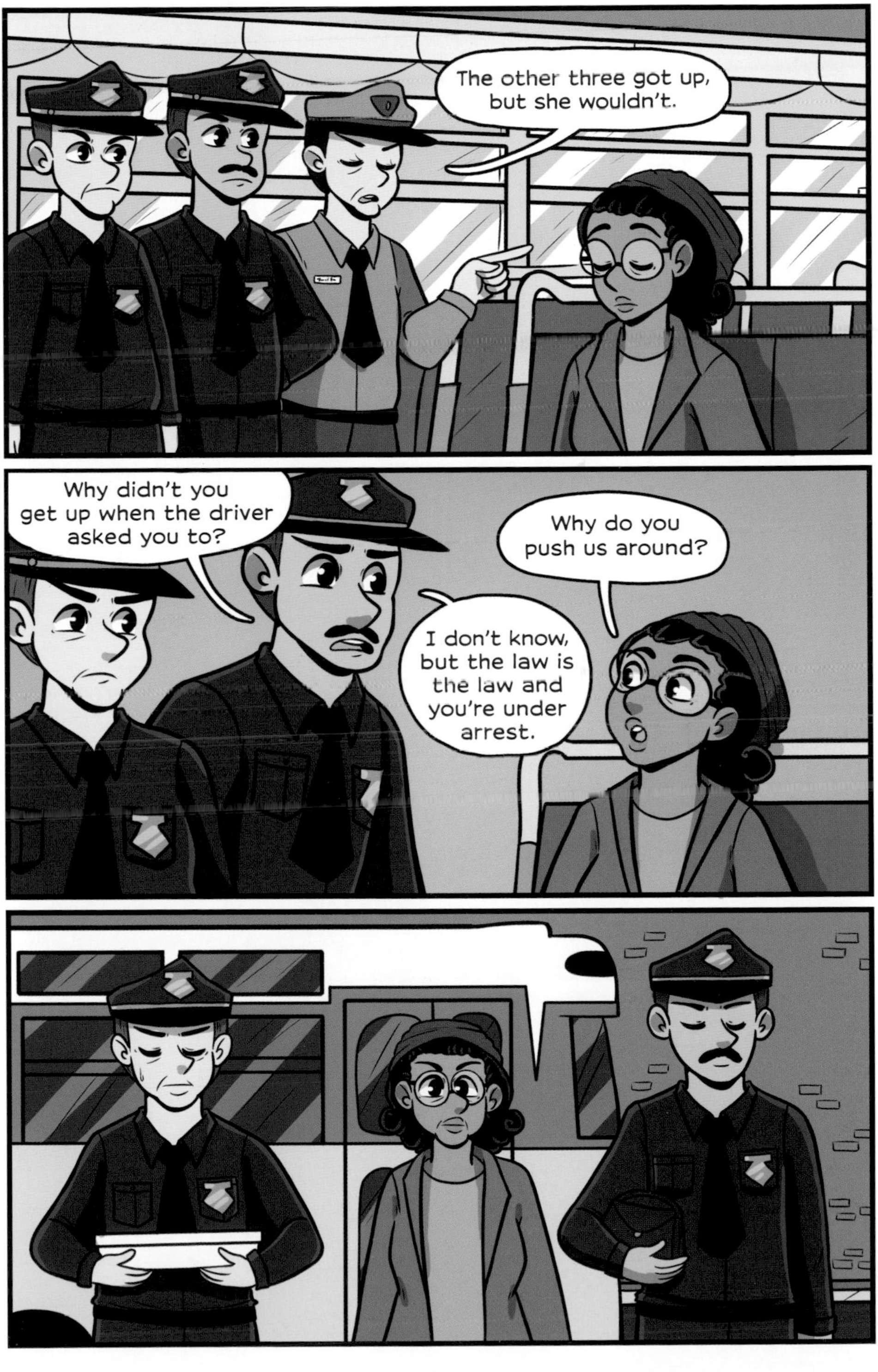

The other three got up, but she wouldn't.
Why didn't you get up when the driver asked you to?
Why do you push us around?
I don't know, but the law is the law and you're under arrest.

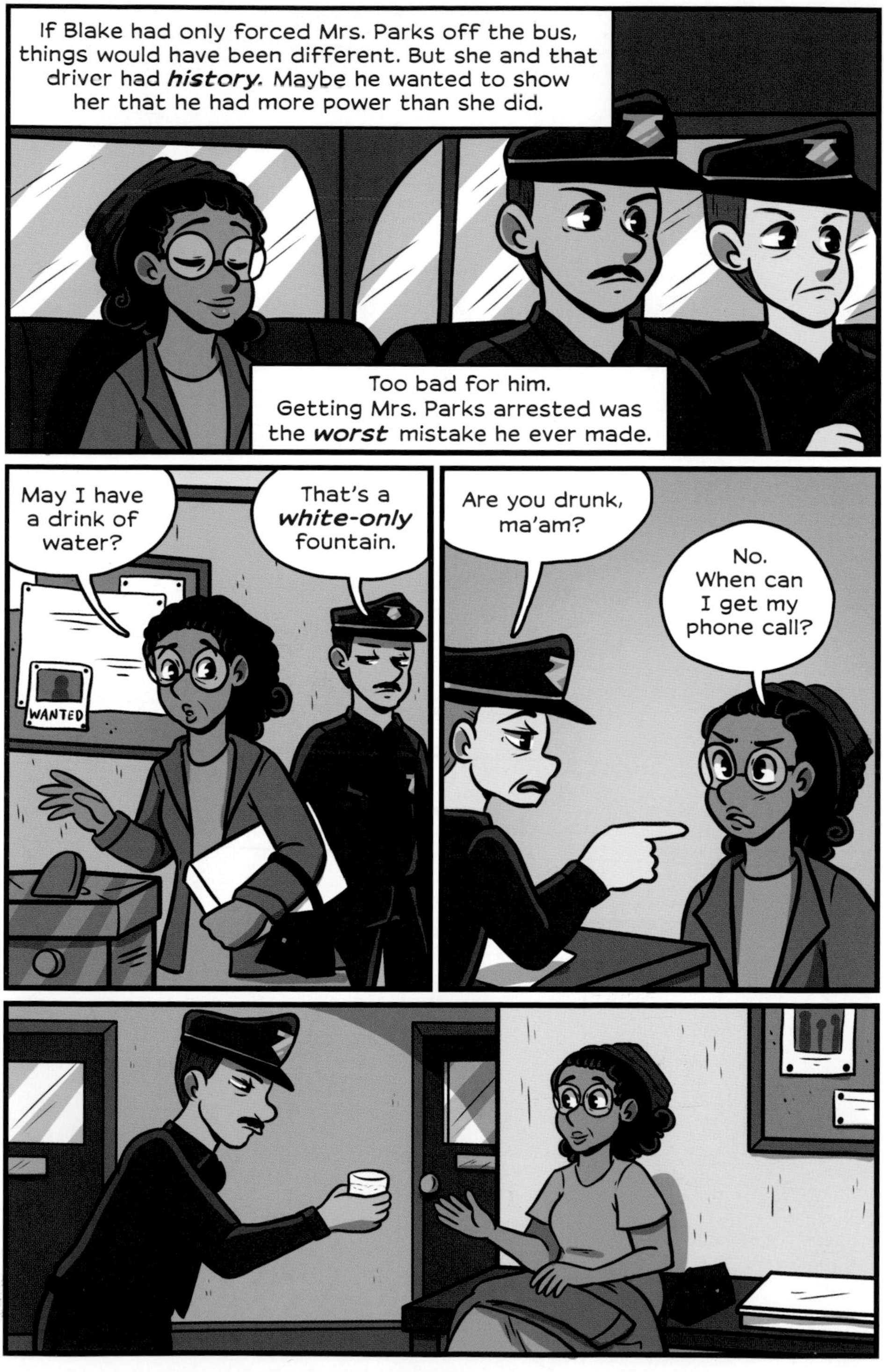
If Blake had only forced Mrs. Parks off the bus, things would have been different. But she and that driver had history. Maybe he wanted to show her that he had more power than she did.
Too bad for him. Getting Mrs. Parks arrested was the worst mistake he ever made.
May I have a drink of water?
That's a white-only fountain.
WANTED
Are you drunk, ma'am?
No. When can I get my phone call?

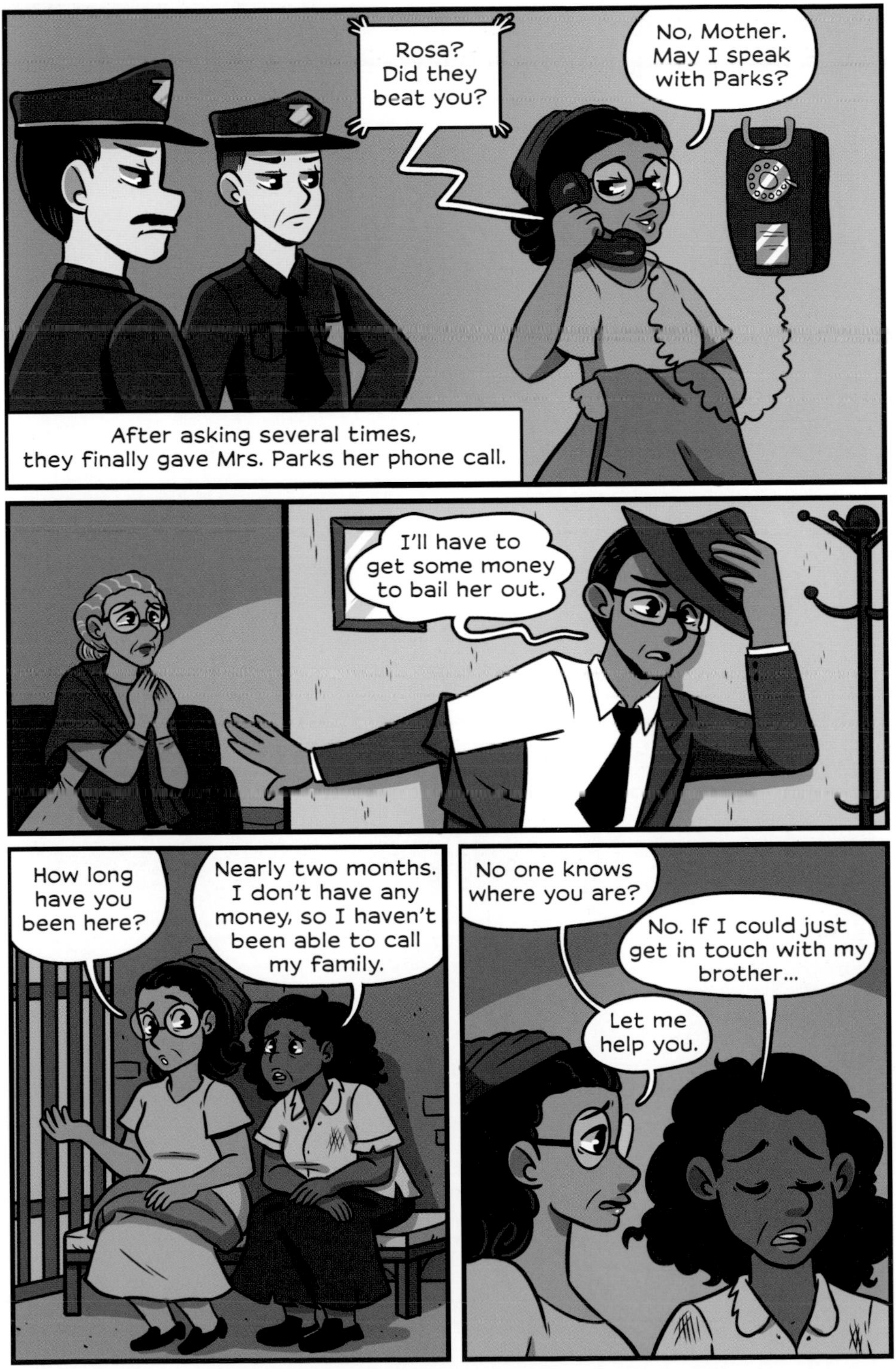

Rosa? Did they beat you?
No, Mother. May I speak with Parks?
After asking several times, they finally gave Mrs. Parks her phone call.
I'll have to get some money to bail her out.
How long have you been here?
Nearly two months. I don't have any money, so I haven't been able to call my family.
No one knows where you are?
No. If I could just get in touch with my brother...
Let me help you.

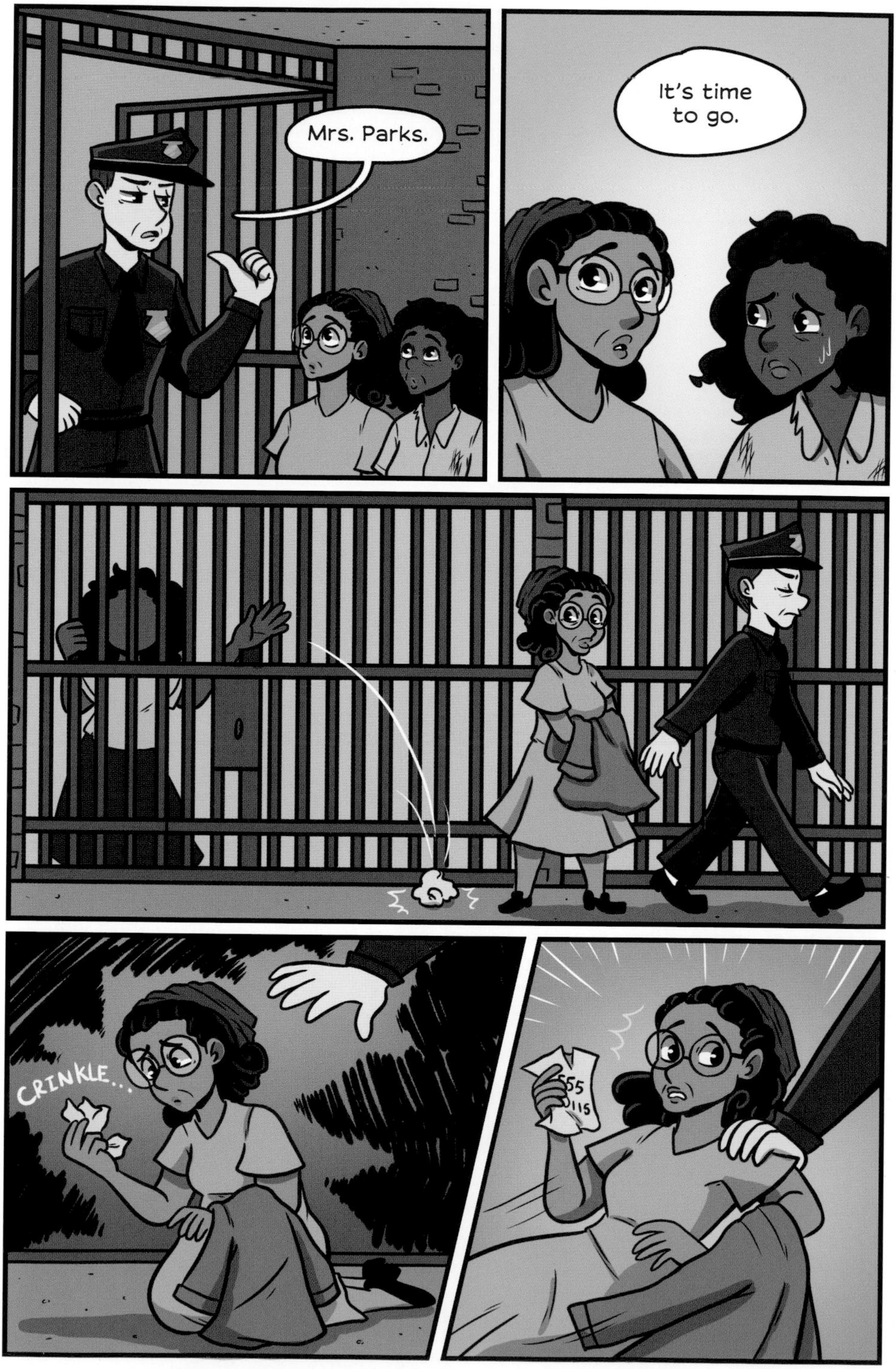
Mrs. Parks.
It's time to go.
CRINKLE...

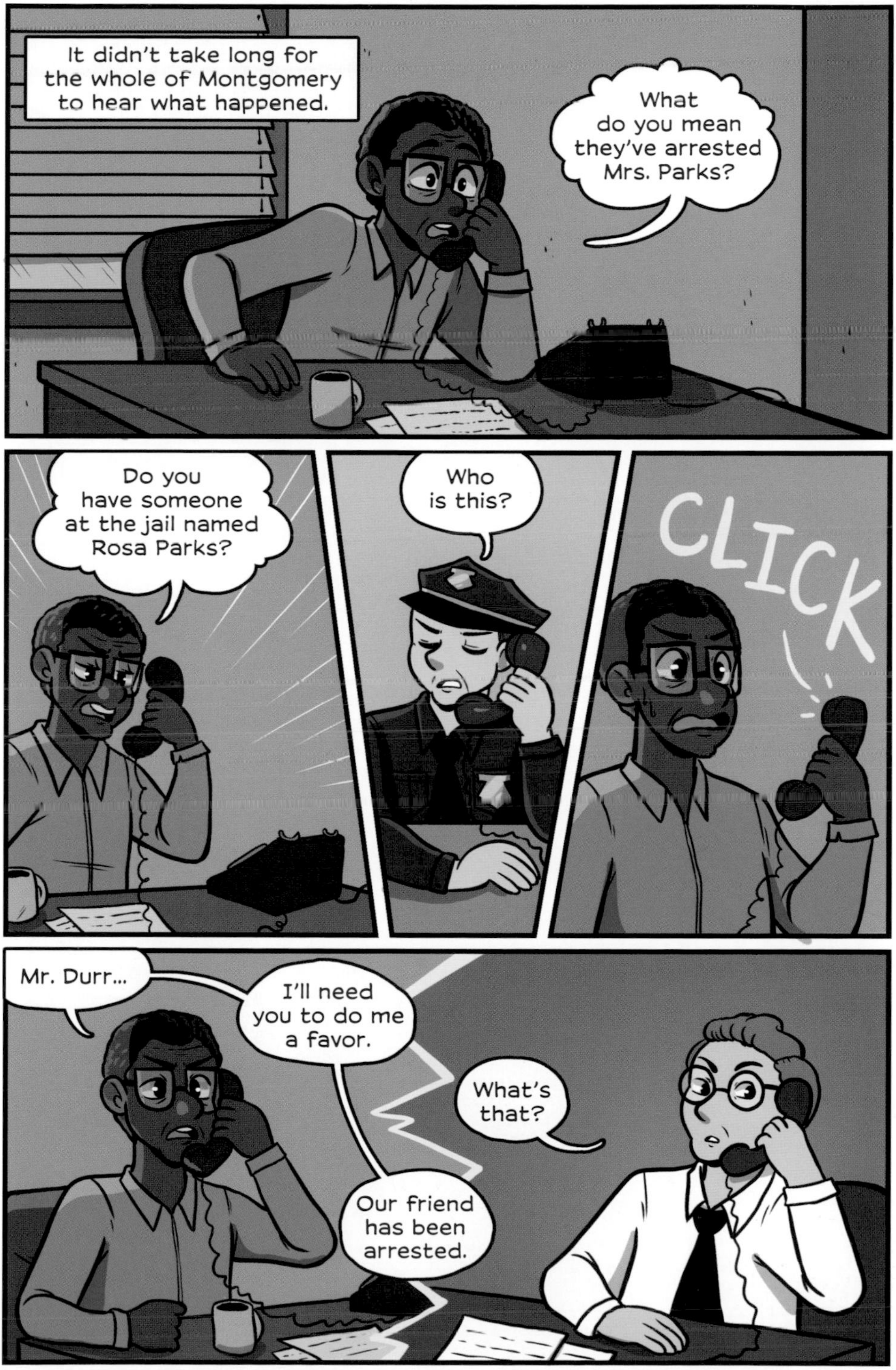

It didn't take long for the whole of Montgomery to hear what happened.
What do you mean they've arrested Mrs. Parks?
Do you have someone at the jail named Rosa Parks?
Who is this?
CLICK
Mr. Durr...
I'll need you to do me a favor.
What's that?
Our friend has been arrested.

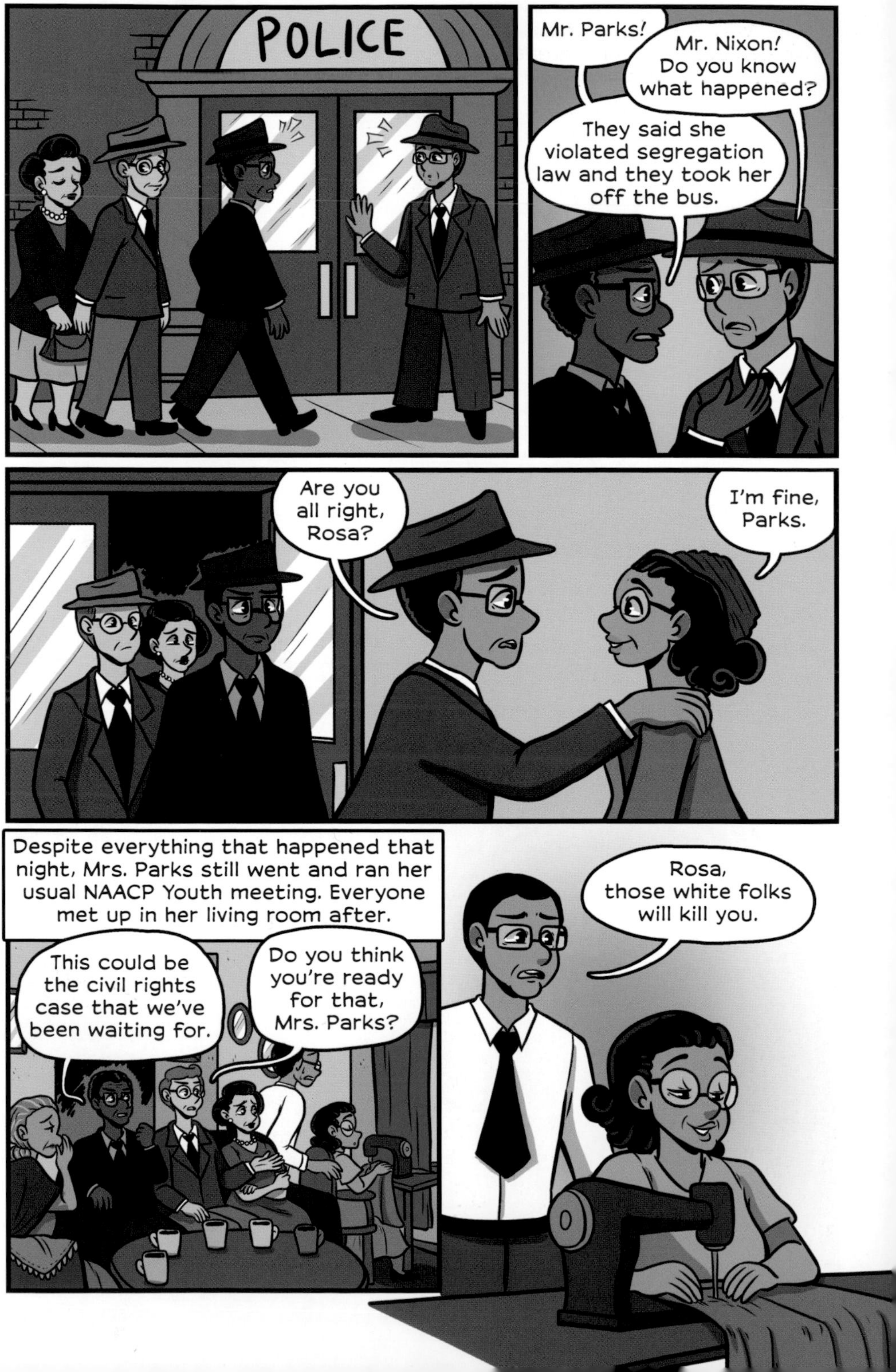
POLICE
Mr. Parks!
Mr. Nixon! Do you know what happened?
They said she violated segregation law and they took her off the bus.
Are you all right, Rosa?
I'm fine, Parks.
Despite everything that happened that night, Mrs. Parks still went and ran her usual NAACP Youth meeting. Everyone met up in her living room after.
This could be the civil rights case that we've been waiting for.
Do you think you're ready for that, Mrs. Parks?
Rosa, those white folks will kill you.

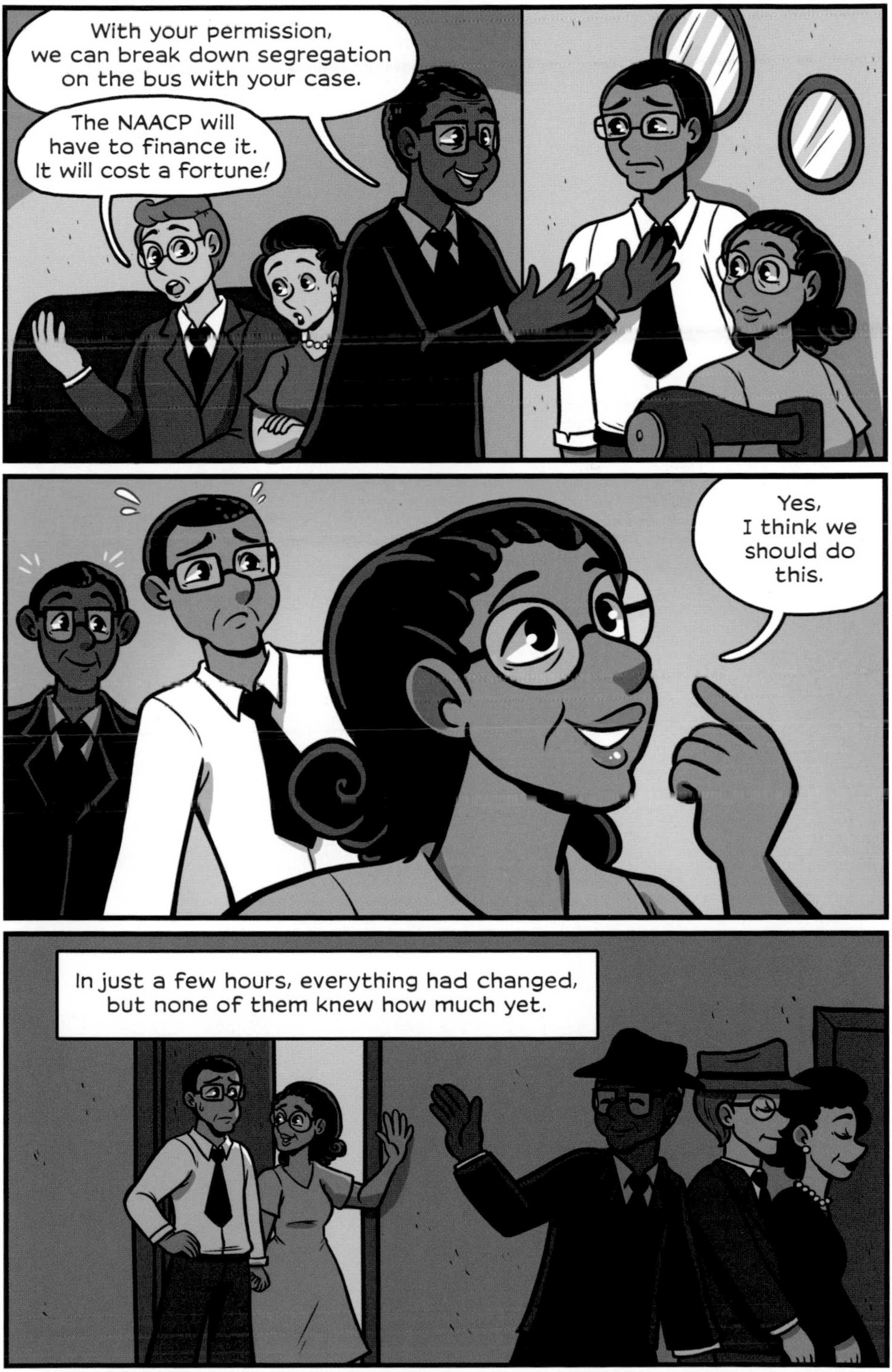

With your permission, we can break down segregation on the bus with your case.
The NAACP will have to finance it. It will cost a fortune!
Yes, I think we should do this.
In just a few hours, everything had changed, but none of them knew how much yet.

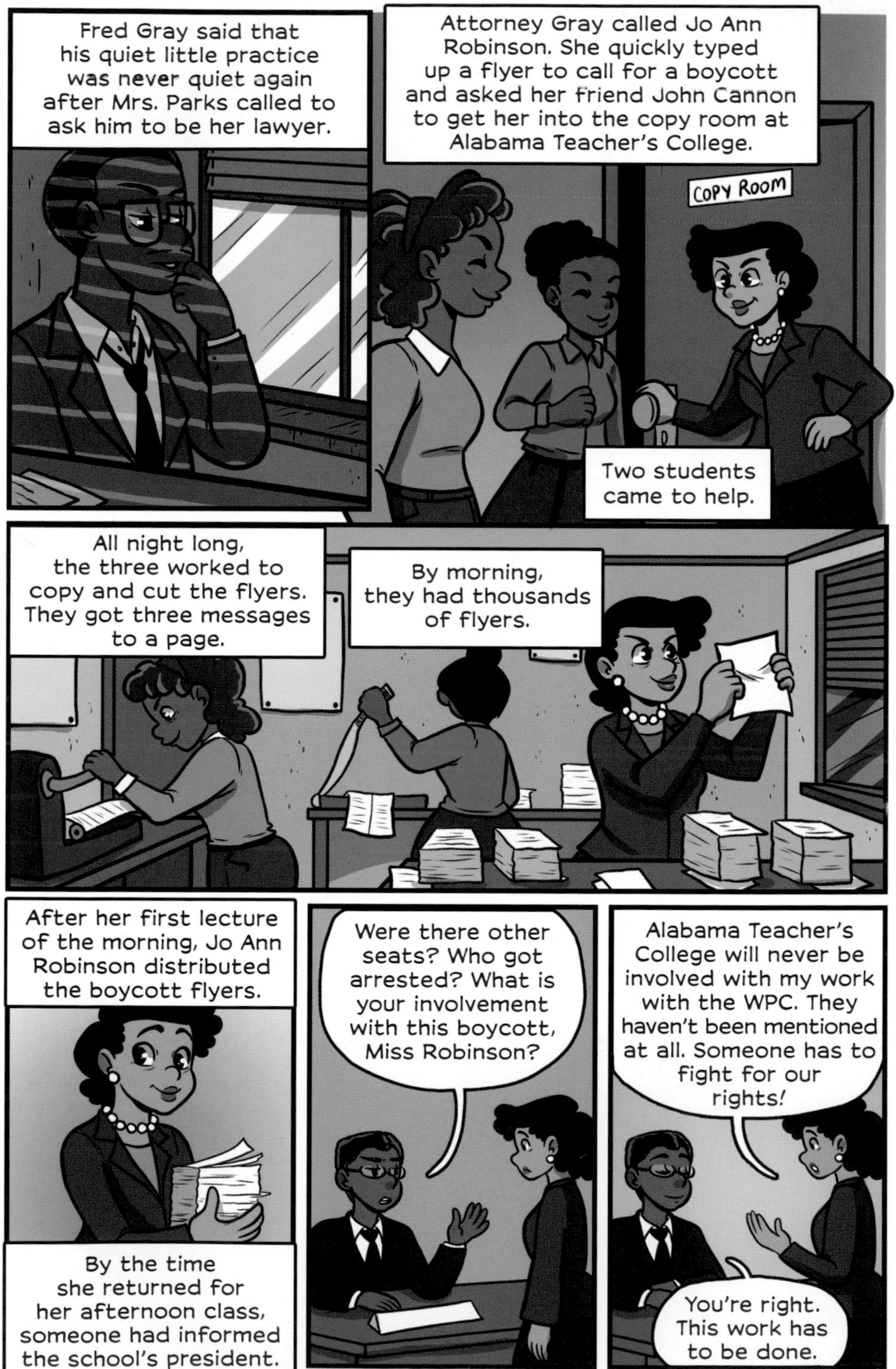
Fred Gray said that his quiet little practice was never quiet again after Mrs. Parks called to ask him to be her lawyer.
Attorney Gray called Jo Ann Robinson. She quickly typed up a flyer to call for a boycott and asked her friend John Cannon to get her into the copy room at Alabama Teacher's College.
COPY ROOM
Two students came to help.
All night long, the three worked to copy and cut the flyers. They got three messages to a page.
By morning, they had thousands of flyers.
After her first lecture of the morning, Jo Ann Robinson distributed the boycott flyers.
By the time she returned for her afternoon class, someone had informed the school's president.
Were there other seats? Who got arrested? What is your involvement with this boycott, Miss Robinson?
Alabama Teacher's College will never be involved with my work with the WPC. They haven't been mentioned at all. Someone has to fight for our rights!
You're right. This work has to be done.

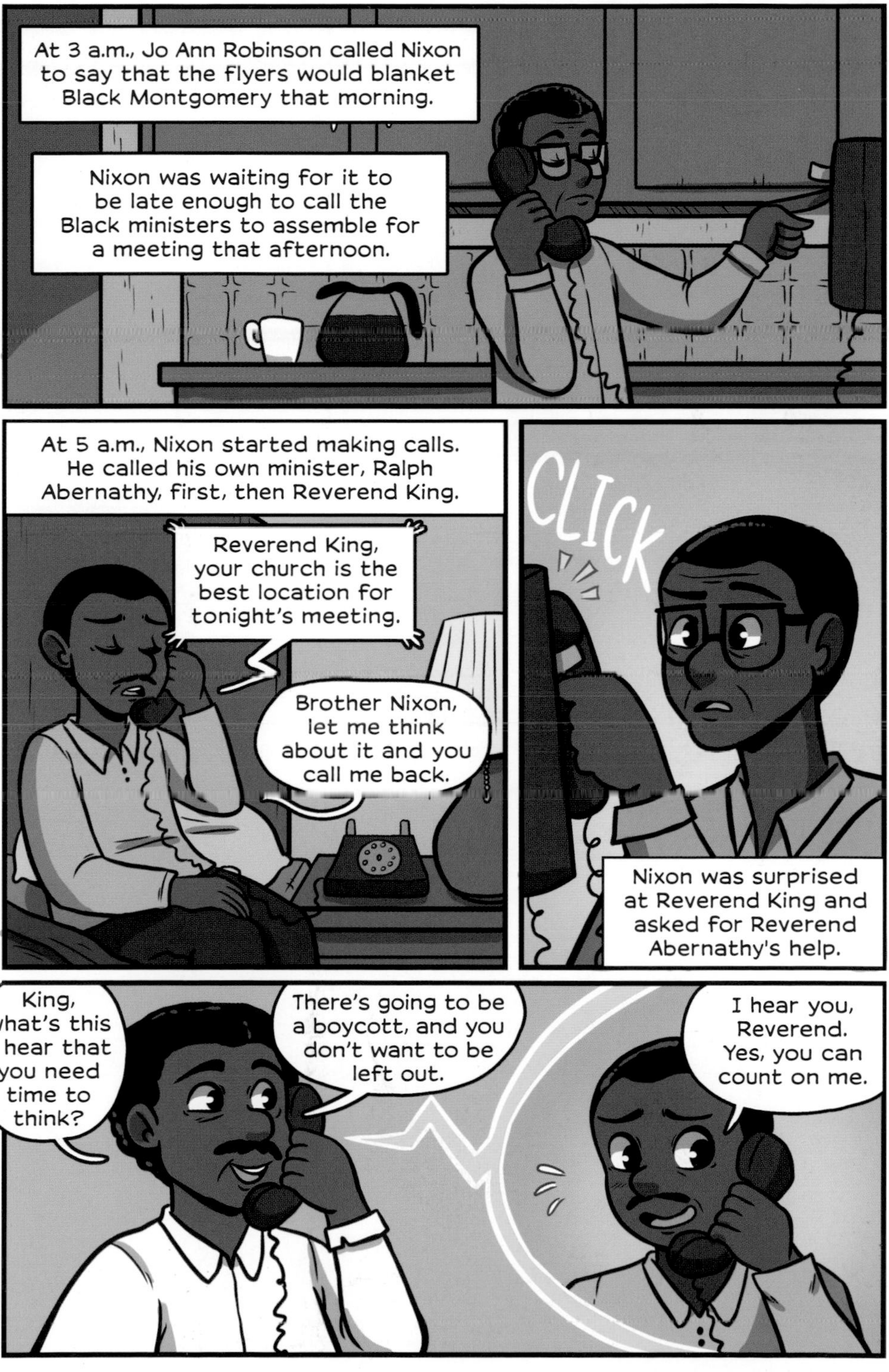
At 3 a.m., Jo Ann Robinson called Nixon to say that the flyers would blanket Black Montgomery that morning.
Nixon was waiting for it to be late enough to call the Black ministers to assemble for a meeting that afternoon.
At 5 a.m., Nixon started making calls. He called his own minister, Ralph Abernathy, first, then Reverend King.
Reverend King, your church is the best location for tonight's meeting.
Brother Nixon, let me think about it and you call me back.
CLICK
Nixon was surprised at Reverend King and asked for Reverend Abernathy's help.
King, what's this I hear that you need time to think?
There's going to be a boycott, and you don't want to be left out.
I hear you, Reverend. Yes, you can count on me.

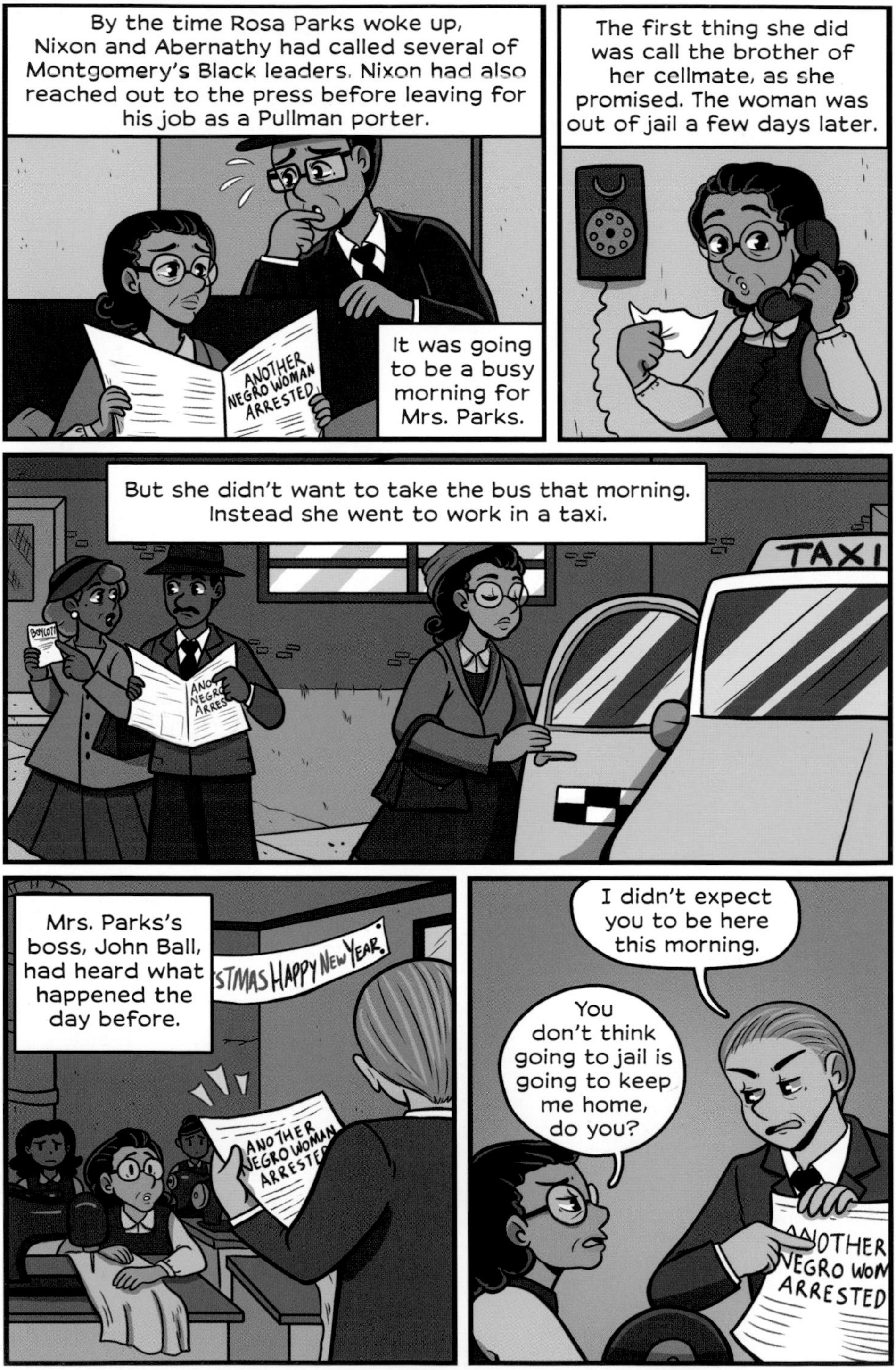
By the time Rosa Parks woke up, Nixon and Abernathy had called several of Montgomery's Black leaders. Nixon had also reached out to the press before leaving for his job as a Pullman porter.
ANOTHER NEGRO WOMAN ARRESTED
It was going to be a busy morning for Mrs. Parks.
The first thing she did was call the brother of her cellmate, as she promised. The woman was out of jail a few days later.
But she didn't want to take the bus that morning. Instead she went to work in a taxi.
TAXI
Mrs. Parks's boss, John Ball, had heard what happened the day before.
I didn't expect you to be here this morning.
You don't think going to jail is going to keep me home, do you?

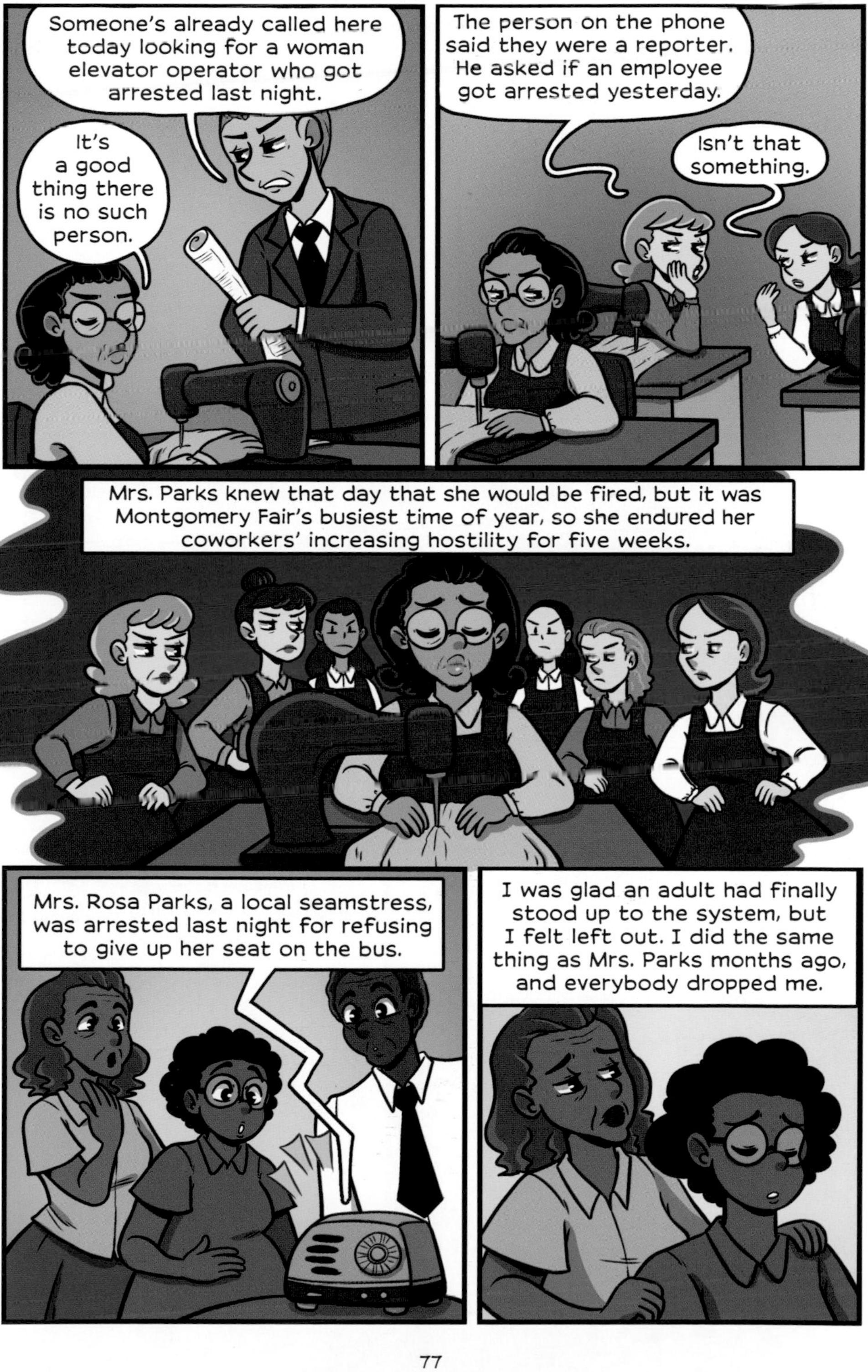
Someone's already called here today looking for a woman elevator operator who got arrested last night.
It's a good thing there is no such person.
The person on the phone said they were a reporter. He asked if an employee got arrested yesterday.
Isn't that something.
Mrs. Parks knew that day that she would be fired, but it was Montgomery Fair's busiest time of year, so she endured her coworkers' increasing hostility for five weeks.
Mrs. Rosa Parks, a local seamstress, was arrested last night for refusing to give up her seat on the bus.
I was glad an adult had finally stood up to the system, but I felt left out. I did the same thing as Mrs. Parks months ago, and everybody dropped me.

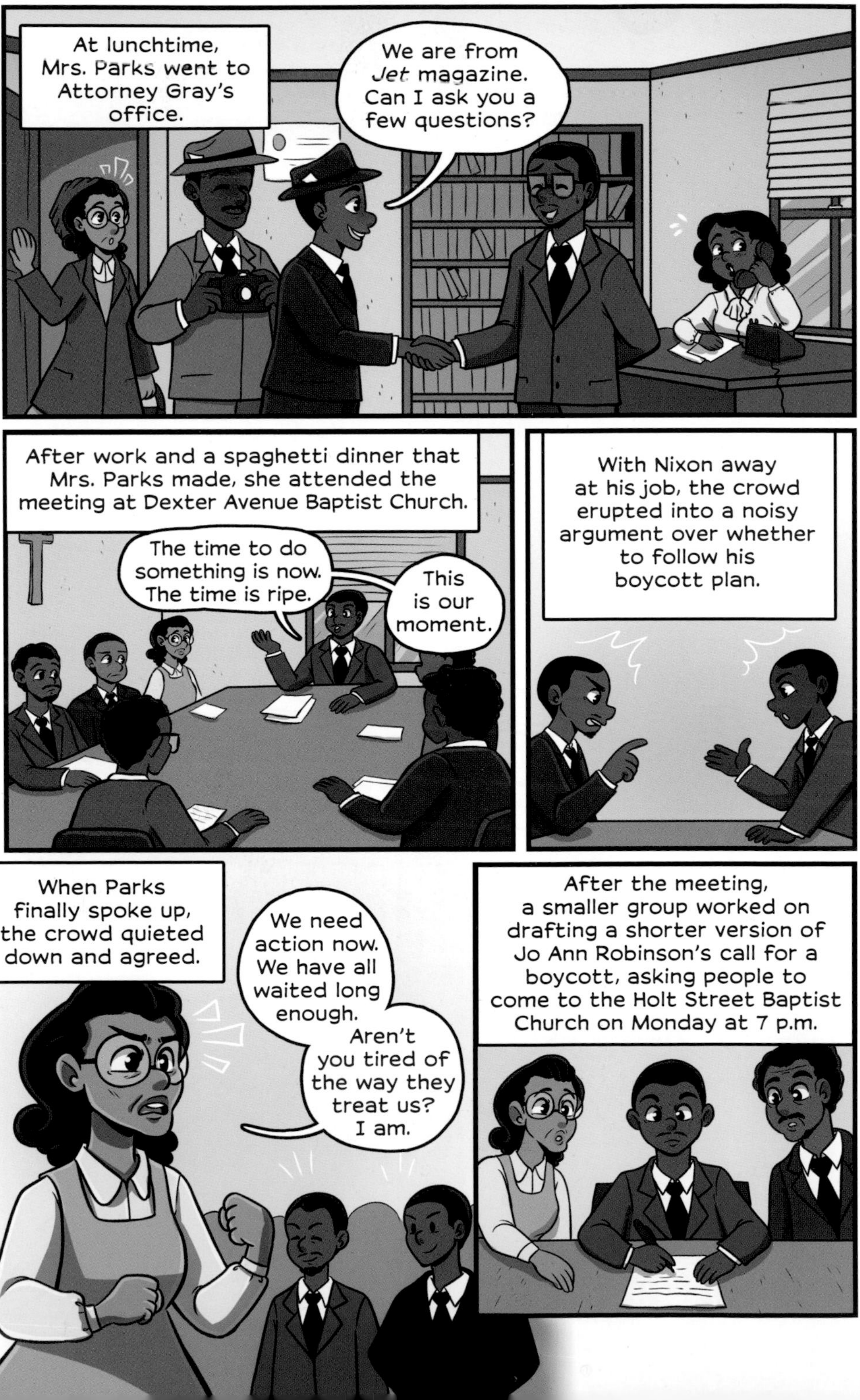
At lunchtime, Mrs. Parks went to Attorney Gray's office.
We are from *Jet* magazine. Can I ask you a few questions?
After work and a spaghetti dinner that Mrs. Parks made, she attended the meeting at Dexter Avenue Baptist Church.
The time to do something is now. The time is ripe.
This is our moment.
With Nixon away at his job, the crowd erupted into a noisy argument over whether to follow his boycott plan.
When Parks finally spoke up, the crowd quieted down and agreed.
We need action now. We have all waited long enough.
Aren't you tired of the way they treat us? I am.
After the meeting, a smaller group worked on drafting a shorter version of Jo Ann Robinson's call for a boycott, asking people to come to the Holt Street Baptist Church on Monday at 7 p.m.

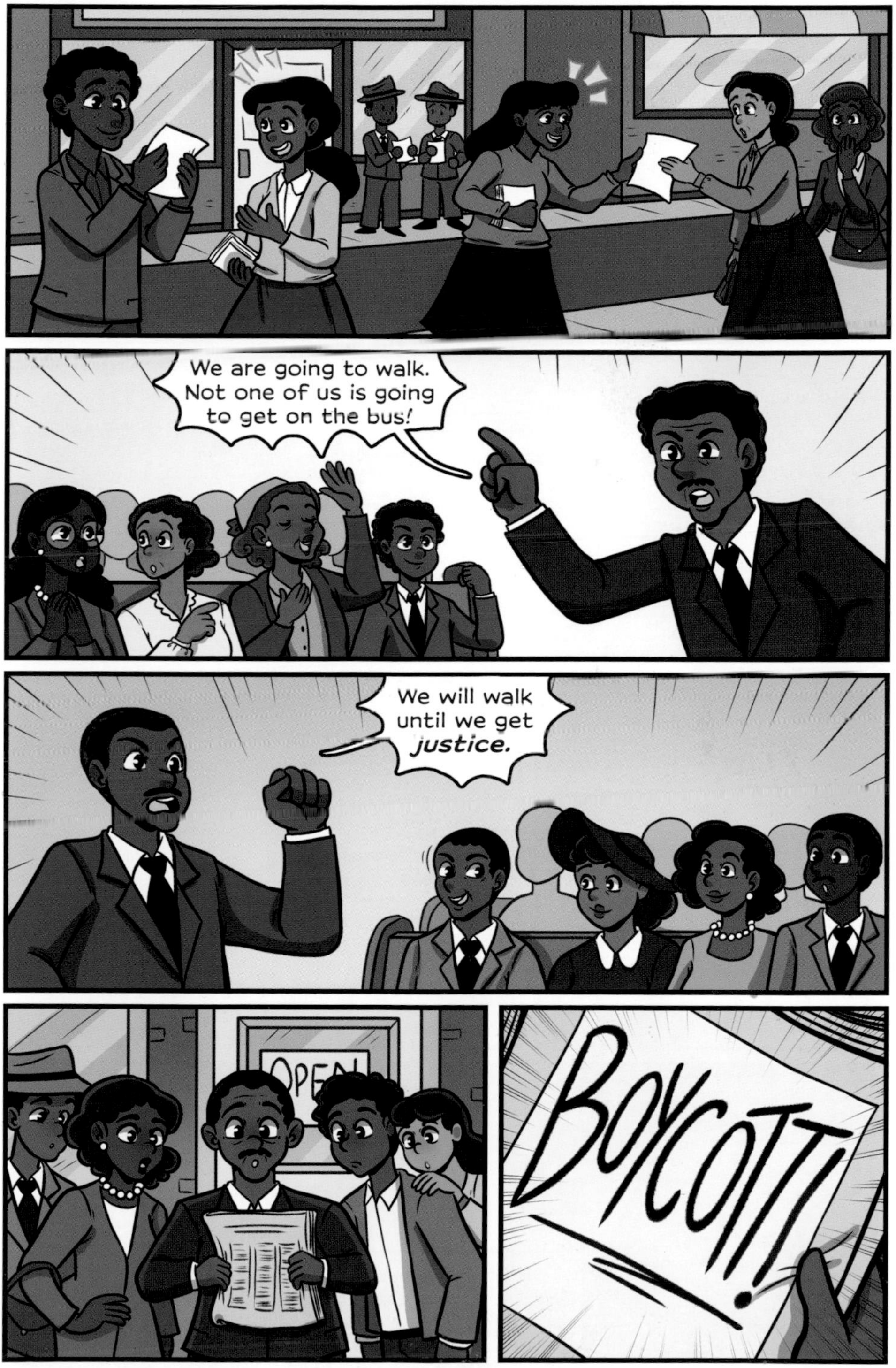
We are going to walk. Not one of us is going to get on the bus!
We will walk until we get *justice.*
OPEN
BOYCOTT!

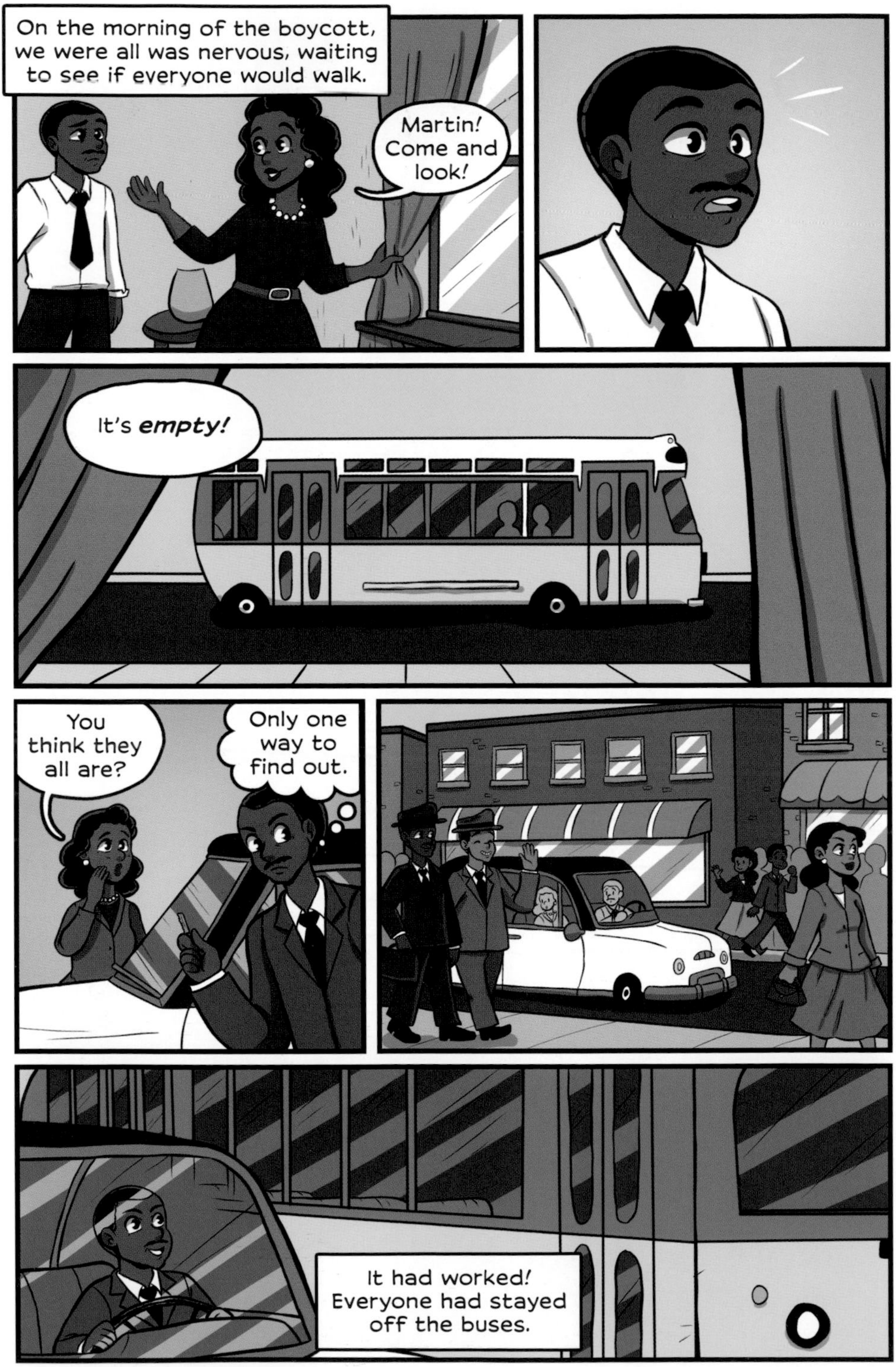
On the morning of the boycott, we were all was nervous, waiting to see if everyone would walk.
Martin! Come and look!
It's ***empty!***
You think they all are?
Only one way to find out.
It had worked! Everyone had stayed off the buses.

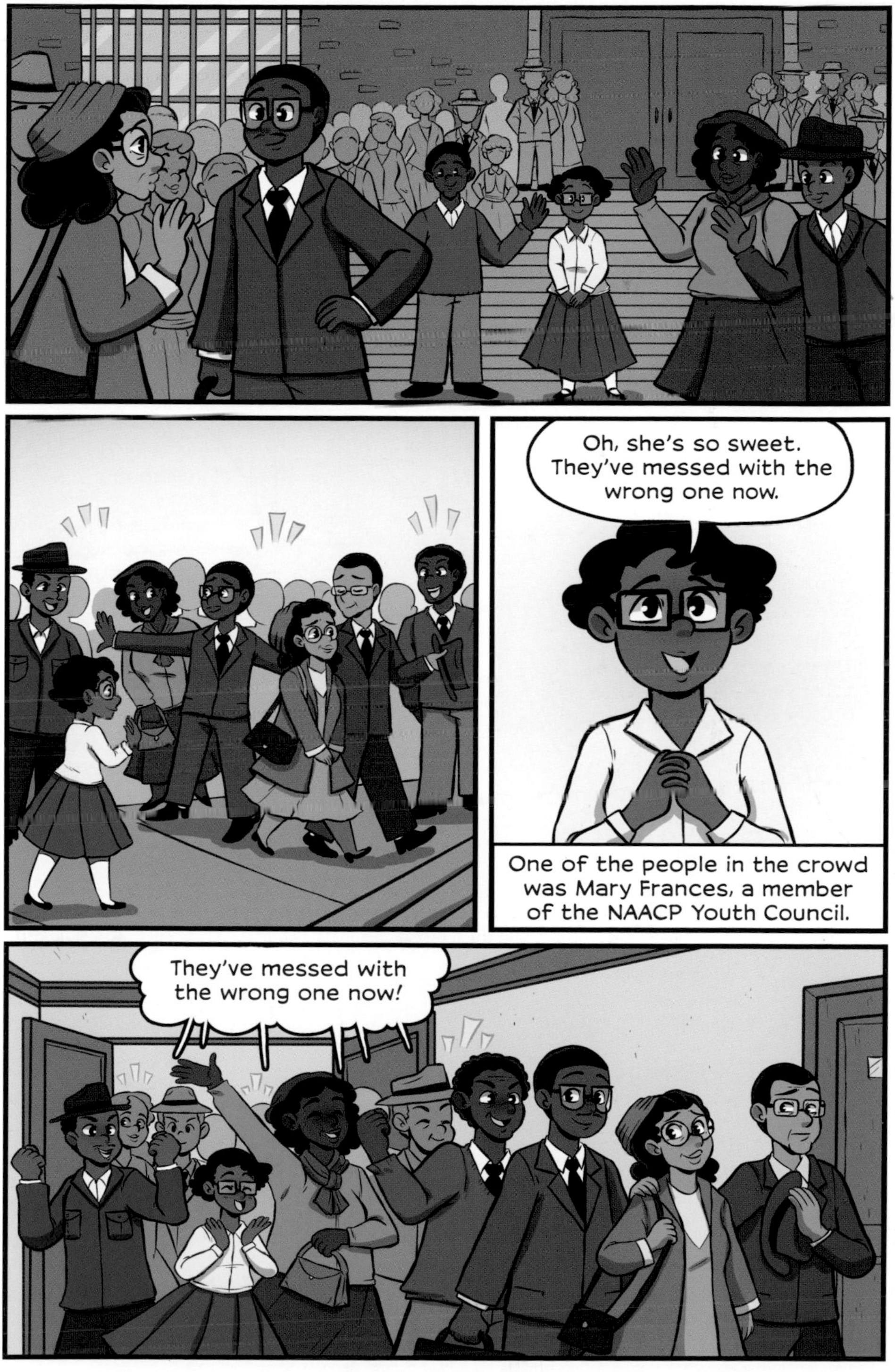
Oh, she's so sweet. They've messed with the wrong one now.
One of the people in the crowd was Mary Frances, a member of the NAACP Youth Council.
They've messed with the wrong one now!

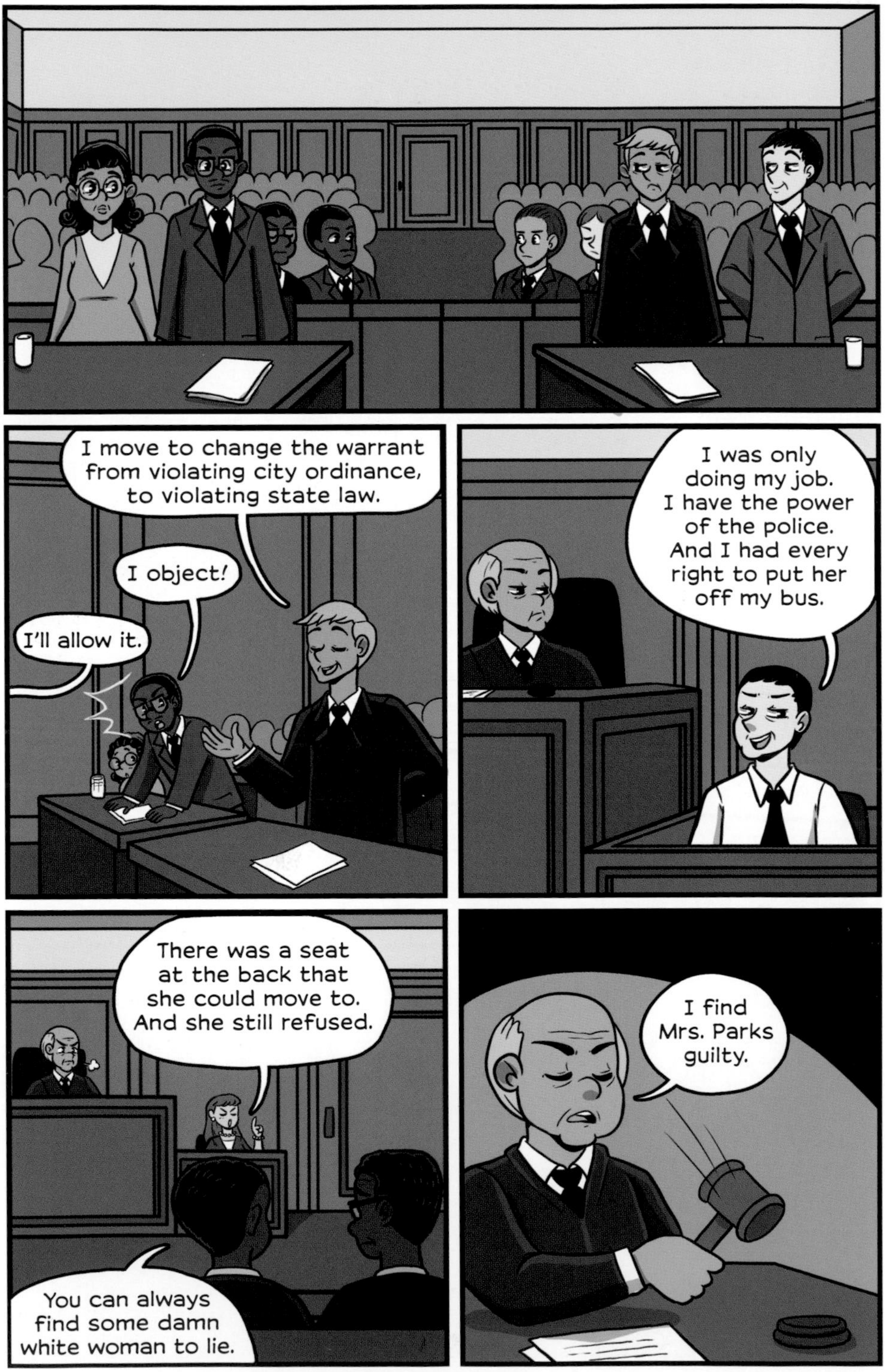
I move to change the warrant from violating city ordinance, to violating state law.
I object!
I'll allow it.
I was only doing my job. I have the power of the police. And I had every right to put her off my bus.
There was a seat at the back that she could move to. And she still refused.
You can always find some damn white woman to lie.
I find Mrs. Parks guilty.

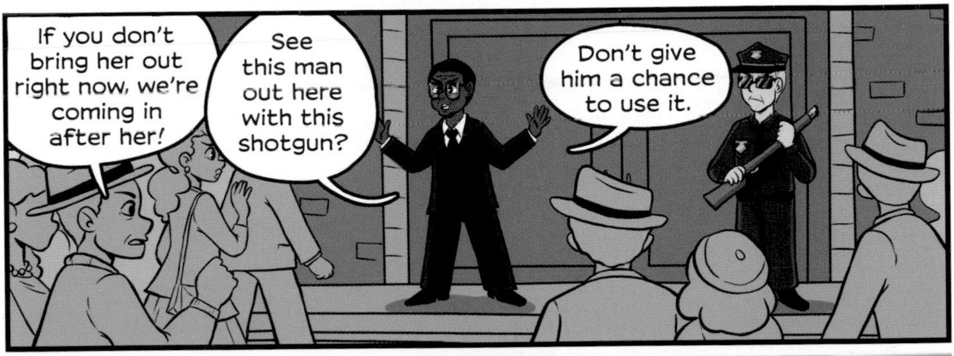
If you don't bring her out right now, we're coming in after her!
See this man out here with this shotgun?
Don't give him a chance to use it.

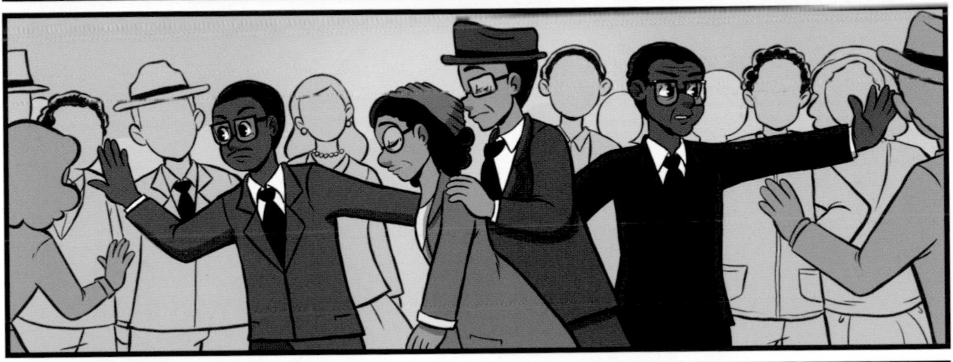

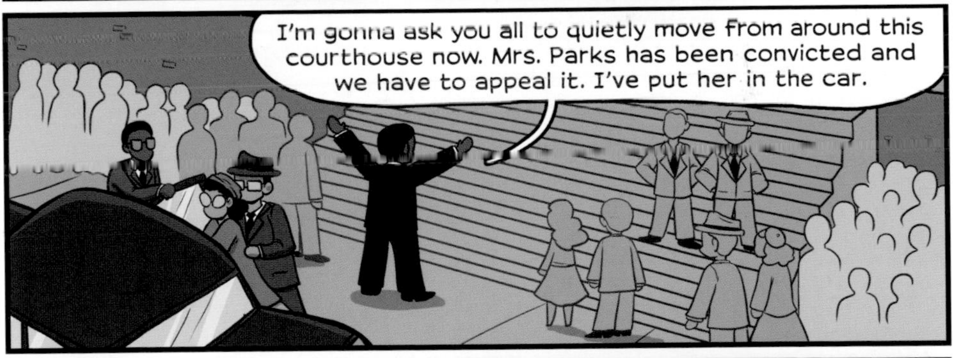
I'm gonna ask you all to quietly move from around this courthouse now. Mrs. Parks has been convicted and we have to appeal it. I've put her in the car.

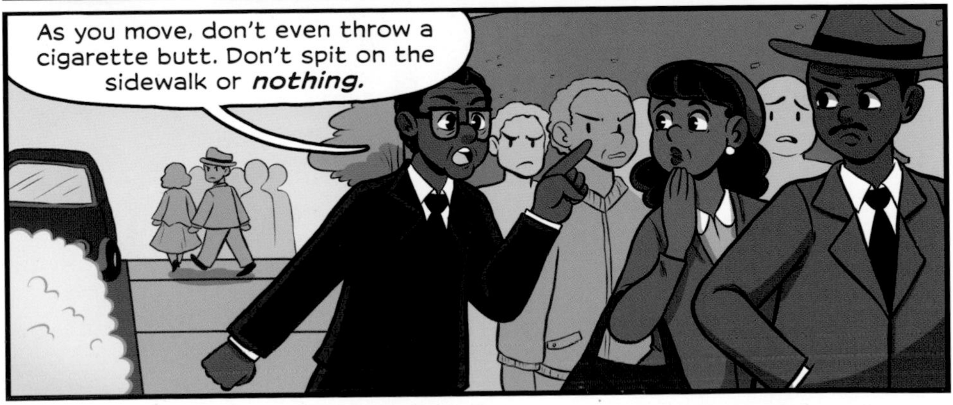
As you move, don't even throw a cigarette butt. Don't spit on the sidewalk or *nothing.*

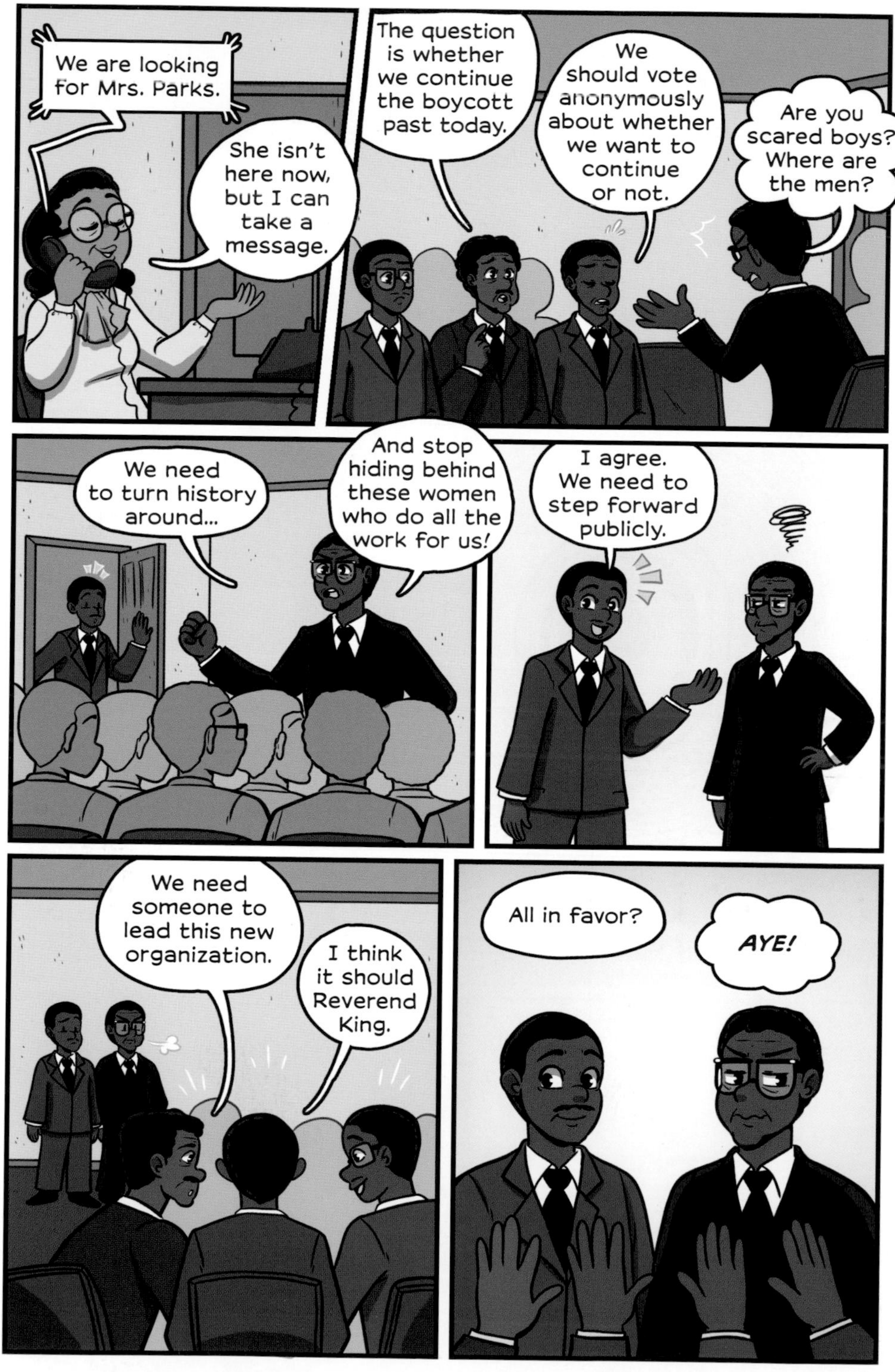
We are looking for Mrs. Parks.
She isn't here now, but I can take a message.
The question is whether we continue the boycott past today.
We should vote anonymously about whether we want to continue or not.
Are you scared boys? Where are the men?
We need to turn history around...
And stop hiding behind these women who do all the work for us!
I agree. We need to step forward publicly.
We need someone to lead this new organization.
I think it should Reverend King.
All in favor?
AYE!

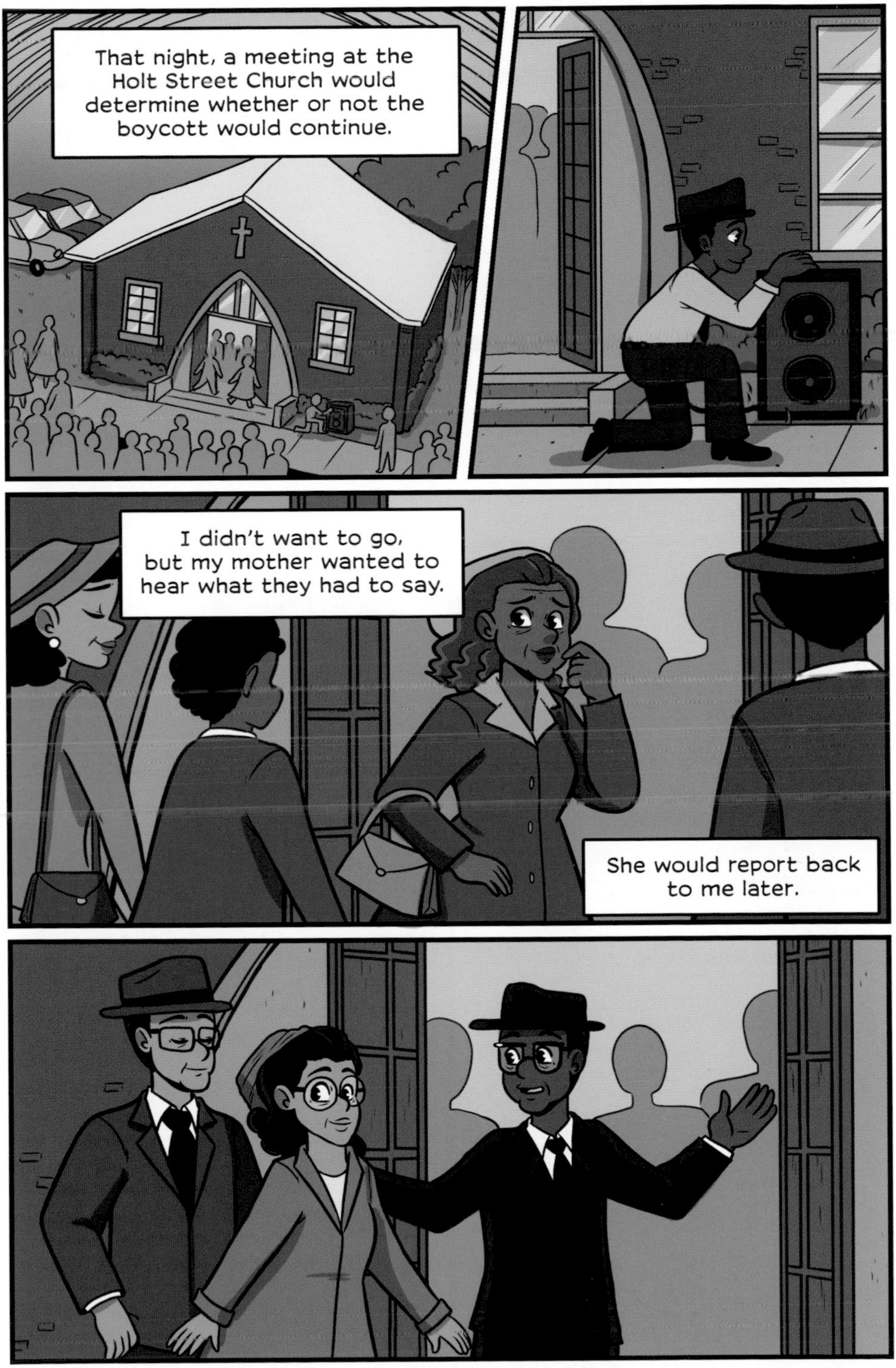
That night, a meeting at the Holt Street Church would determine whether or not the boycott would continue.
I didn't want to go, but my mother wanted to hear what they had to say.
She would report back to me later.

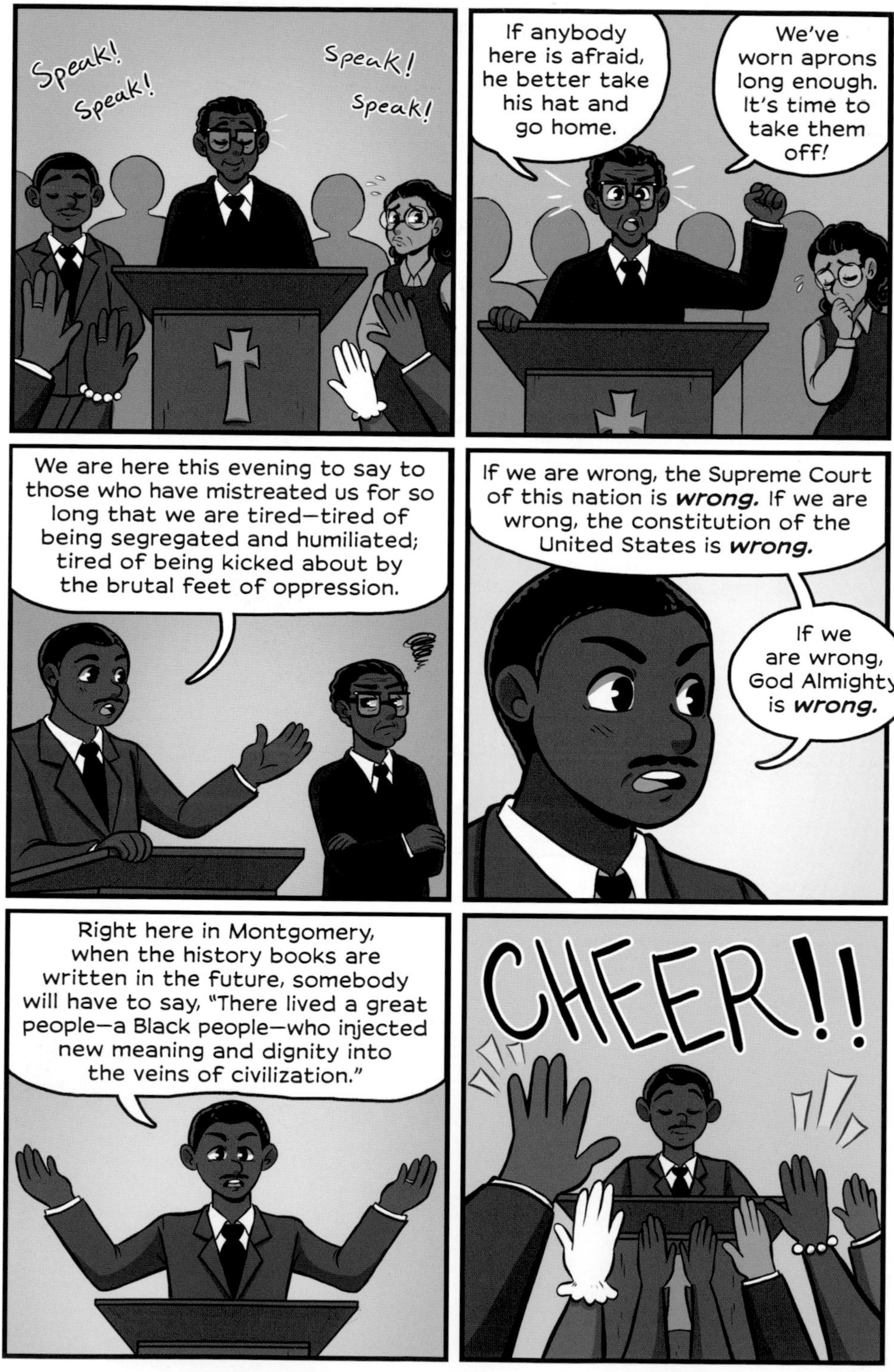
Speak!
Speak!
Speak!
Speak!
If anybody here is afraid, he better take his hat and go home.
We've worn aprons long enough. It's time to take them off!
We are here this evening to say to those who have mistreated us for so long that we are tired—tired of being segregated and humiliated; tired of being kicked about by the brutal feet of oppression.
If we are wrong, the Supreme Court of this nation is ***wrong.*** If we are wrong, the constitution of the United States is ***wrong.***
If we are wrong, God Almighty is ***wrong.***
Right here in Montgomery, when the history books are written in the future, somebody will have to say, "There lived a great people—a Black people—who injected new meaning and dignity into the veins of civilization."
CHEER!!

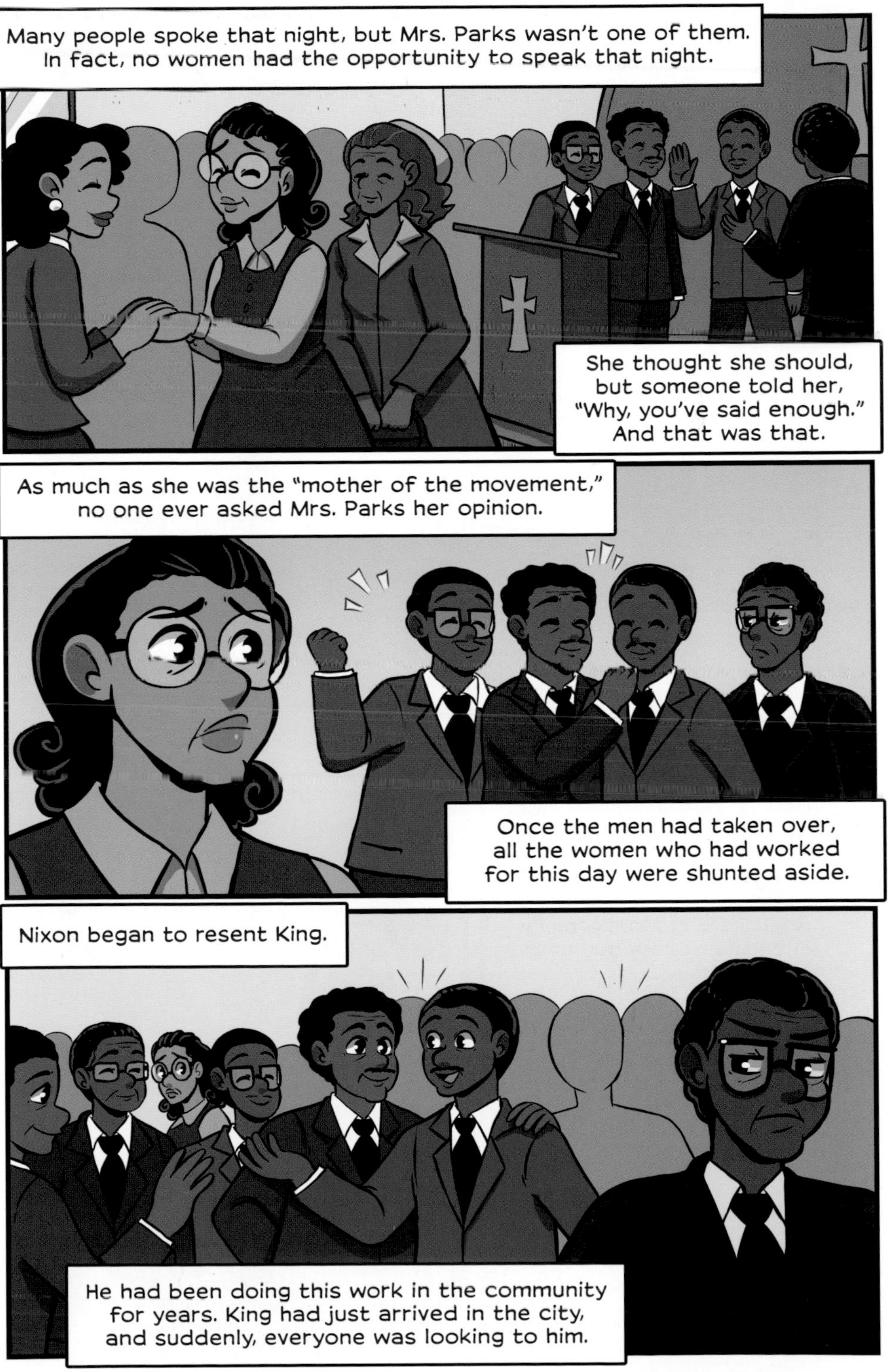
Many people spoke that night, but Mrs. Parks wasn't one of them. In fact, no women had the opportunity to speak that night.
She thought she should, but someone told her, "Why, you've said enough." And that was that.
As much as she was the "mother of the movement," no one ever asked Mrs. Parks her opinion.
Once the men had taken over, all the women who had worked for this day were shunted aside.
Nixon began to resent King.
He had been doing this work in the community for years. King had just arrived in the city, and suddenly, everyone was looking to him.

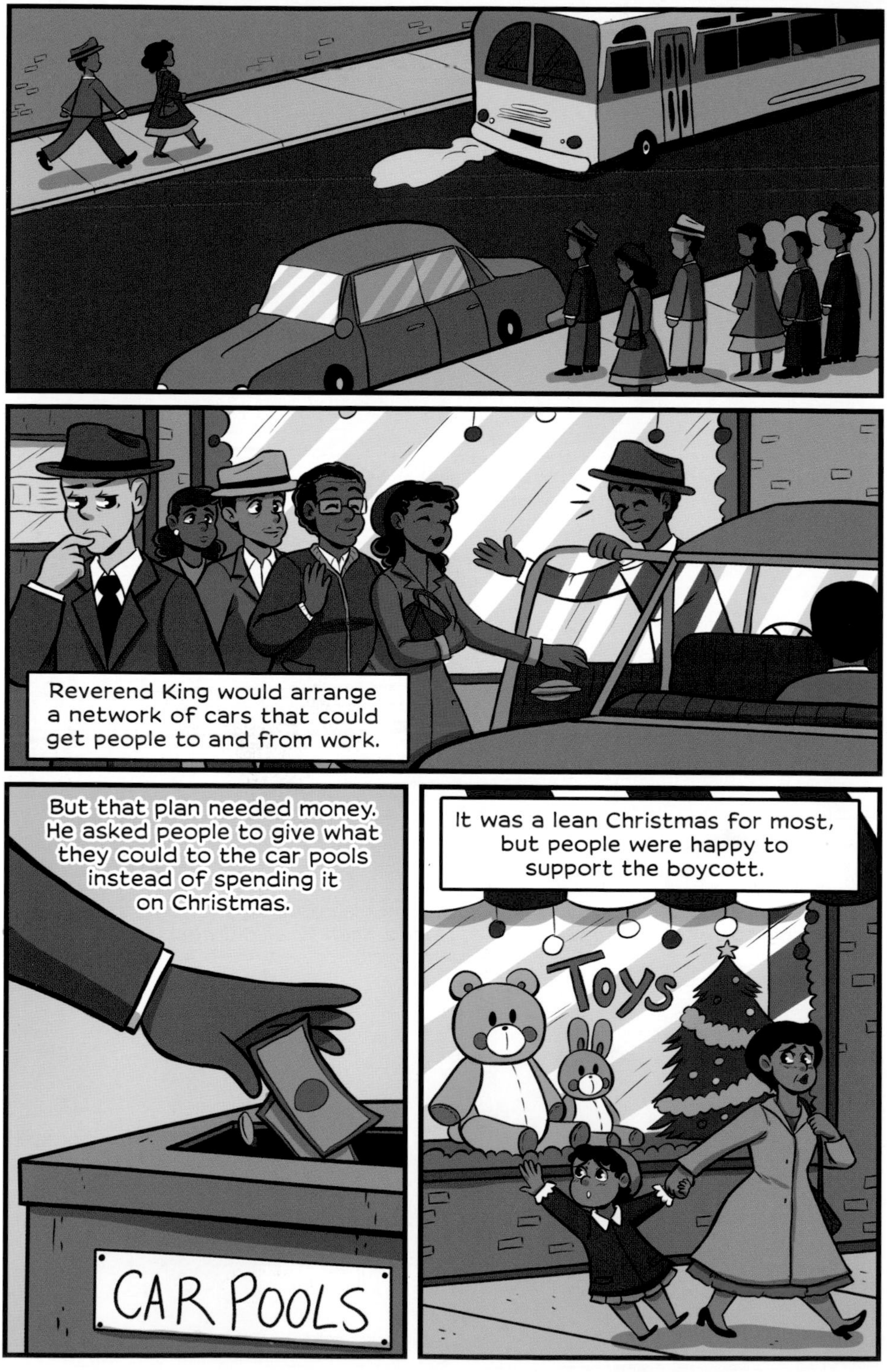
Reverend King would arrange a network of cars that could get people to and from work.
But that plan needed money. He asked people to give what they could to the car pools instead of spending it on Christmas.
CAR POOLS
It was a lean Christmas for most, but people were happy to support the boycott.
TOYS

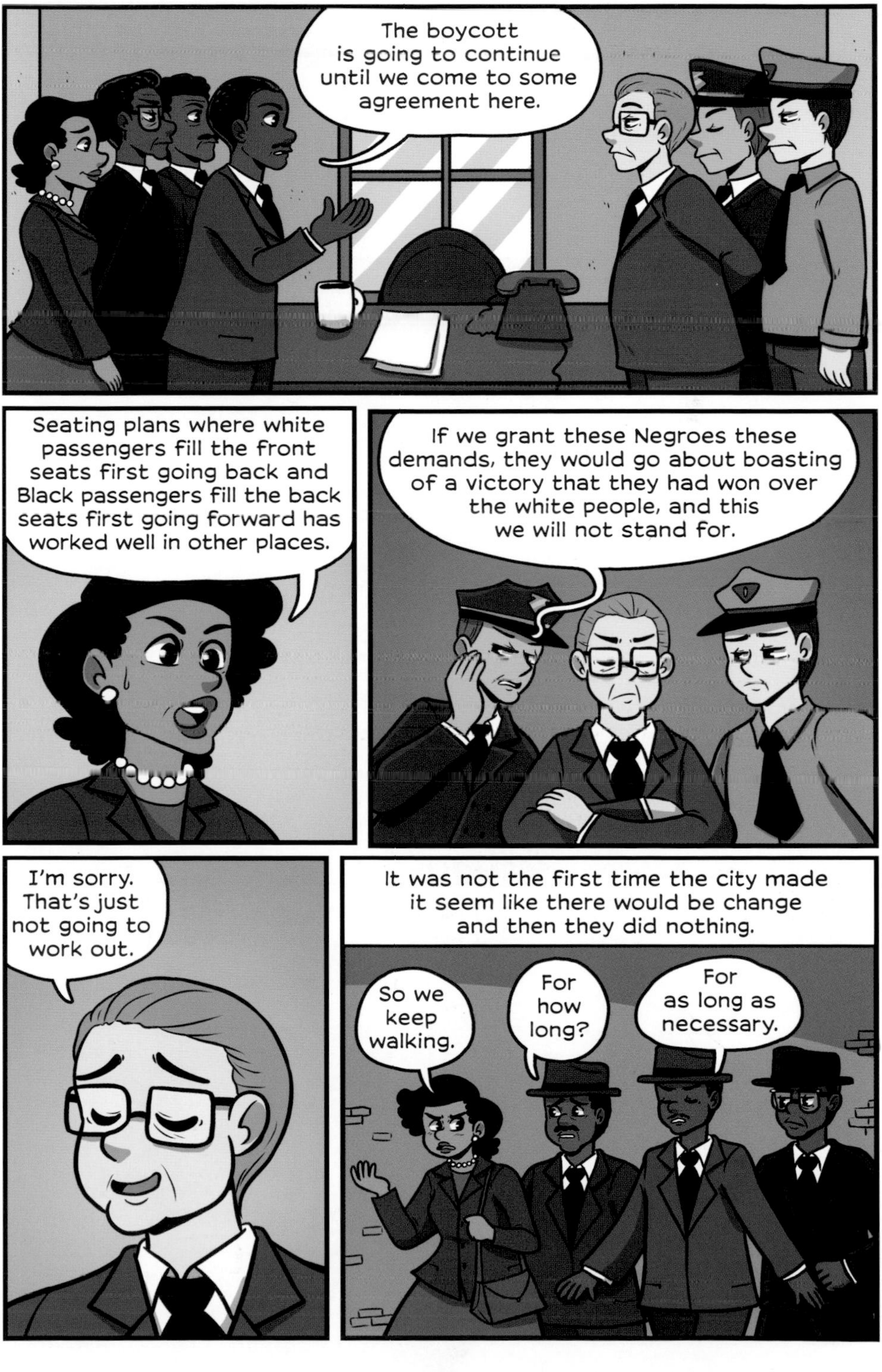
The boycott is going to continue until we come to some agreement here.
Seating plans where white passengers fill the front seats first going back and Black passengers fill the back seats first going forward has worked well in other places.
If we grant these Negroes these demands, they would go about boasting of a victory that they had won over the white people, and this we will not stand for.
I'm sorry. That's just not going to work out.
It was not the first time the city made it seem like there would be change and then they did nothing.
So we keep walking.
For how long?
For as long as necessary.

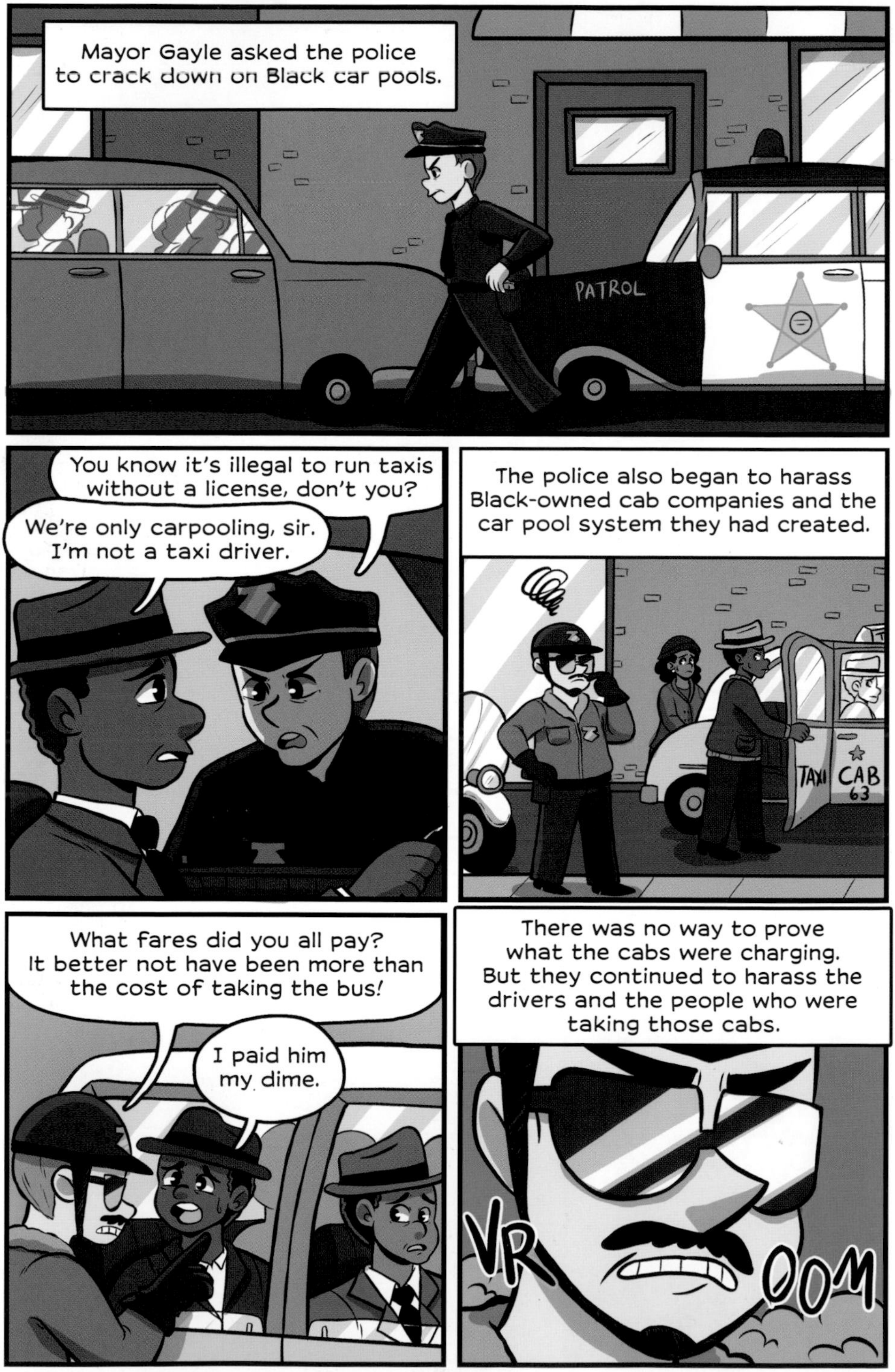
Mayor Gayle asked the police to crack down on Black car pools.
PATROL
You know it's illegal to run taxis without a license, don't you?
We're only carpooling, sir. I'm not a taxi driver.
The police also began to harass Black-owned cab companies and the car pool system they had created.
TAXI CAB 63
What fares did you all pay? It better not have been more than the cost of taking the bus!
I paid him my dime.
There was no way to prove what the cabs were charging. But they continued to harass the drivers and the people who were taking those cabs.
VROOM

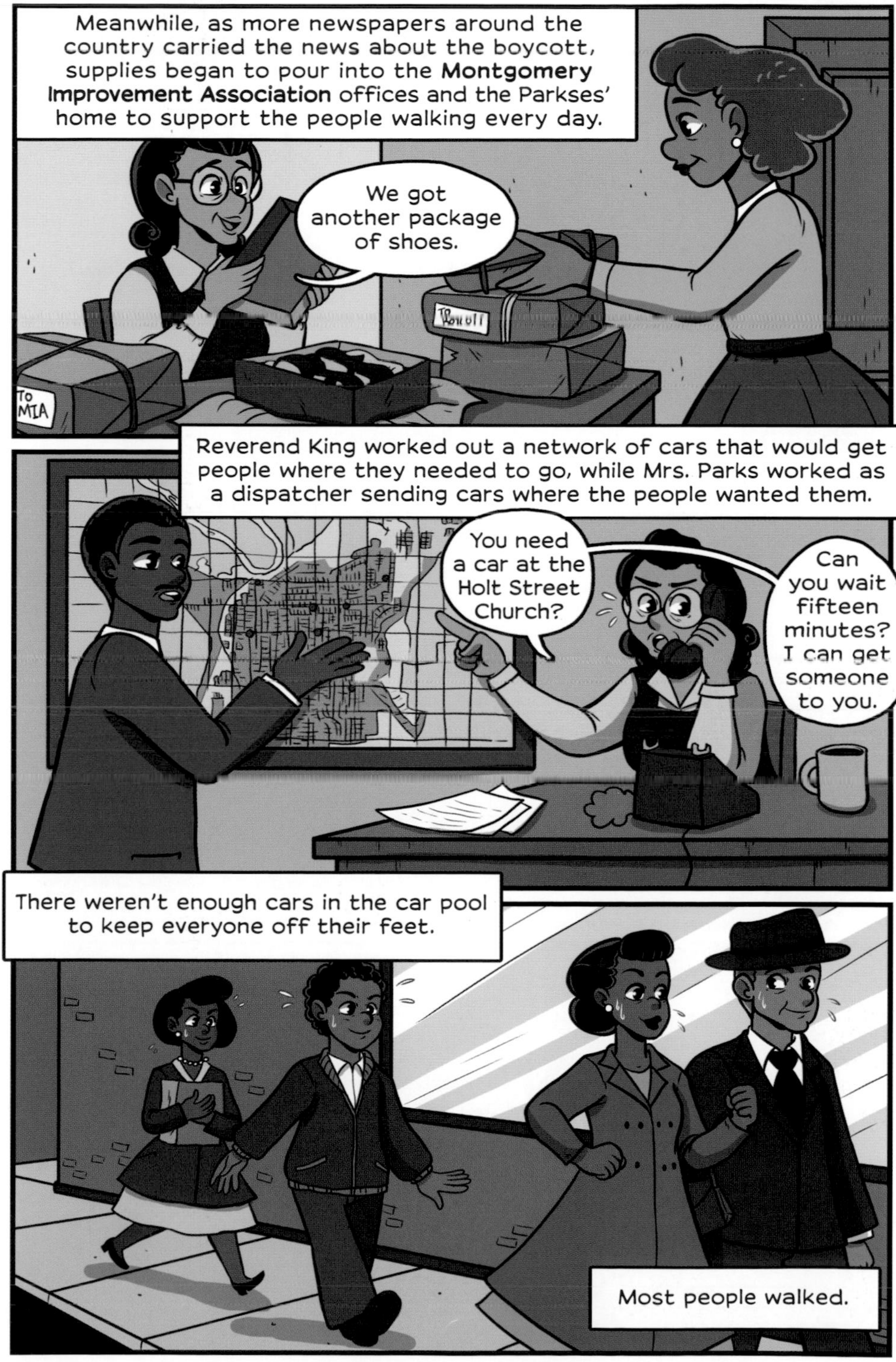
Meanwhile, as more newspapers around the country carried the news about the boycott, supplies began to pour into the **Montgomery Improvement Association** offices and the Parkses' home to support the people walking every day.
We got another package of shoes.
TO MIA
Reverend King worked out a network of cars that would get people where they needed to go, while Mrs. Parks worked as a dispatcher sending cars where the people wanted them.
You need a car at the Holt Street Church?
Can you wait fifteen minutes? I can get someone to you.
There weren't enough cars in the car pool to keep everyone off their feet.
Most people walked.

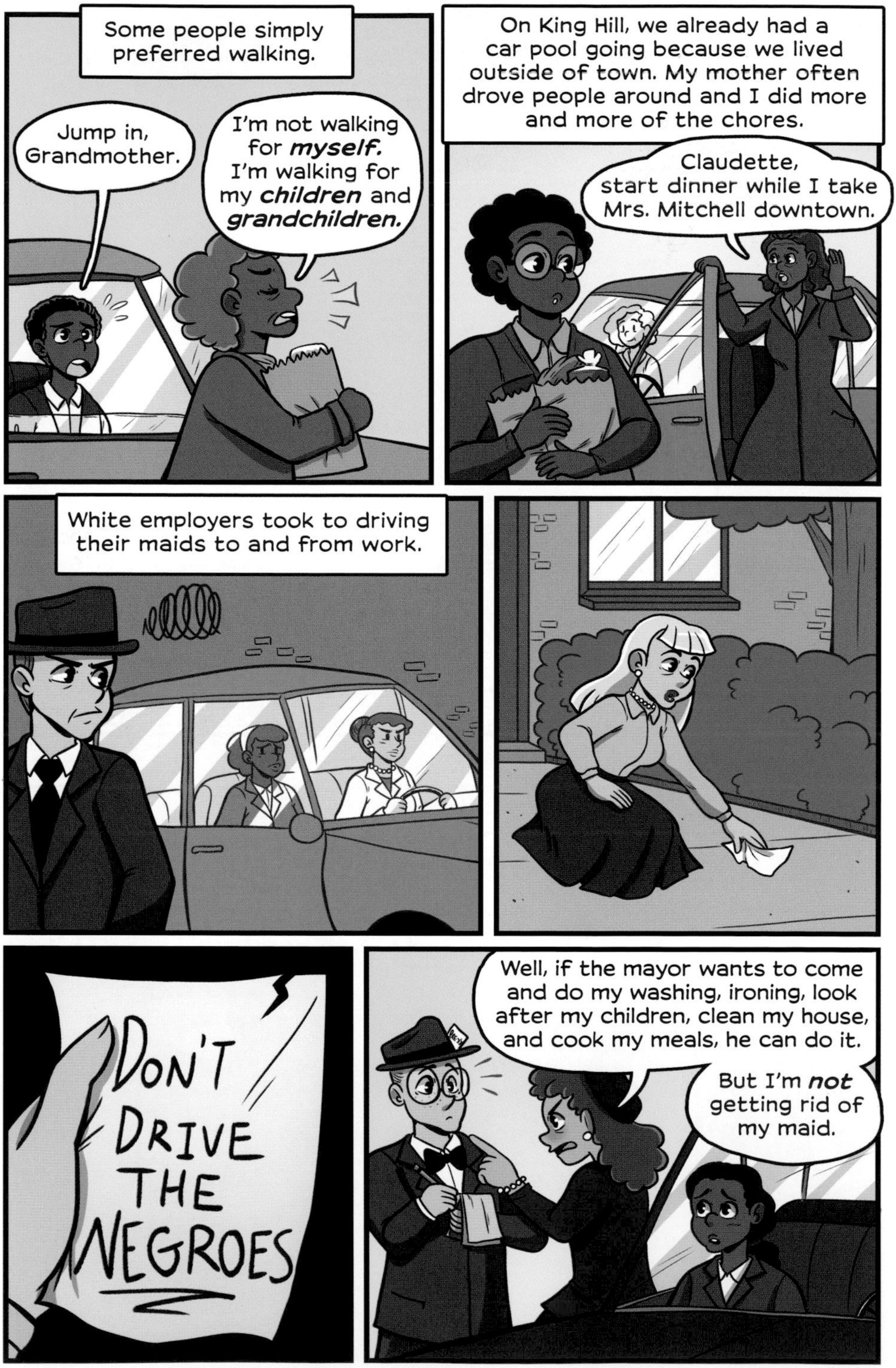
Some people simply preferred walking.
Jump in, Grandmother.
I'm not walking for *myself.* I'm walking for my *children* and *grandchildren.*
On King Hill, we already had a car pool going because we lived outside of town. My mother often drove people around and I did more and more of the chores.
Claudette, start dinner while I take Mrs. Mitchell downtown.
White employers took to driving their maids to and from work.
DON'T DRIVE THE NEGROES
Well, if the mayor wants to come and do my washing, ironing, look after my children, clean my house, and cook my meals, he can do it.
But I'm *not* getting rid of my maid.

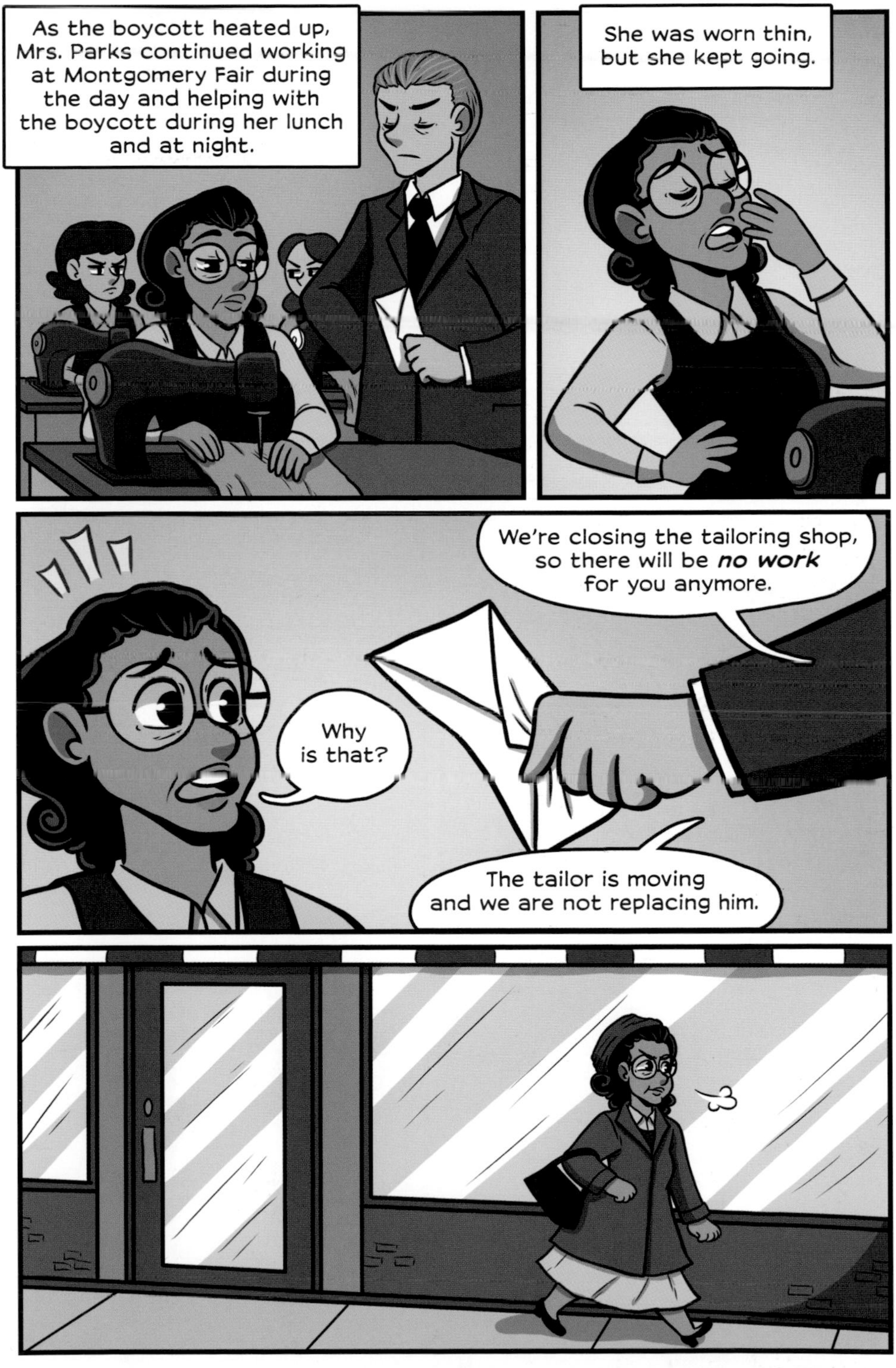
As the boycott heated up, Mrs. Parks continued working at Montgomery Fair during the day and helping with the boycott during her lunch and at night.
She was worn thin, but she kept going.
We're closing the tailoring shop, so there will be ***no work*** for you anymore.
Why is that?
The tailor is moving and we are not replacing him.

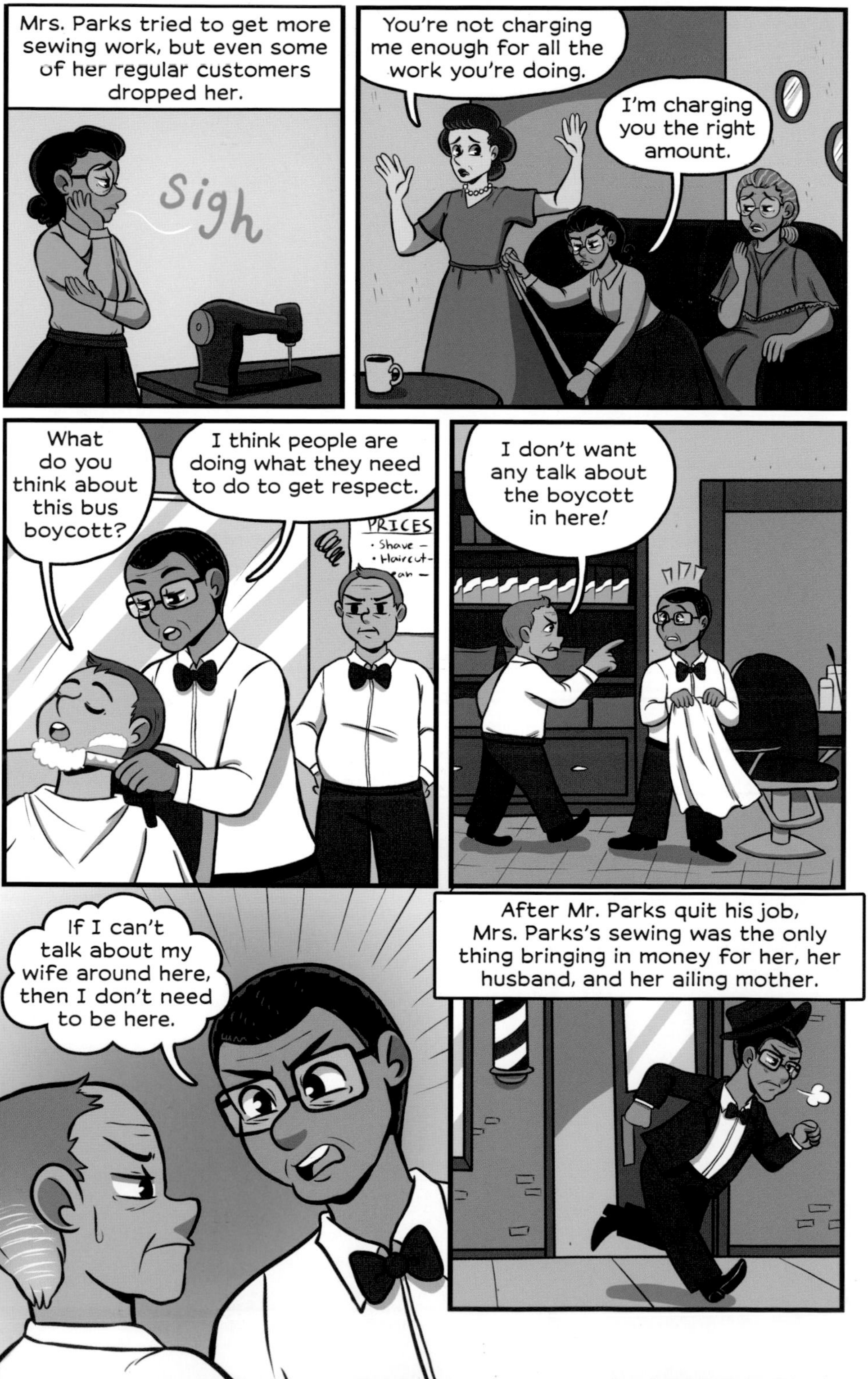

Mrs. Parks tried to get more sewing work, but even some of her regular customers dropped her.
Sigh
You're not charging me enough for all the work you're doing.
I'm charging you the right amount.
What do you think about this bus boycott?
I think people are doing what they need to do to get respect.
PRICES
• Shave –
• Haircut –
I don't want any talk about the boycott in here!
If I can't talk about my wife around here, then I don't need to be here.
After Mr. Parks quit his job, Mrs. Parks's sewing was the only thing bringing in money for her, her husband, and her ailing mother.

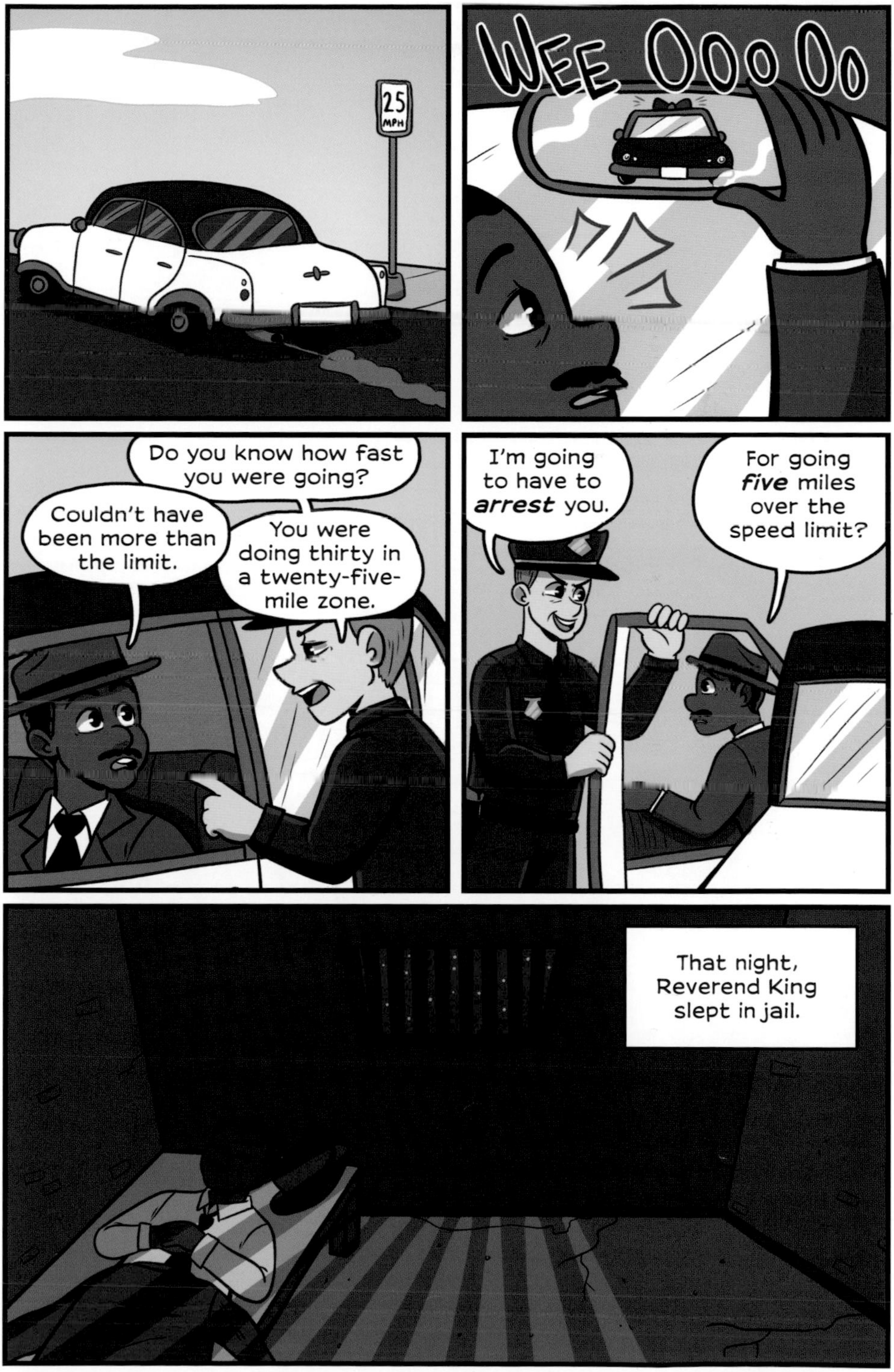

25 MPH
WEE OOO OO
Do you know how fast you were going?
Couldn't have been more than the limit.
You were doing thirty in a twenty-five-mile zone.
I'm going to have to *arrest* you.
For going *five* miles over the speed limit?
That night, Reverend King slept in jail.

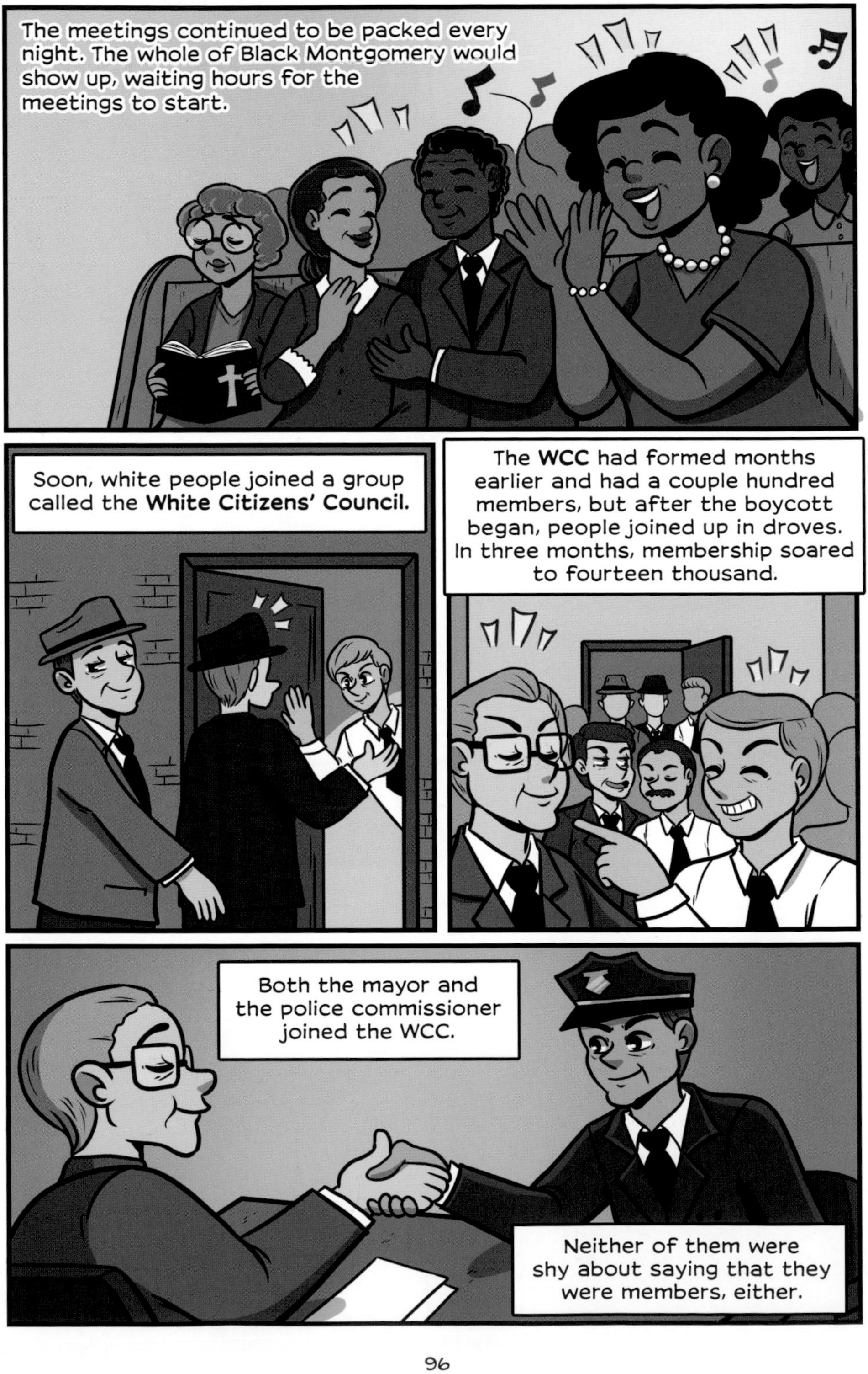
The meetings continued to be packed every night. The whole of Black Montgomery would show up, waiting hours for the meetings to start.
Soon, white people joined a group called the **White Citizens' Council.**
The **WCC** had formed months earlier and had a couple hundred members, but after the boycott began, people joined up in droves. In three months, membership soared to fourteen thousand.
Both the mayor and the police commissioner joined the WCC.
Neither of them were shy about saying that they were members, either.

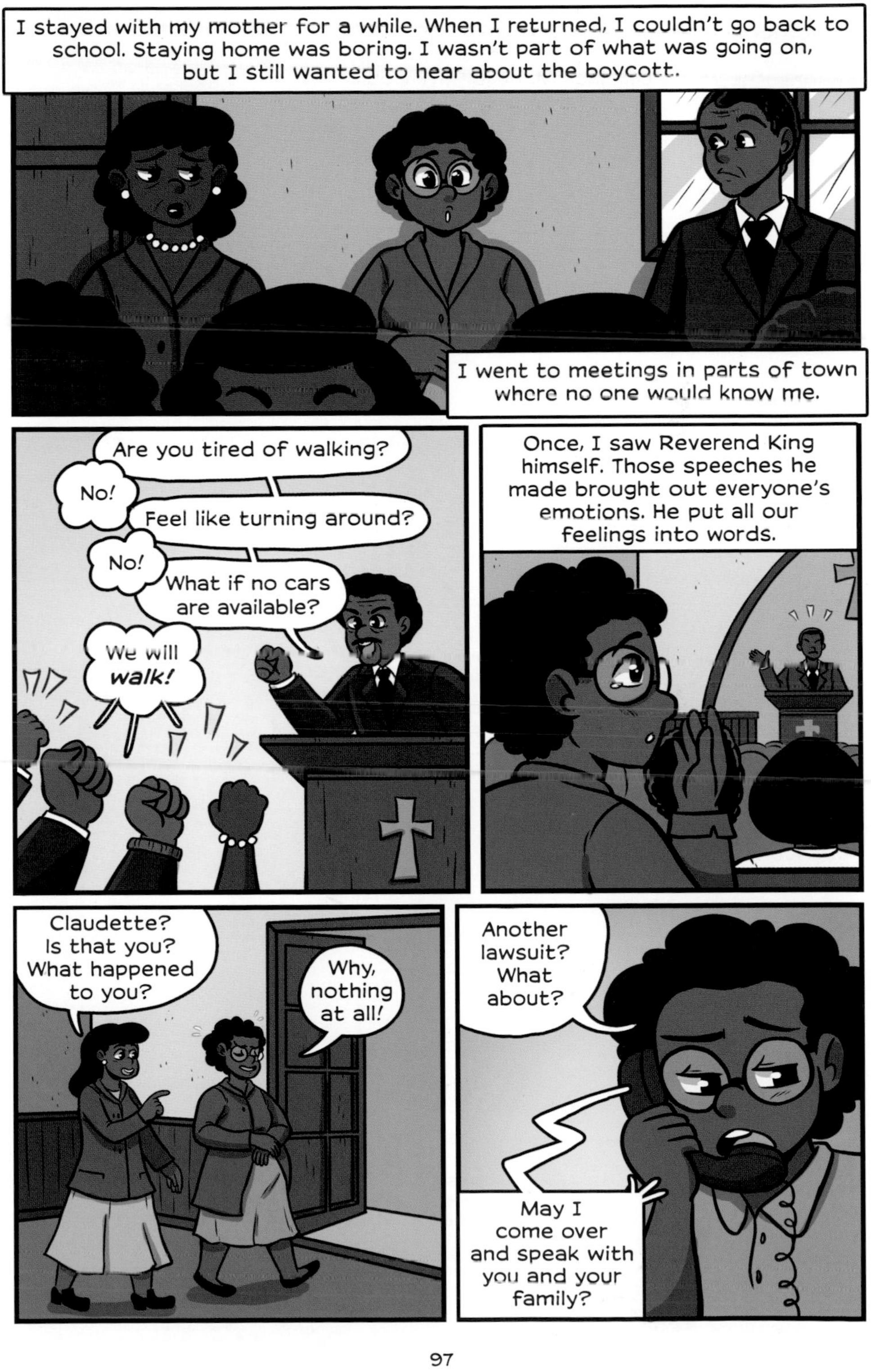

I stayed with my mother for a while. When I returned, I couldn't go back to school. Staying home was boring. I wasn't part of what was going on, but I still wanted to hear about the boycott.
I went to meetings in parts of town where no one would know me.
Are you tired of walking?
No!
Feel like turning around?
No!
What if no cars are available?
We will *walk!*
Once, I saw Reverend King himself. Those speeches he made brought out everyone's emotions. He put all our feelings into words.
Claudette? Is that you? What happened to you?
Why, nothing at all!
Another lawsuit? What about?
May I come over and speak with you and your family?

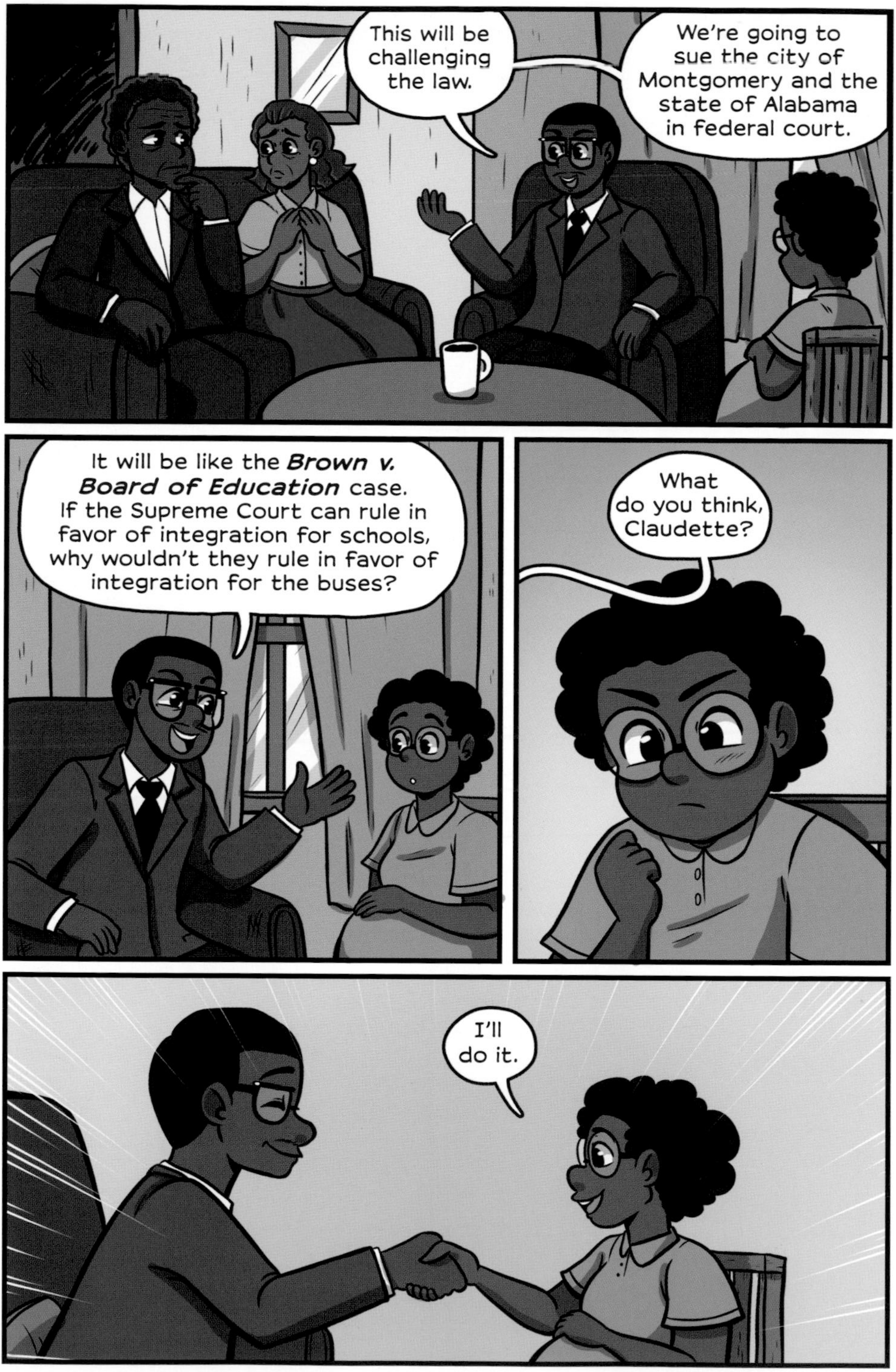
This will be challenging the law.
We're going to sue the city of Montgomery and the state of Alabama in federal court.
It will be like the ***Brown v. Board of Education*** case. If the Supreme Court can rule in favor of integration for schools, why wouldn't they rule in favor of integration for the buses?
What do you think, Claudette?
I'll do it.

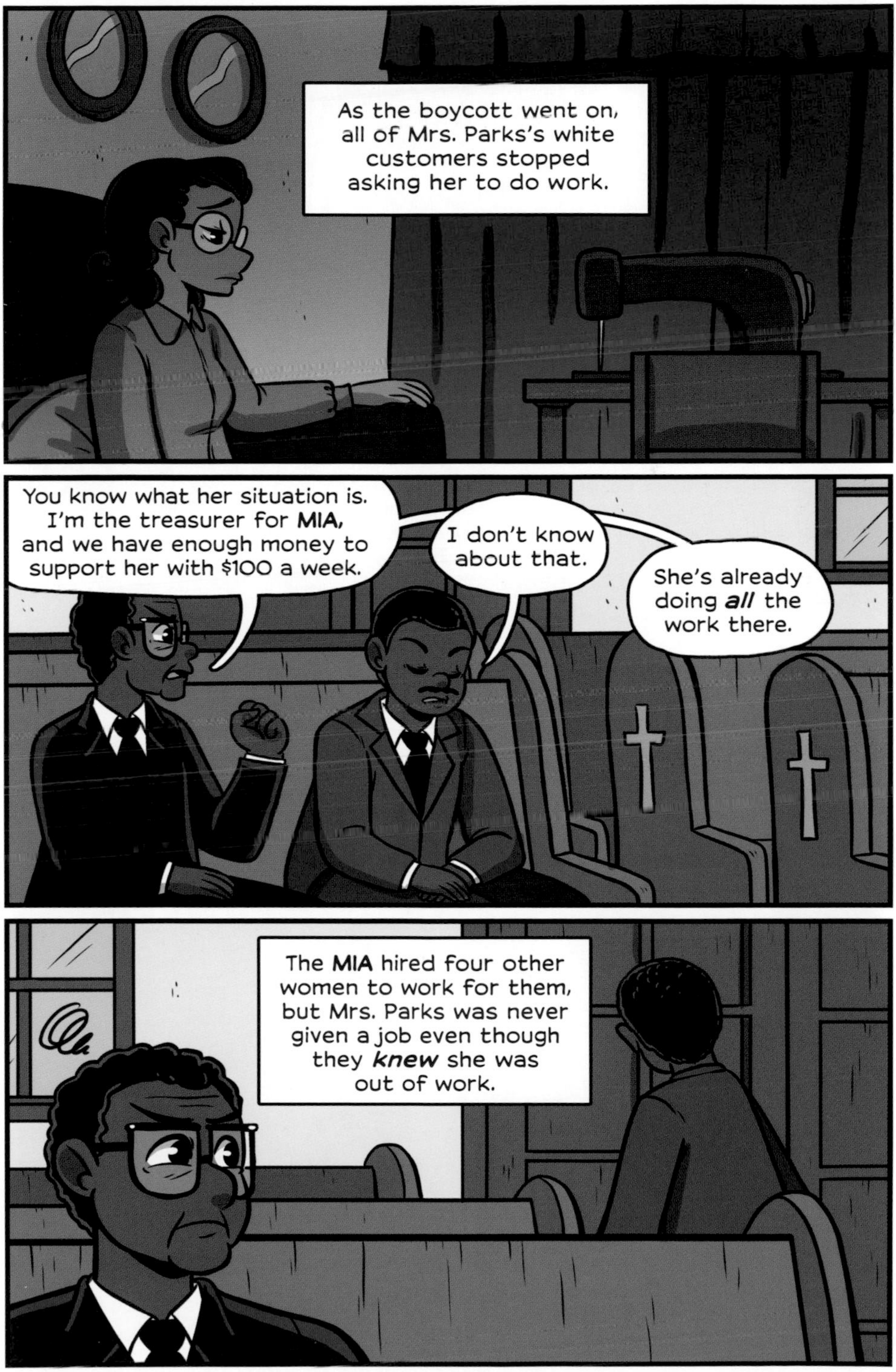
As the boycott went on, all of Mrs. Parks's white customers stopped asking her to do work.
You know what her situation is. I'm the treasurer for **MIA**, and we have enough money to support her with $100 a week.
I don't know about that.
She's already doing ***all*** the work there.
The **MIA** hired four other women to work for them, but Mrs. Parks was never given a job even though they ***knew*** she was out of work.

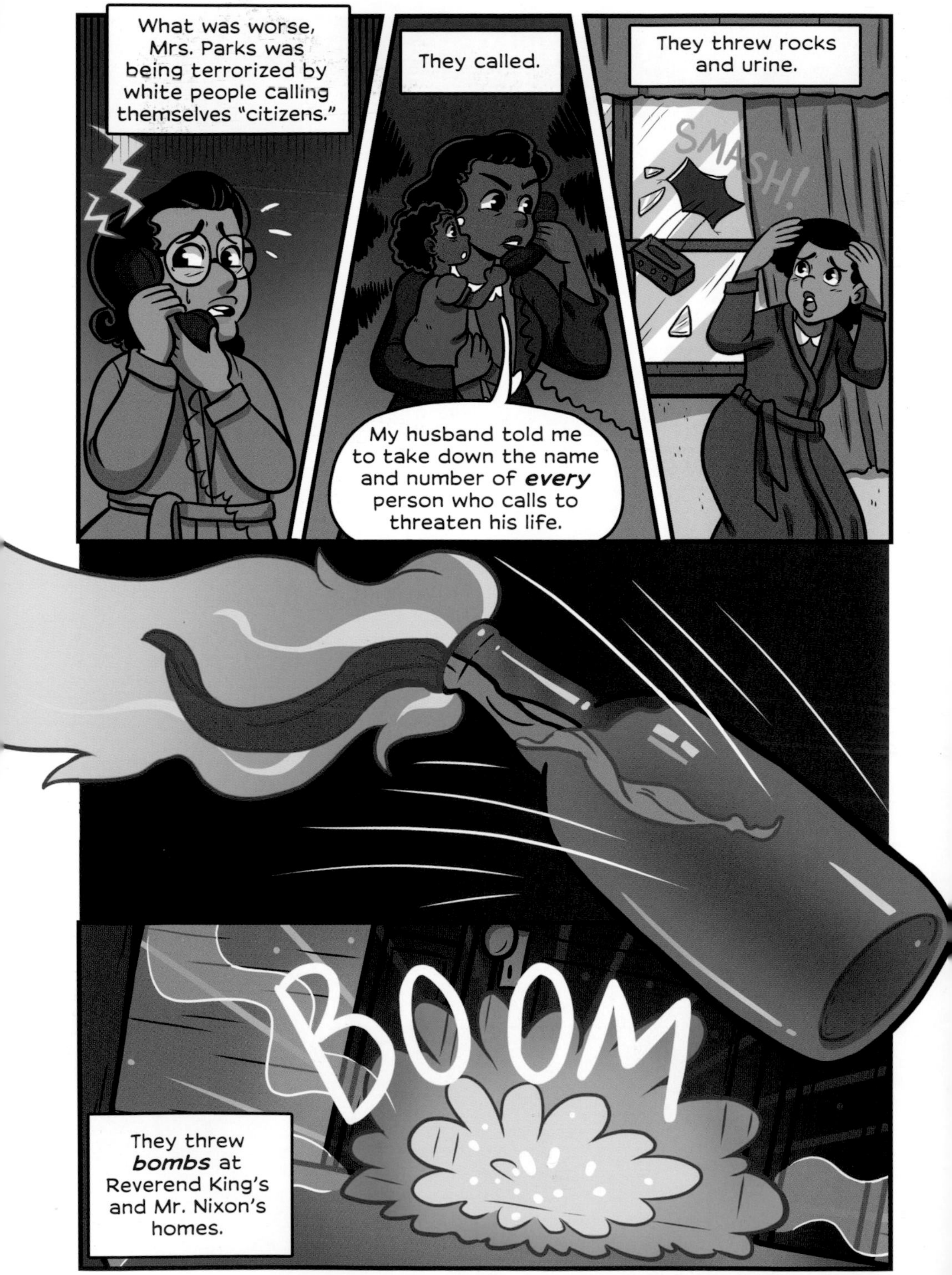
What was worse, Mrs. Parks was being terrorized by white people calling themselves "citizens."
They called.
My husband told me to take down the name and number of ***every*** person who calls to threaten his life.
They threw rocks and urine.
SMASH!
BOOM
They threw ***bombs*** at Reverend King's and Mr. Nixon's homes.

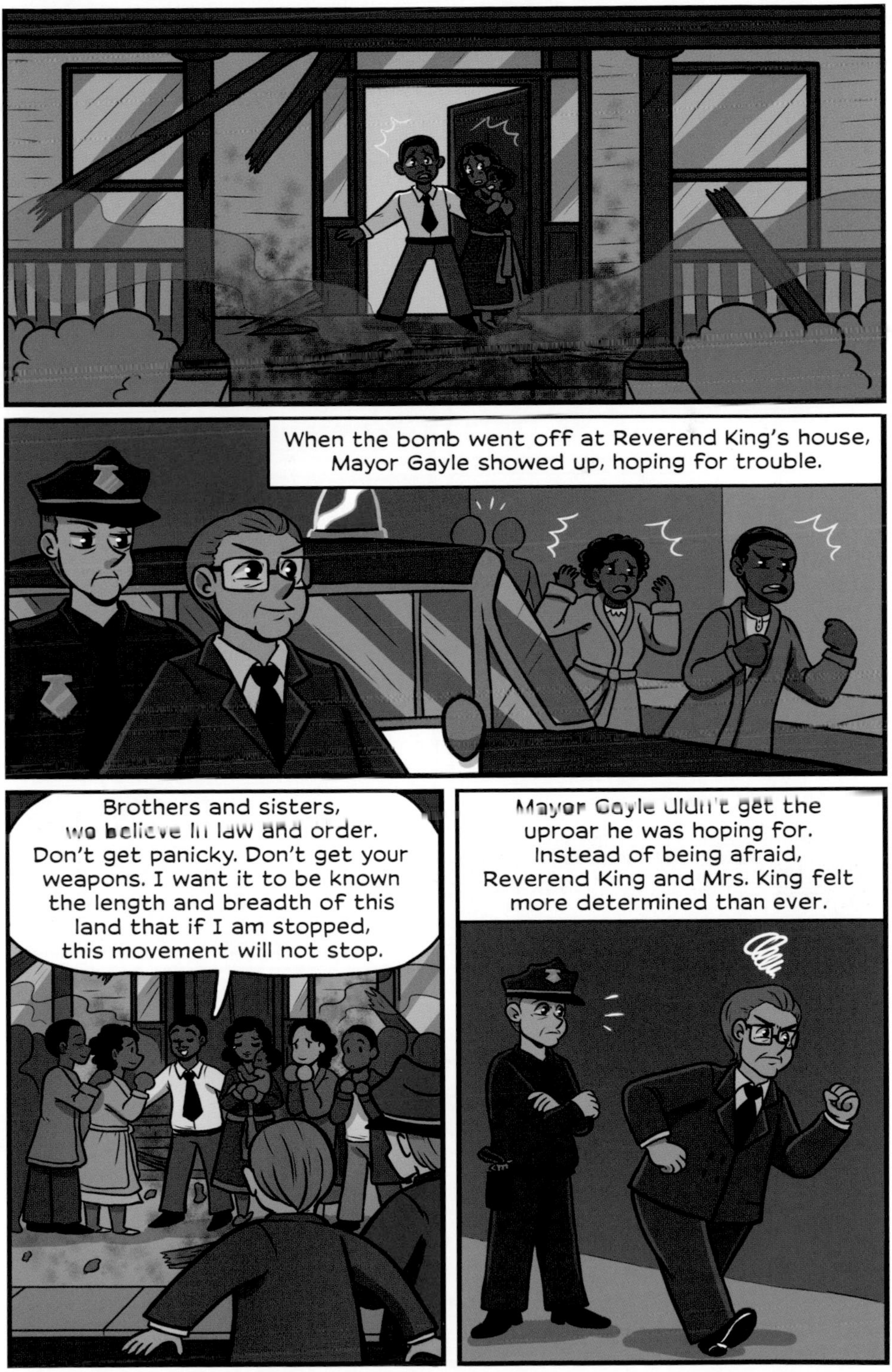
When the bomb went off at Reverend King's house, Mayor Gayle showed up, hoping for trouble.
Brothers and sisters, we believe in law and order. Don't get panicky. Don't get your weapons. I want it to be known the length and breadth of this land that if I am stopped, this movement will not stop.
Mayor Gayle didn't get the uproar he was hoping for. Instead of being afraid, Reverend King and Mrs. King felt more determined than ever.

We're going to pay for a bodyguard for his house to the tune of $30 a week.

There have been some people coming around my neighborhood asking about me...

Don't worry, we can get someone to watch over your house, too.

Bombings began to be so frequent that Mrs. Parks and her husband became part of a regular bomb clean-up crew.

Since intimidation wasn't working, Mayor Gayle tried another tactic: *lying.*

That's right. The bus boycott is over.

We'll be sure to print that up in the next edition. Thank you, Mayor Gayle!

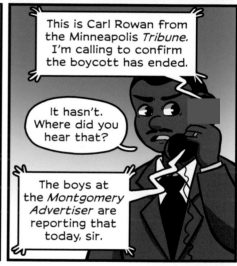

This is Carl Rowan from the Minneapolis *Tribune.* I'm calling to confirm the boycott has ended.

It hasn't. Where did you hear that?

The boys at the *Montgomery Advertiser* are reporting that today, sir.

Be sure to tell everyone that despite what's being reported in the *Montgomery Advertiser,* the boycott is not over. They need to stay off the buses!

Will everyone get the message?

We'll have to make sure they do.

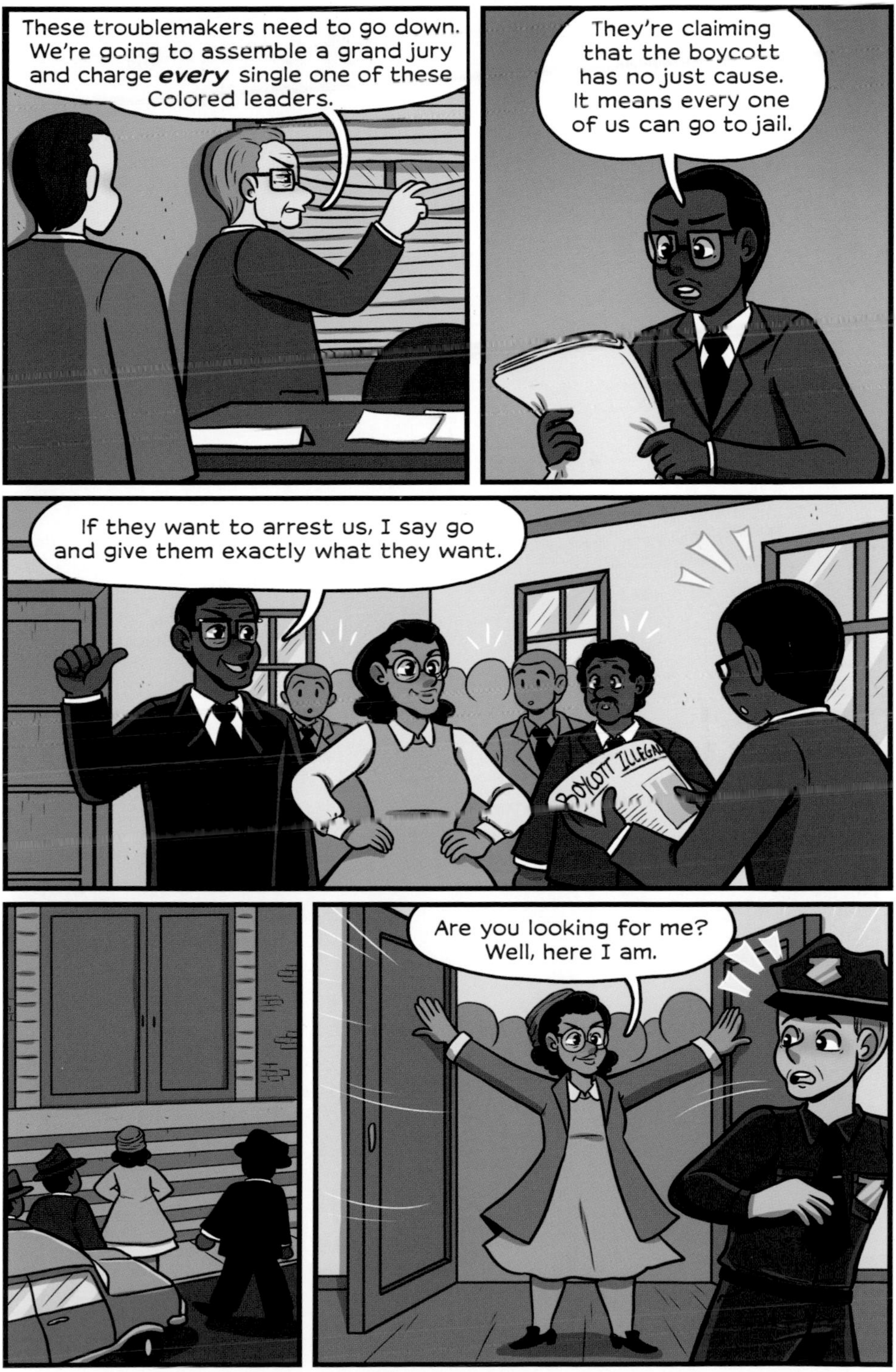
These troublemakers need to go down. We're going to assemble a grand jury and charge ***every*** single one of these Colored leaders.
They're claiming that the boycott has no just cause. It means every one of us can go to jail.
If they want to arrest us, I say go and give them exactly what they want.
Are you looking for me? Well, here I am.

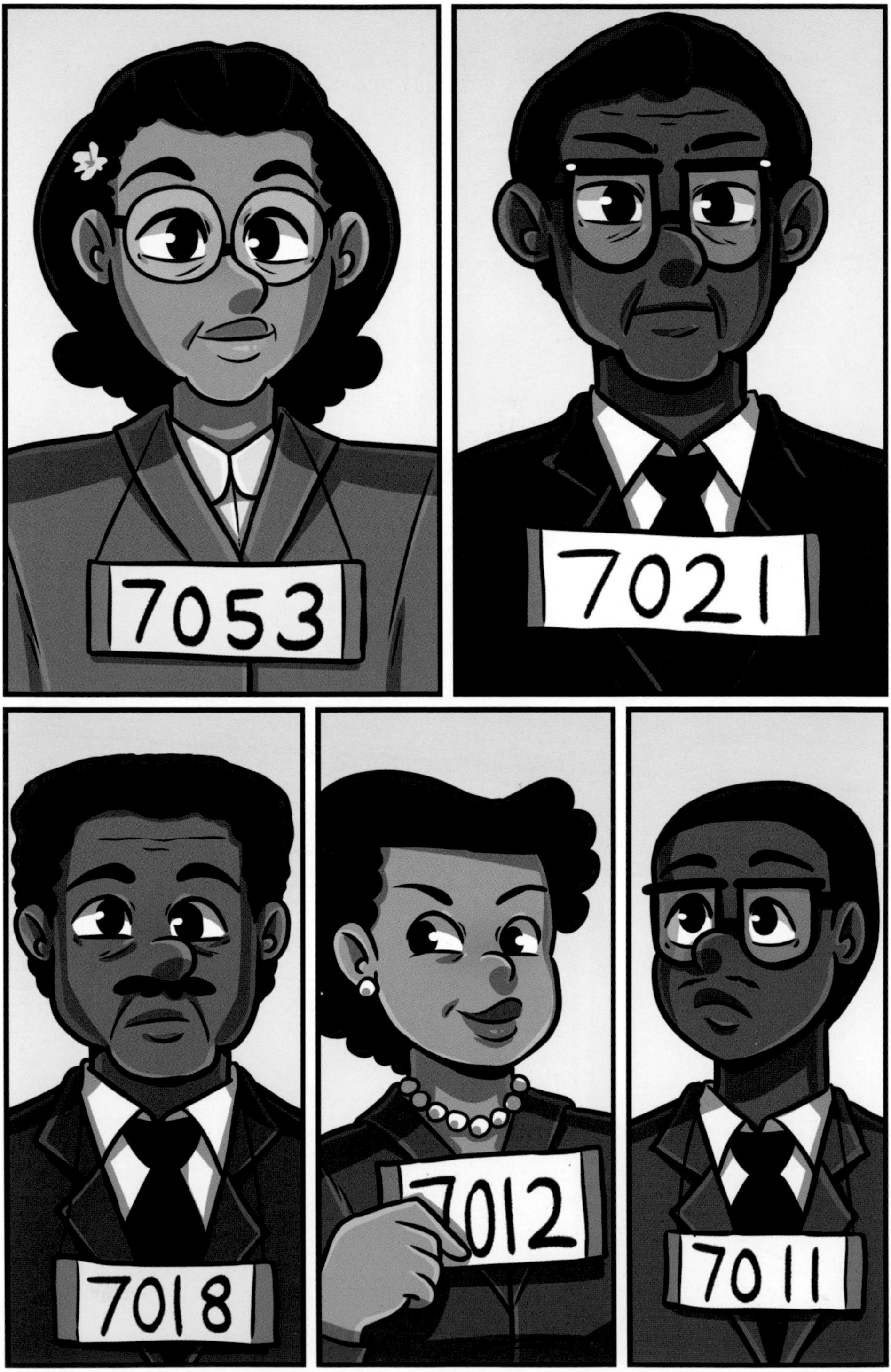
7053
7021
7018
7012
7011

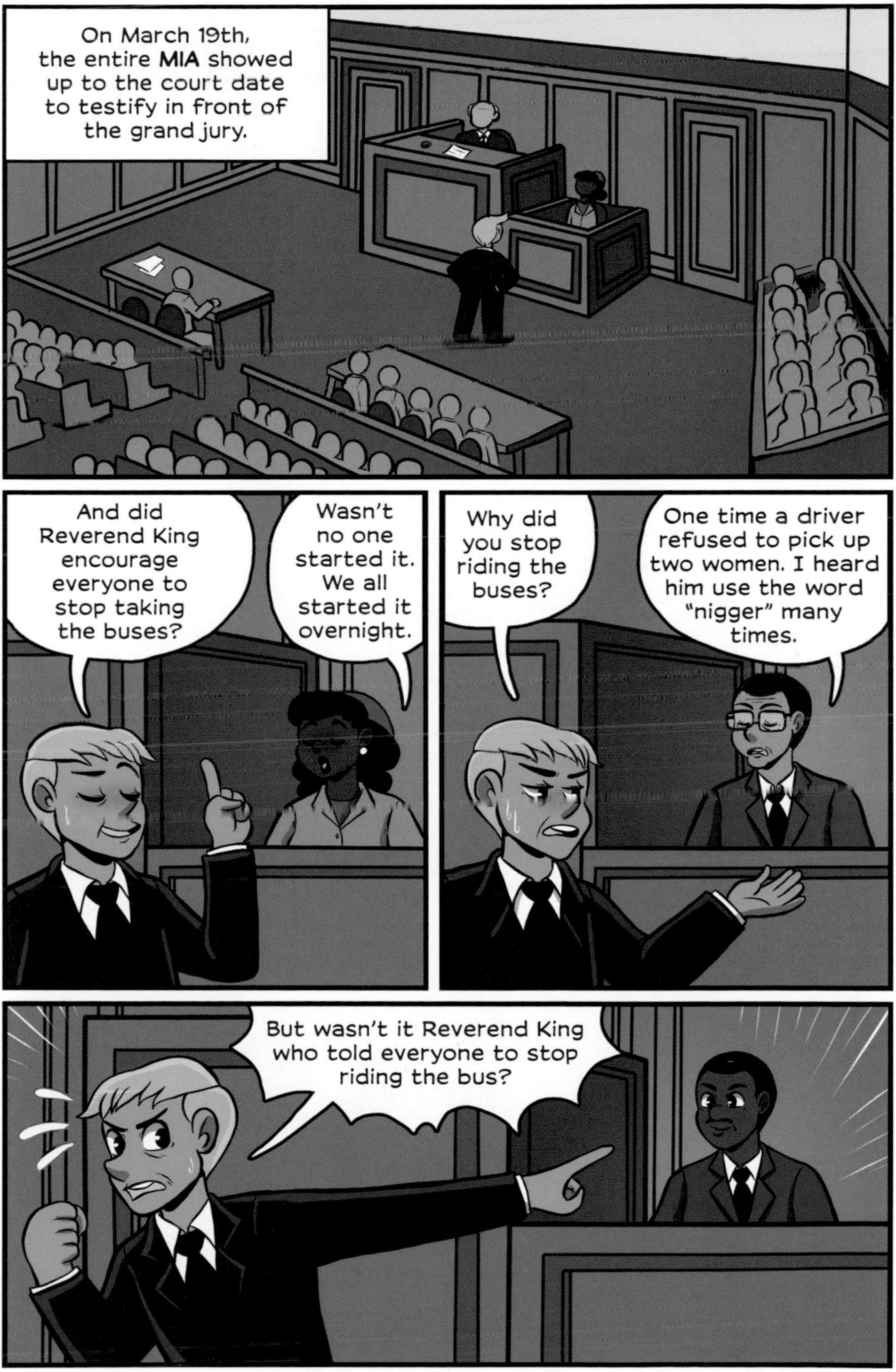
On March 19th, the entire **MIA** showed up to the court date to testify in front of the grand jury.
And did Reverend King encourage everyone to stop taking the buses?
Wasn't no one started it. We all started it overnight.
Why did you stop riding the buses?
One time a driver refused to pick up two women. I heard him use the word "nigger" many times.
But wasn't it Reverend King who told everyone to stop riding the bus?

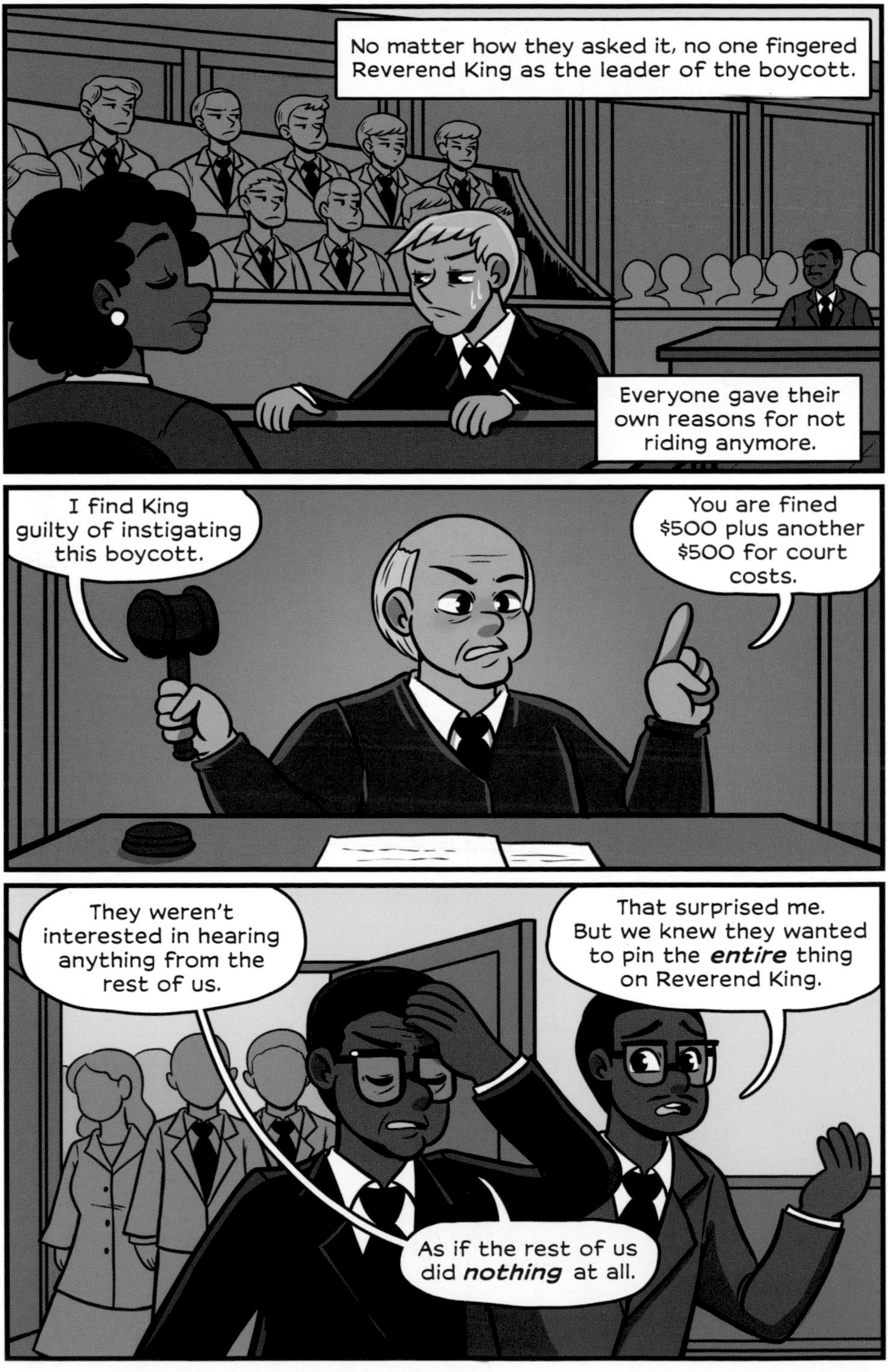
No matter how they asked it, no one fingered Reverend King as the leader of the boycott.
Everyone gave their own reasons for not riding anymore.
I find King guilty of instigating this boycott.
You are fined $500 plus another $500 for court costs.
They weren't interested in hearing anything from the rest of us.
That surprised me. But we knew they wanted to pin the ***entire*** thing on Reverend King.
As if the rest of us did ***nothing*** at all.

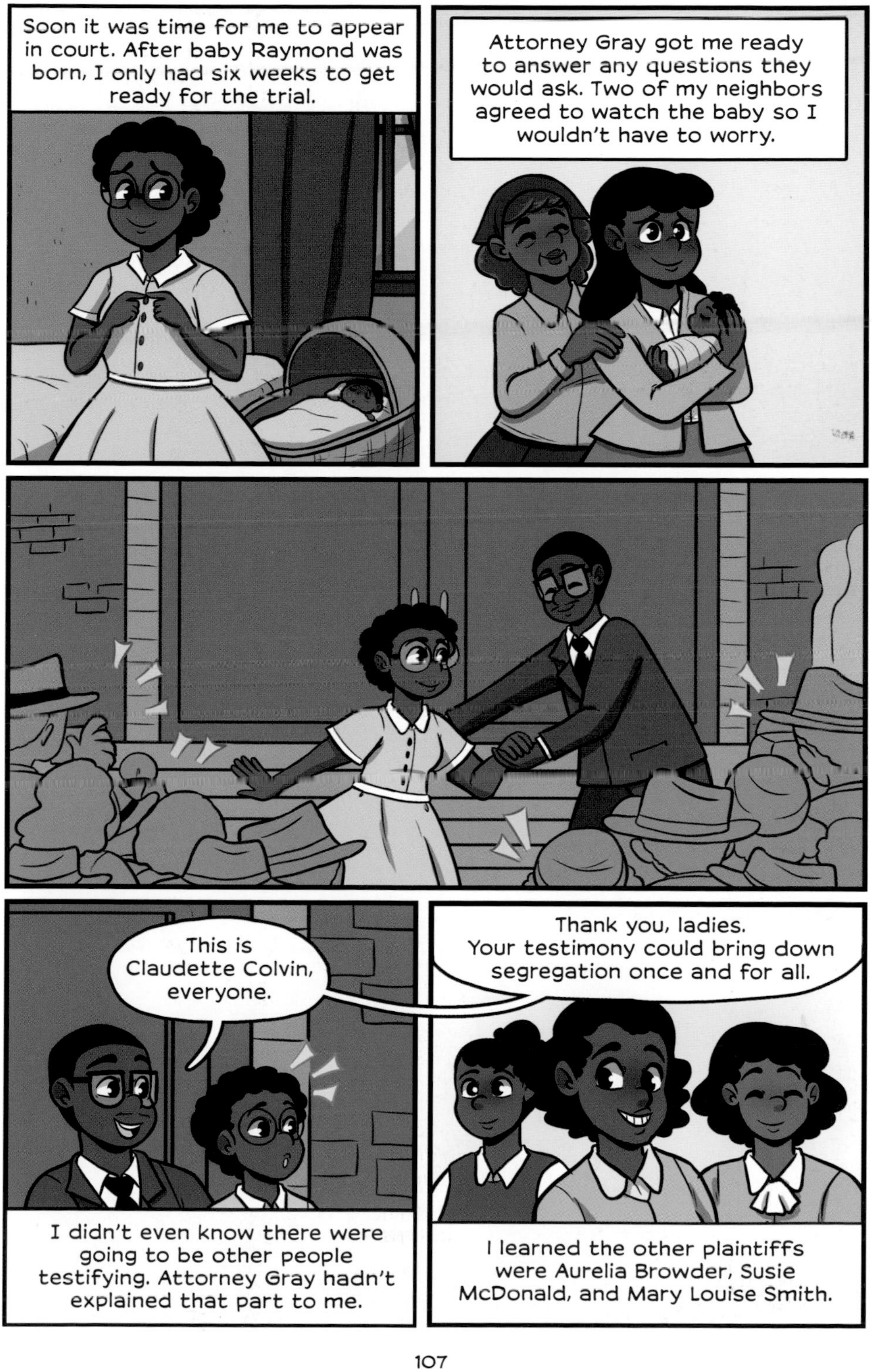

Soon it was time for me to appear in court. After baby Raymond was born, I only had six weeks to get ready for the trial.
Attorney Gray got me ready to answer any questions they would ask. Two of my neighbors agreed to watch the baby so I wouldn't have to worry.
This is Claudette Colvin, everyone.
I didn't even know there were going to be other people testifying. Attorney Gray hadn't explained that part to me.
Thank you, ladies. Your testimony could bring down segregation once and for all.
I learned the other plaintiffs were Aurelia Browder, Susie McDonald, and Mary Louise Smith.

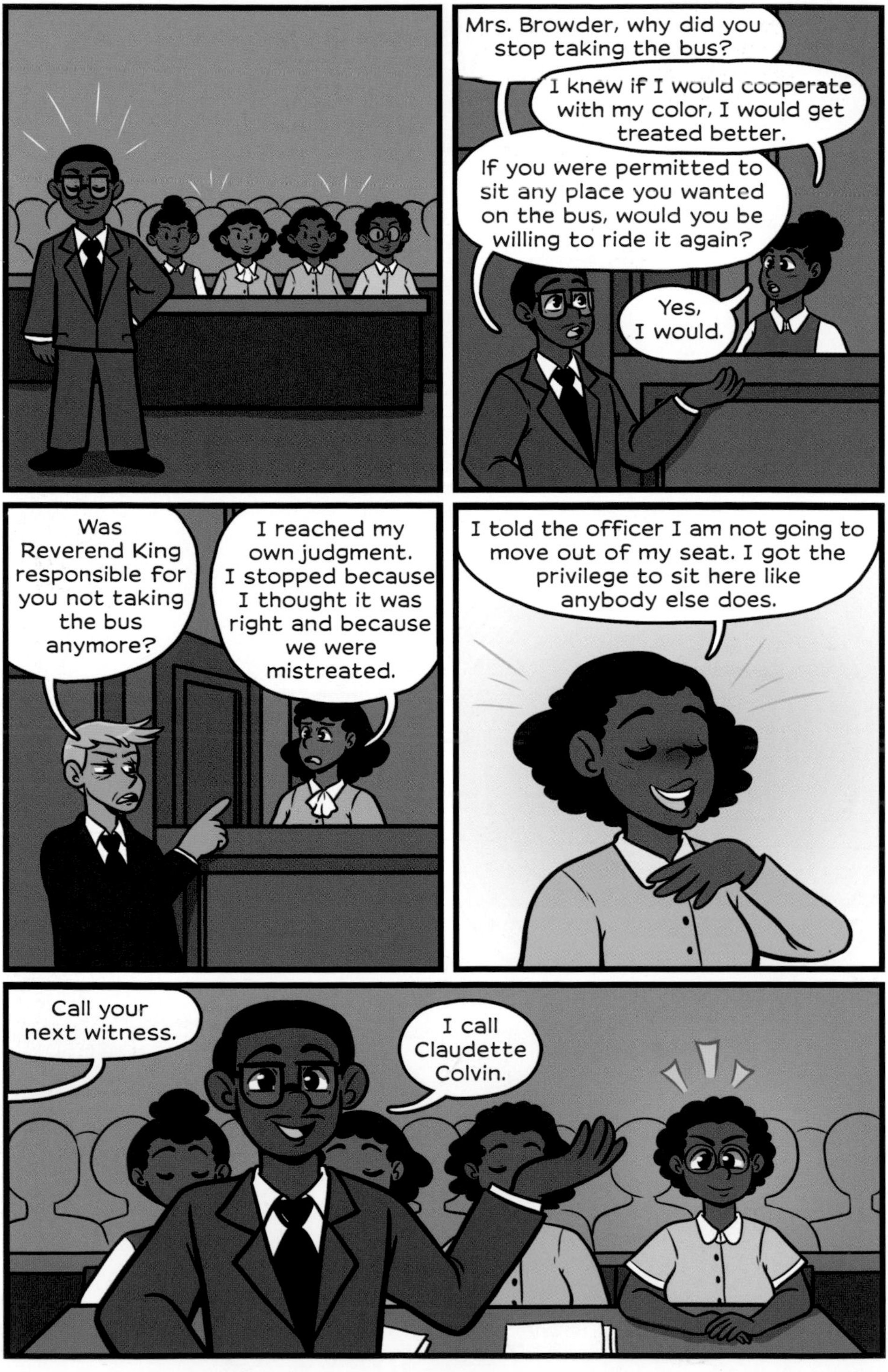
Mrs. Browder, why did you stop taking the bus?
I knew if I would cooperate with my color, I would get treated better.
If you were permitted to sit any place you wanted on the bus, would you be willing to ride it again?
Yes, I would.
Was Reverend King responsible for you not taking the bus anymore?
I reached my own judgment. I stopped because I thought it was right and because we were mistreated.
I told the officer I am not going to move out of my seat. I got the privilege to sit here like anybody else does.
Call your next witness.
I call Claudette Colvin.

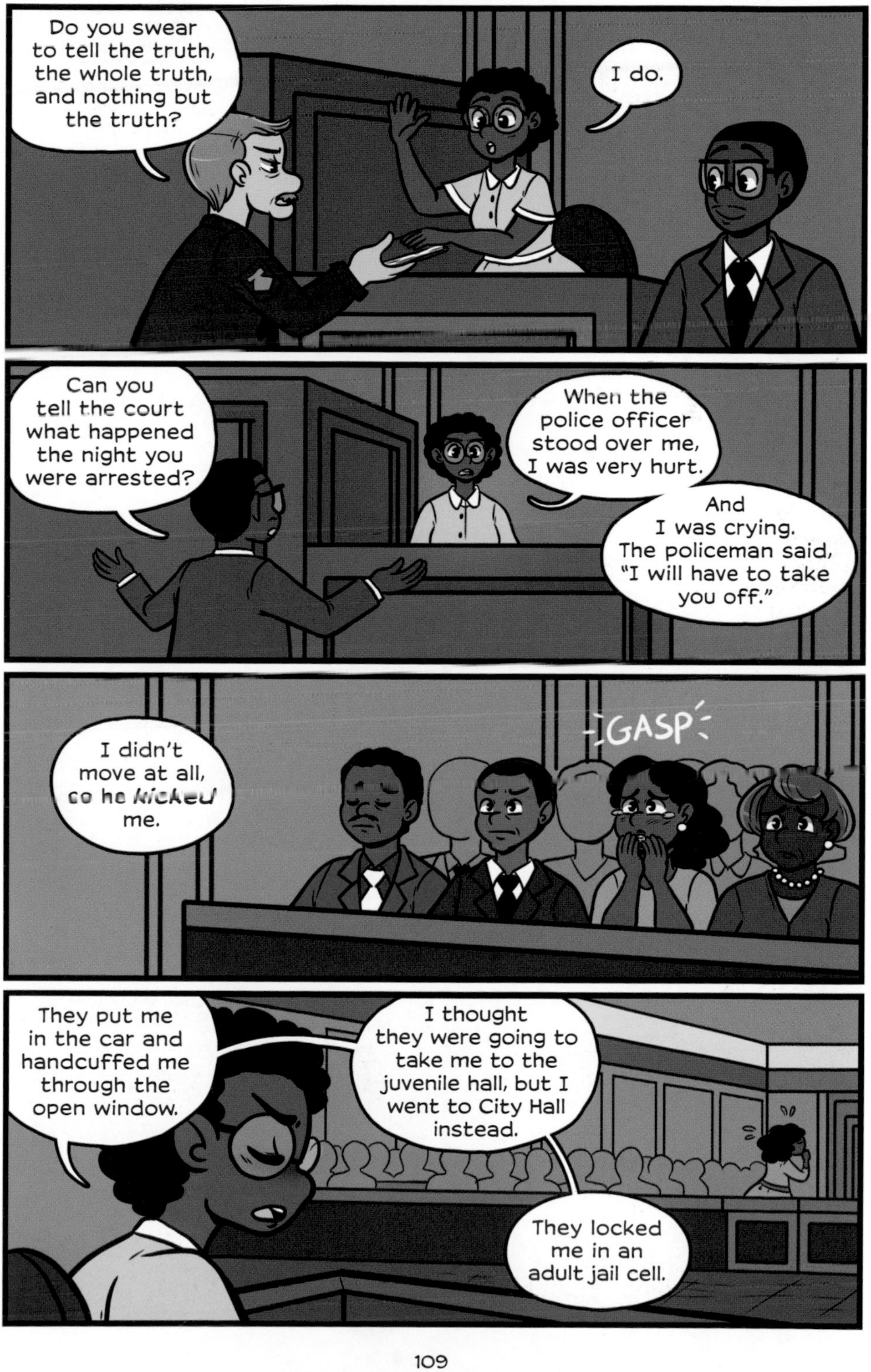
Do you swear to tell the truth, the whole truth, and nothing but the truth?
I do.
Can you tell the court what happened the night you were arrested?
When the police officer stood over me, I was very hurt.
And I was crying. The policeman said, "I will have to take you off."
I didn't move at all, so he *kicked* me.
GASP
They put me in the car and handcuffed me through the open window.
I thought they were going to take me to the juvenile hall, but I went to City Hall instead.
They locked me in an adult jail cell.

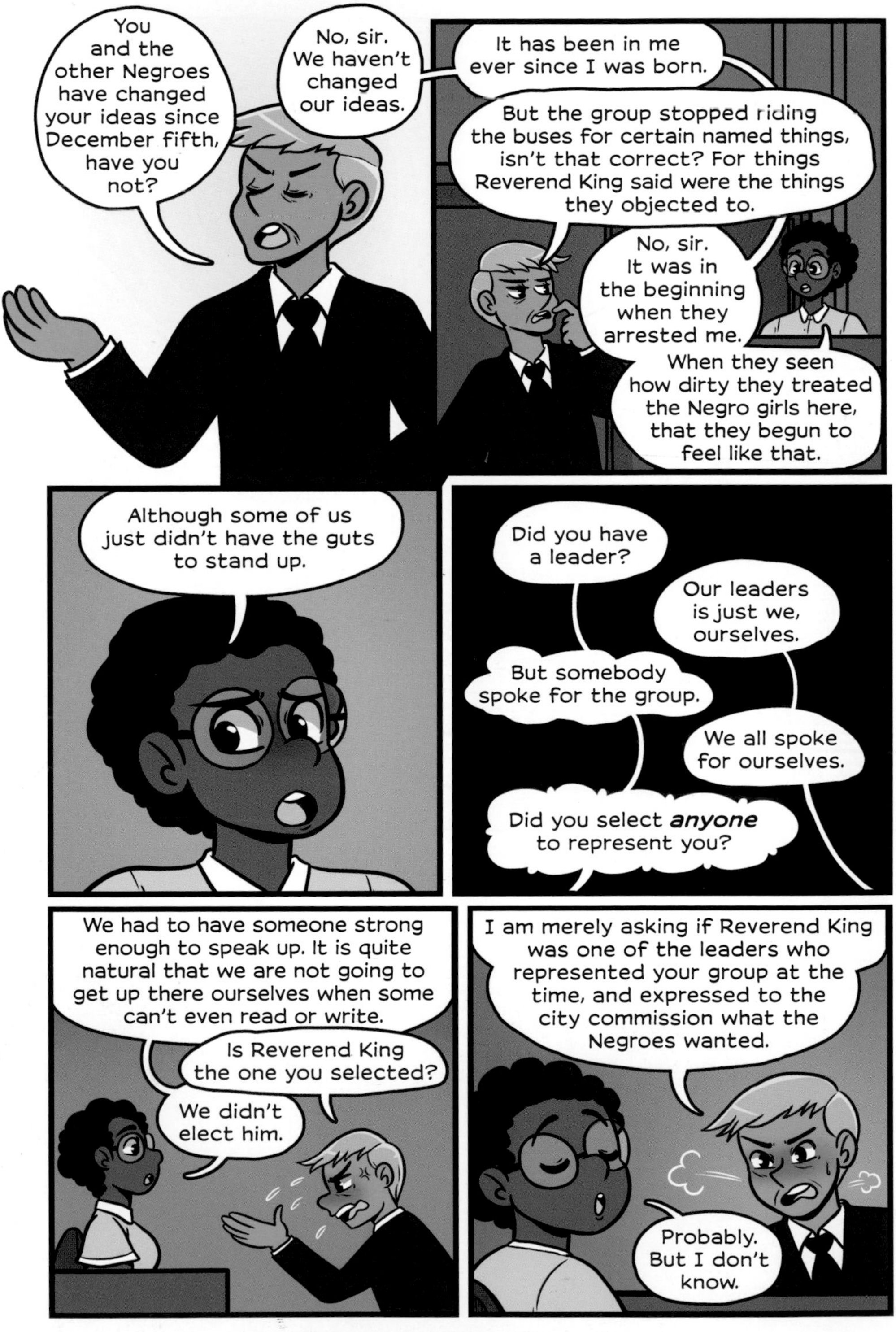
You and the other Negroes have changed your ideas since December fifth, have you not?
No, sir. We haven't changed our ideas.
It has been in me ever since I was born.
But the group stopped riding the buses for certain named things, isn't that correct? For things Reverend King said were the things they objected to.
No, sir. It was in the beginning when they arrested me.
When they seen how dirty they treated the Negro girls here, that they begun to feel like that.
Although some of us just didn't have the guts to stand up.
Did you have a leader?
Our leaders is just we, ourselves.
But somebody spoke for the group.
We all spoke for ourselves.
Did you select *anyone* to represent you?
We had to have someone strong enough to speak up. It is quite natural that we are not going to get up there ourselves when some can't even read or write.
Is Reverend King the one you selected?
We didn't elect him.
I am merely asking if Reverend King was one of the leaders who represented your group at the time, and expressed to the city commission what the Negroes wanted.
Probably. But I don't know.

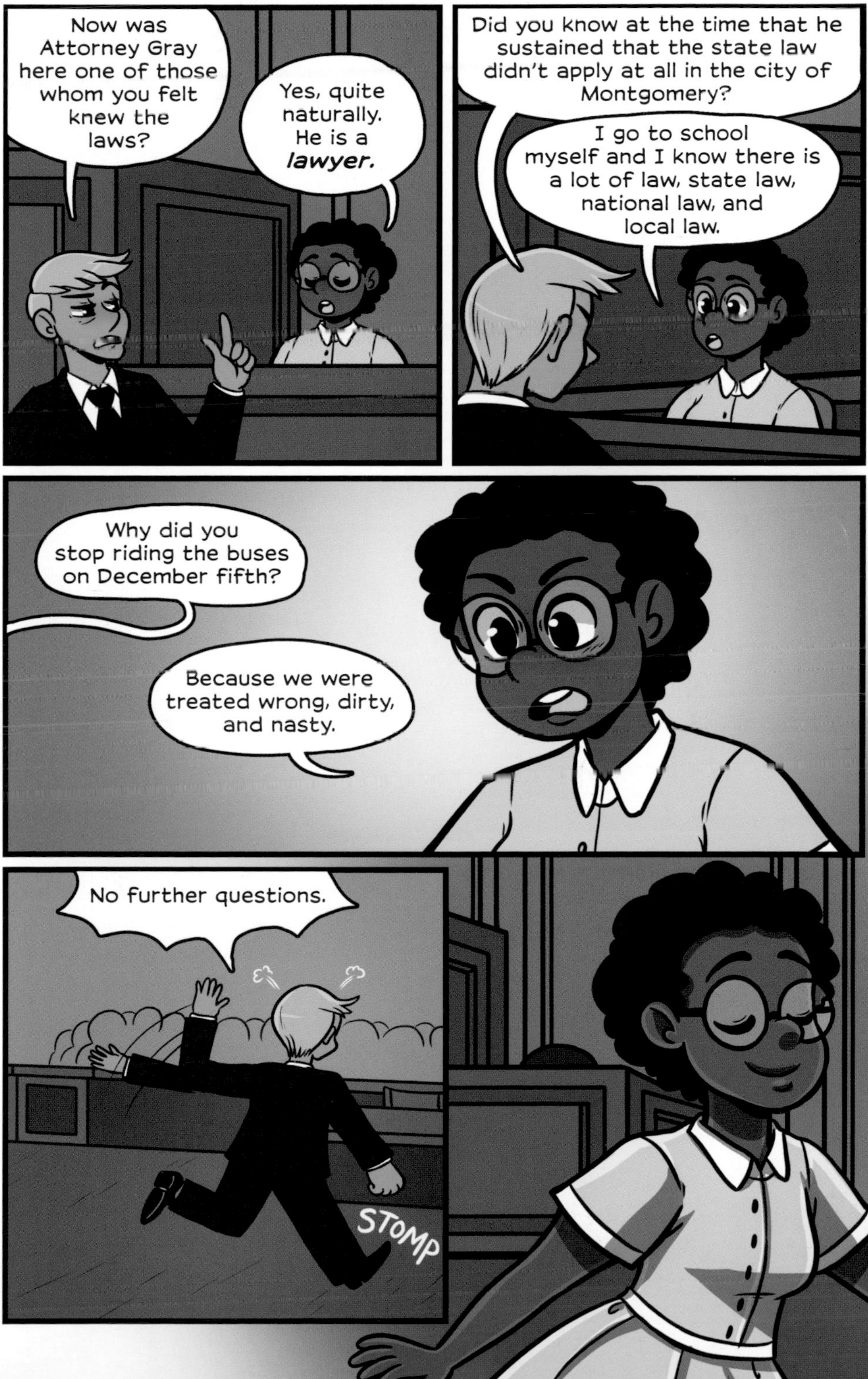
Now was Attorney Gray here one of those whom you felt knew the laws?
Yes, quite naturally. He is a *lawyer.*
Did you know at the time that he sustained that the state law didn't apply at all in the city of Montgomery?
I go to school myself and I know there is a lot of law, state law, national law, and local law.
Why did you stop riding the buses on December fifth?
Because we were treated wrong, dirty, and nasty.
No further questions.
STOMP

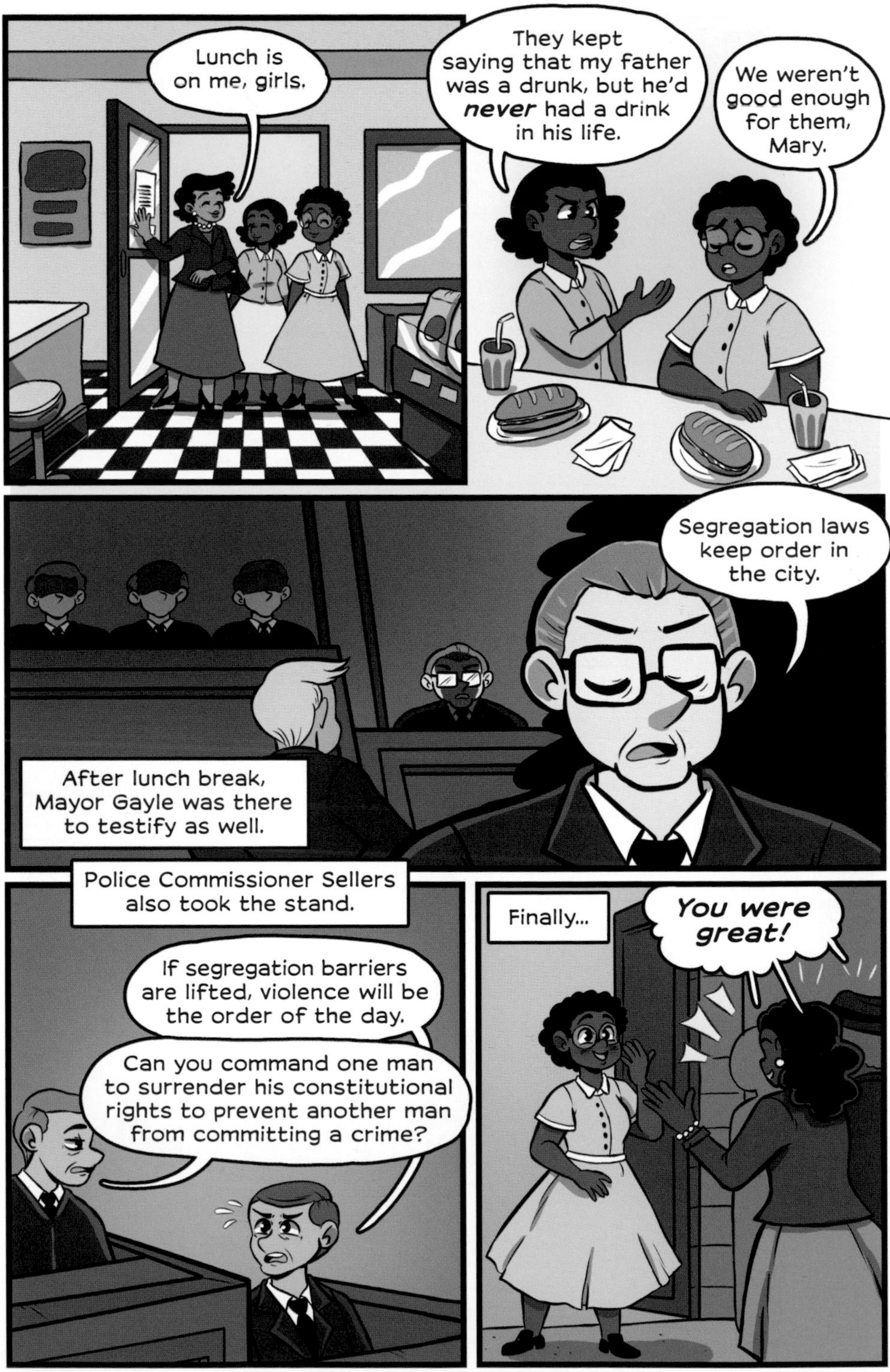

Lunch is on me, girls.
They kept saying that my father was a drunk, but he'd *never* had a drink in his life.
We weren't good enough for them, Mary.
Segregation laws keep order in the city.
After lunch break, Mayor Gayle was there to testify as well.
Police Commissioner Sellers also took the stand.
If segregation barriers are lifted, violence will be the order of the day.
Can you command one man to surrender his constitutional rights to prevent another man from committing a crime?
Finally...
You were great!

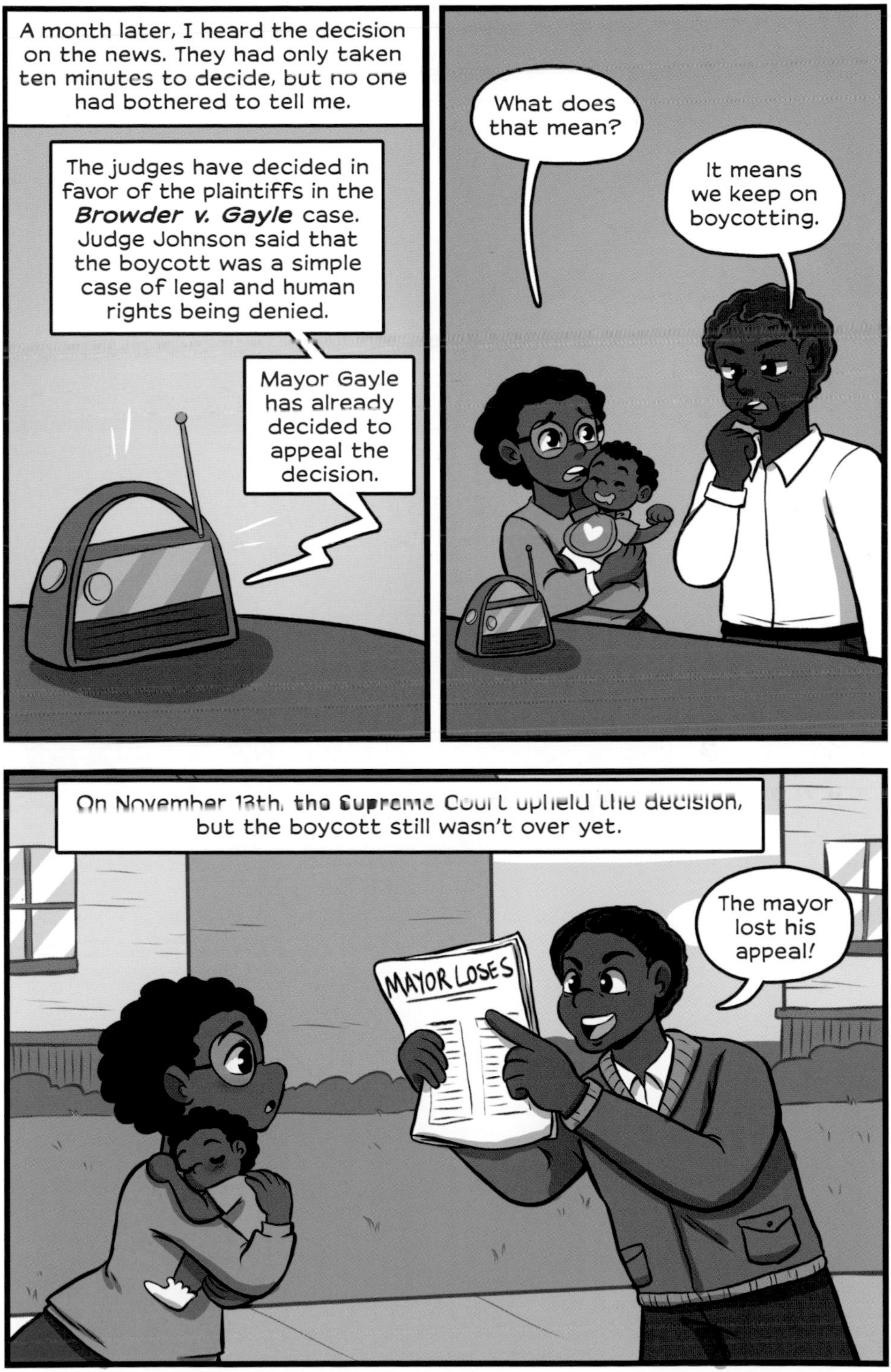
A month later, I heard the decision on the news. They had only taken ten minutes to decide, but no one had bothered to tell me.
The judges have decided in favor of the plaintiffs in the *Browder v. Gayle* case. Judge Johnson said that the boycott was a simple case of legal and human rights being denied.
Mayor Gayle has already decided to appeal the decision.
What does that mean?
It means we keep on boycotting.
On November 13th, the Supreme Court upheld the decision, but the boycott still wasn't over yet.
MAYOR LOSES
The mayor lost his appeal!

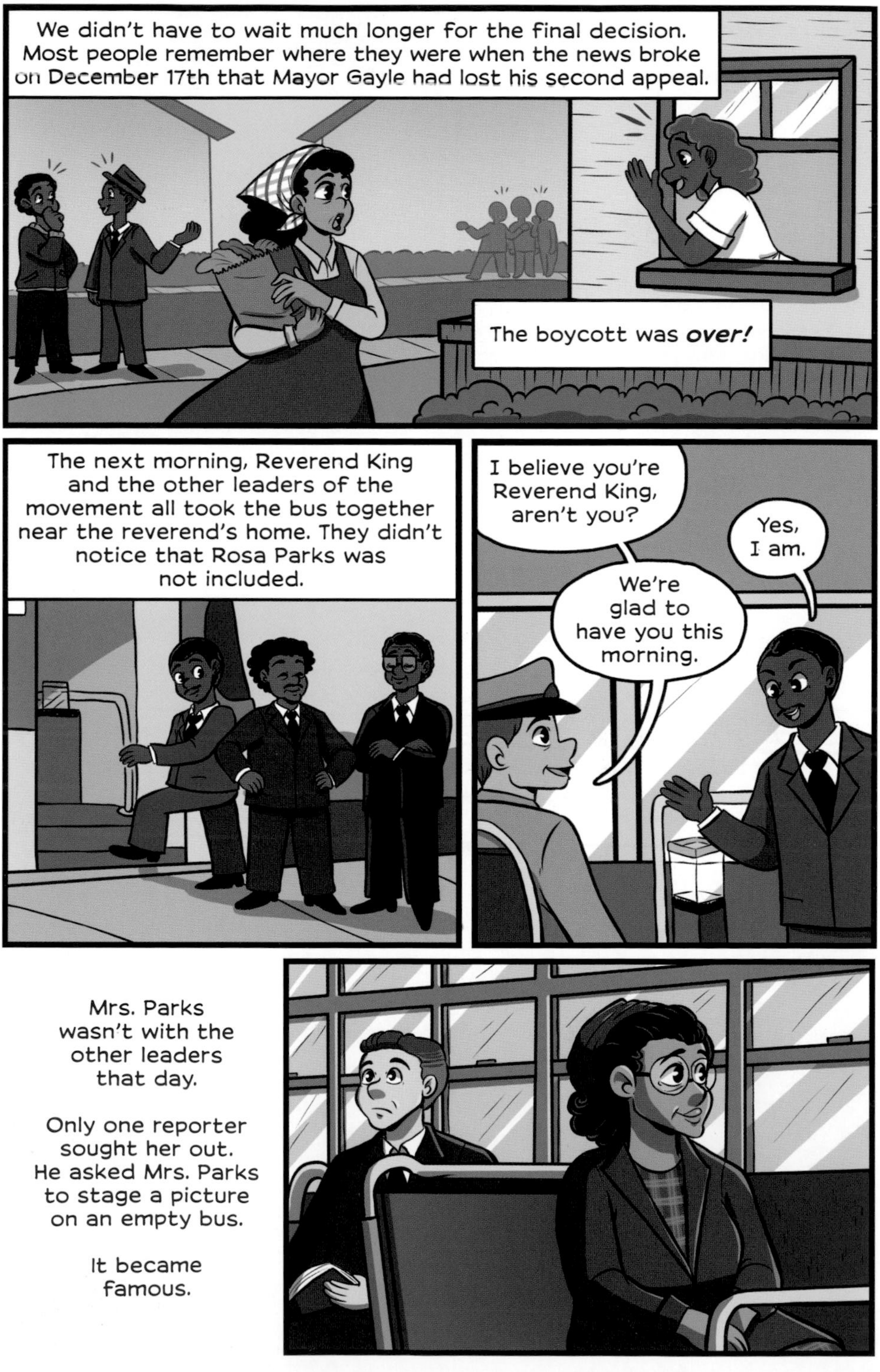
We didn't have to wait much longer for the final decision. Most people remember where they were when the news broke on December 17th that Mayor Gayle had lost his second appeal.
The boycott was *over!*
The next morning, Reverend King and the other leaders of the movement all took the bus together near the reverend's home. They didn't notice that Rosa Parks was not included.
I believe you're Reverend King, aren't you?
Yes, I am.
We're glad to have you this morning.
Mrs. Parks wasn't with the other leaders that day.
Only one reporter sought her out. He asked Mrs. Parks to stage a picture on an empty bus.
It became famous.

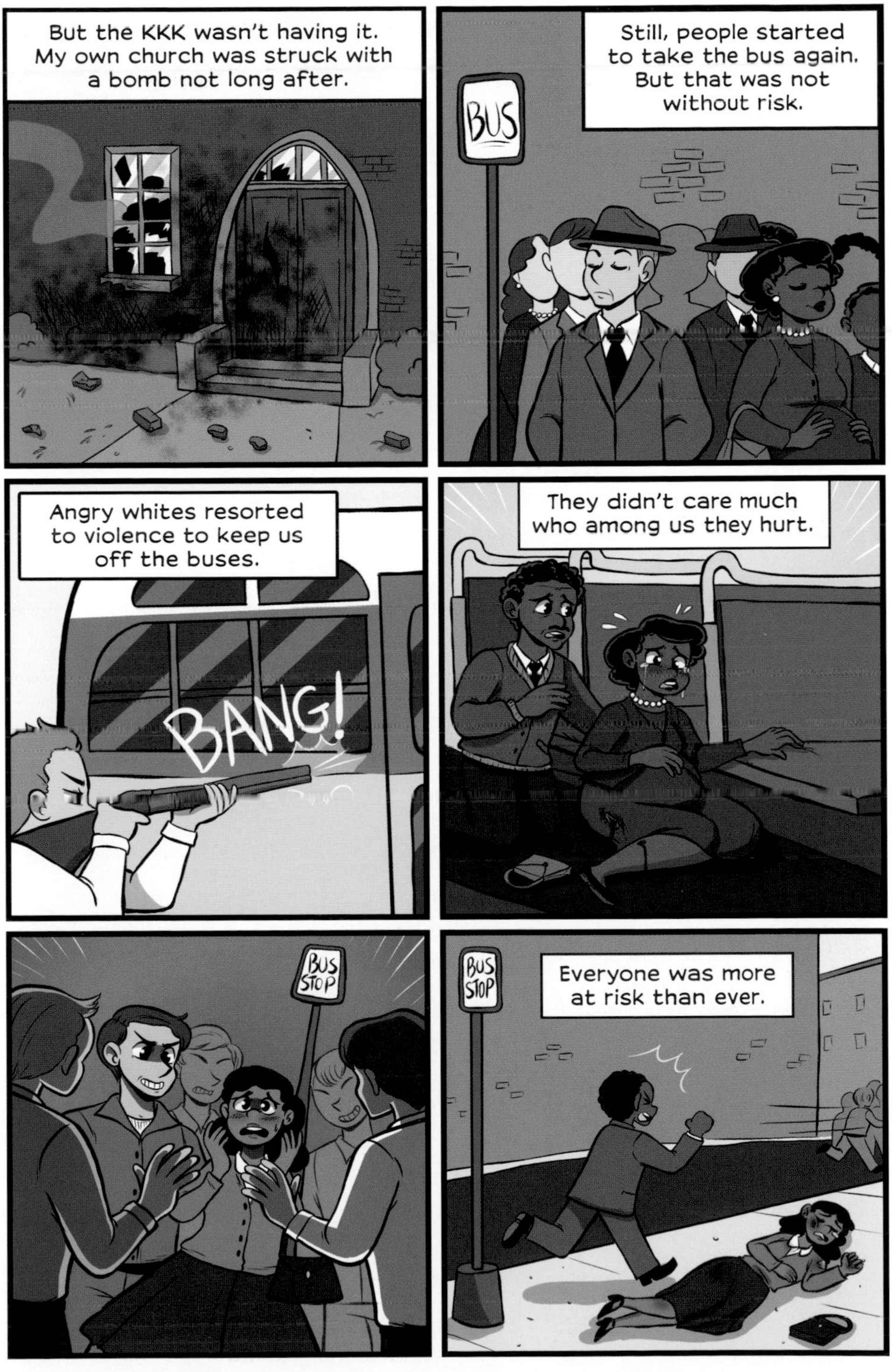

But the KKK wasn't having it. My own church was struck with a bomb not long after.
BUS
Still, people started to take the bus again. But that was not without risk.
Angry whites resorted to violence to keep us off the buses.
BANG!
They didn't care much who among us they hurt.
BUS STOP
BUS STOP
Everyone was more at risk than ever.

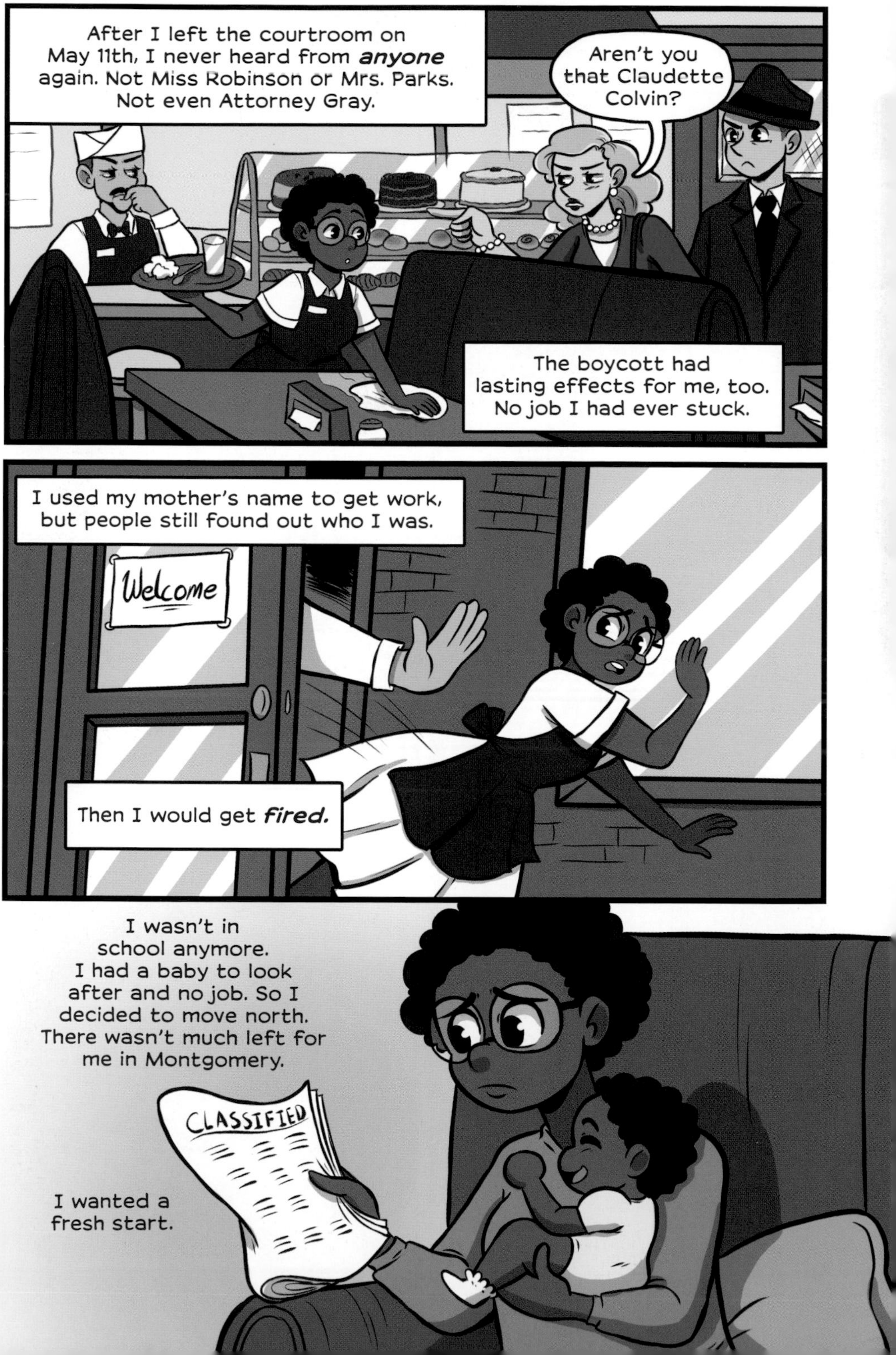
After I left the courtroom on May 11th, I never heard from *anyone* again. Not Miss Robinson or Mrs. Parks. Not even Attorney Gray.
Aren't you that Claudette Colvin?
The boycott had lasting effects for me, too. No job I had ever stuck.
I used my mother's name to get work, but people still found out who I was.
Welcome
Then I would get *fired.*
I wasn't in school anymore. I had a baby to look after and no job. So I decided to move north. There wasn't much left for me in Montgomery.
CLASSIFIED
I wanted a fresh start.

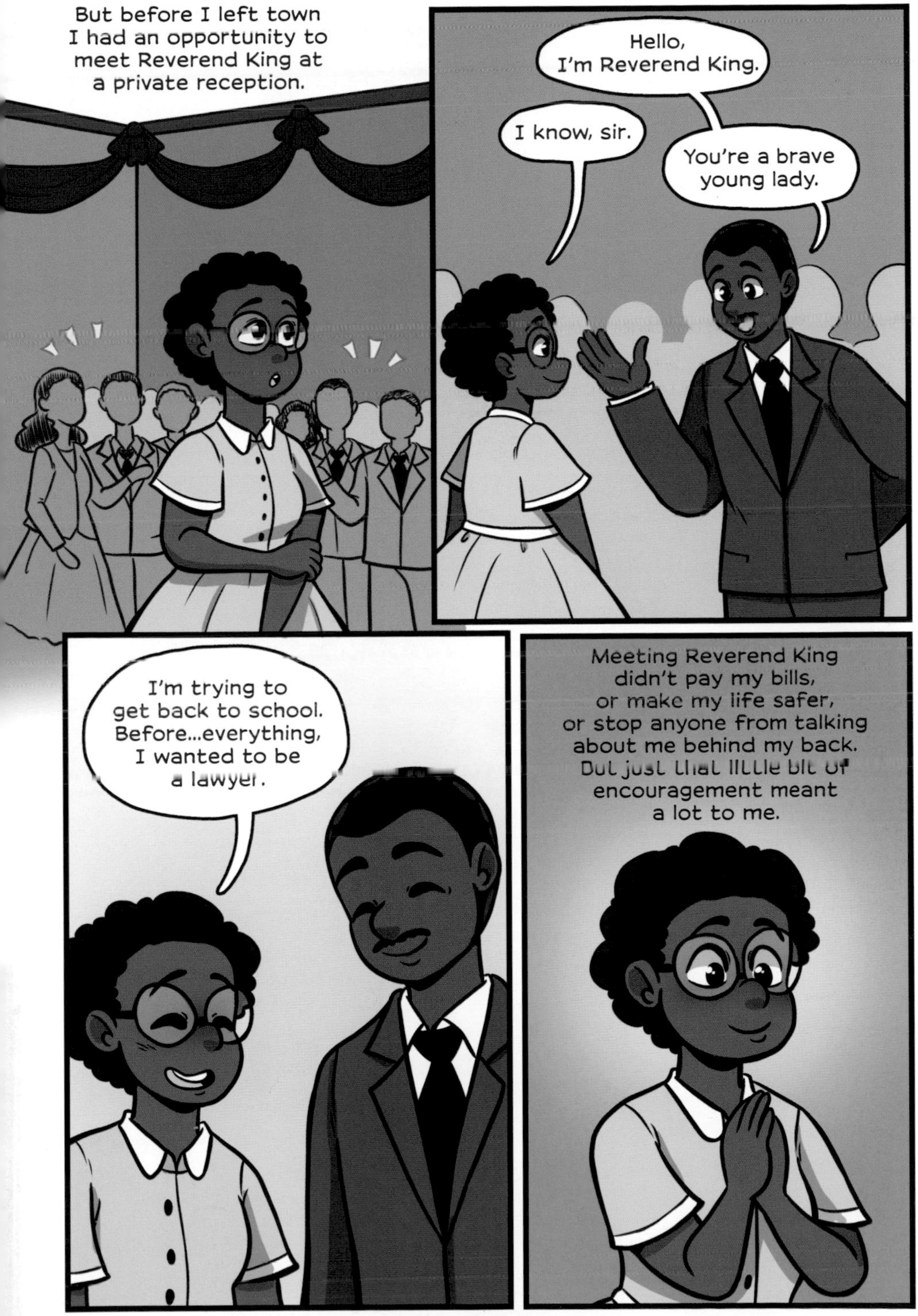
But before I left town I had an opportunity to meet Reverend King at a private reception.
Hello, I'm Reverend King.
I know, sir.
You're a brave young lady.
I'm trying to get back to school. Before...everything, I wanted to be a lawyer.
Meeting Reverend King didn't pay my bills, or make my life safer, or stop anyone from talking about me behind my back. But just that little bit of encouragement meant a lot to me.

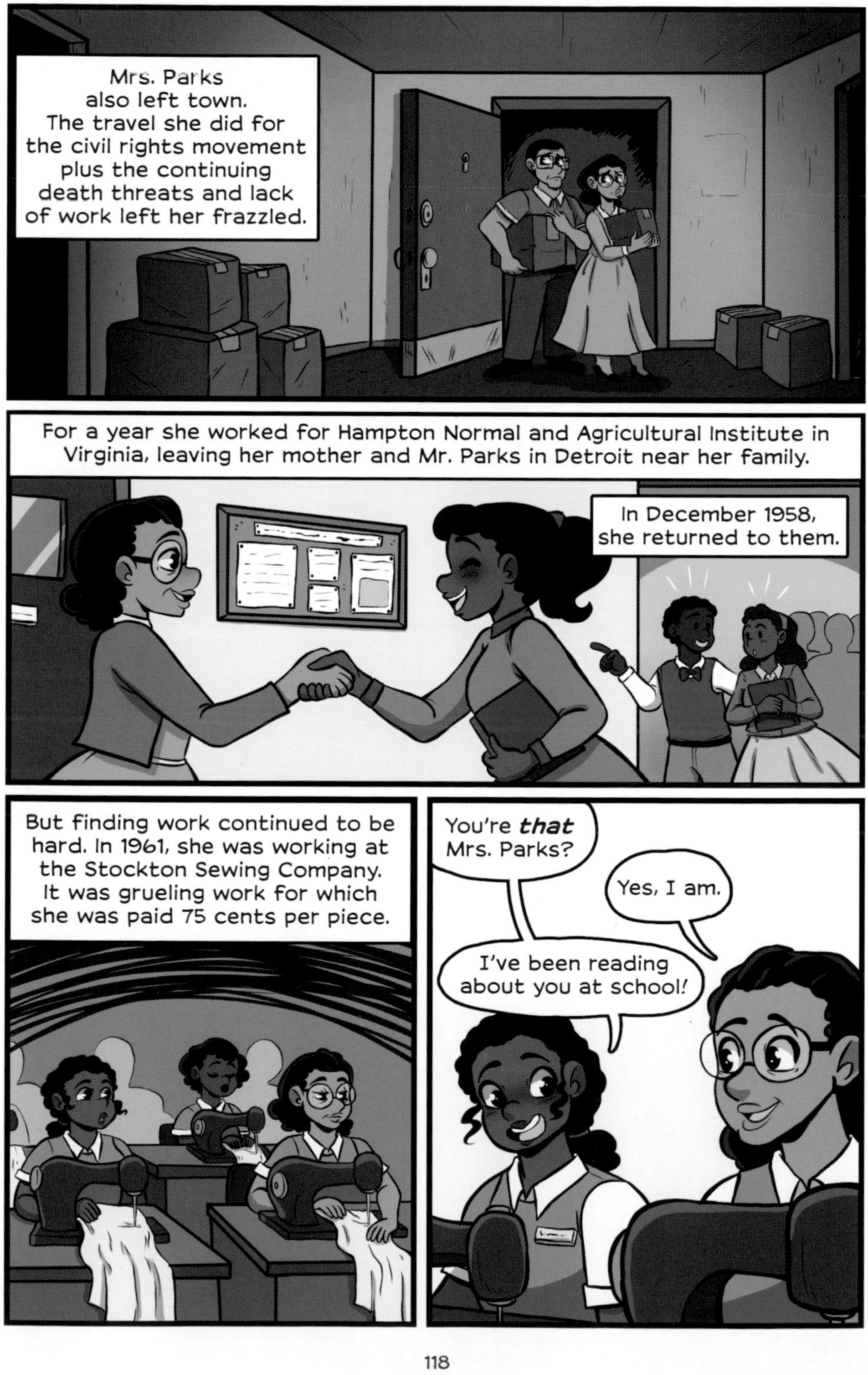
Mrs. Parks also left town. The travel she did for the civil rights movement plus the continuing death threats and lack of work left her frazzled.
For a year she worked for Hampton Normal and Agricultural Institute in Virginia, leaving her mother and Mr. Parks in Detroit near her family.
In December 1958, she returned to them.
But finding work continued to be hard. In 1961, she was working at the Stockton Sewing Company. It was grueling work for which she was paid 75 cents per piece.
You're *that* Mrs. Parks?
Yes, I am.
I've been reading about you at school!

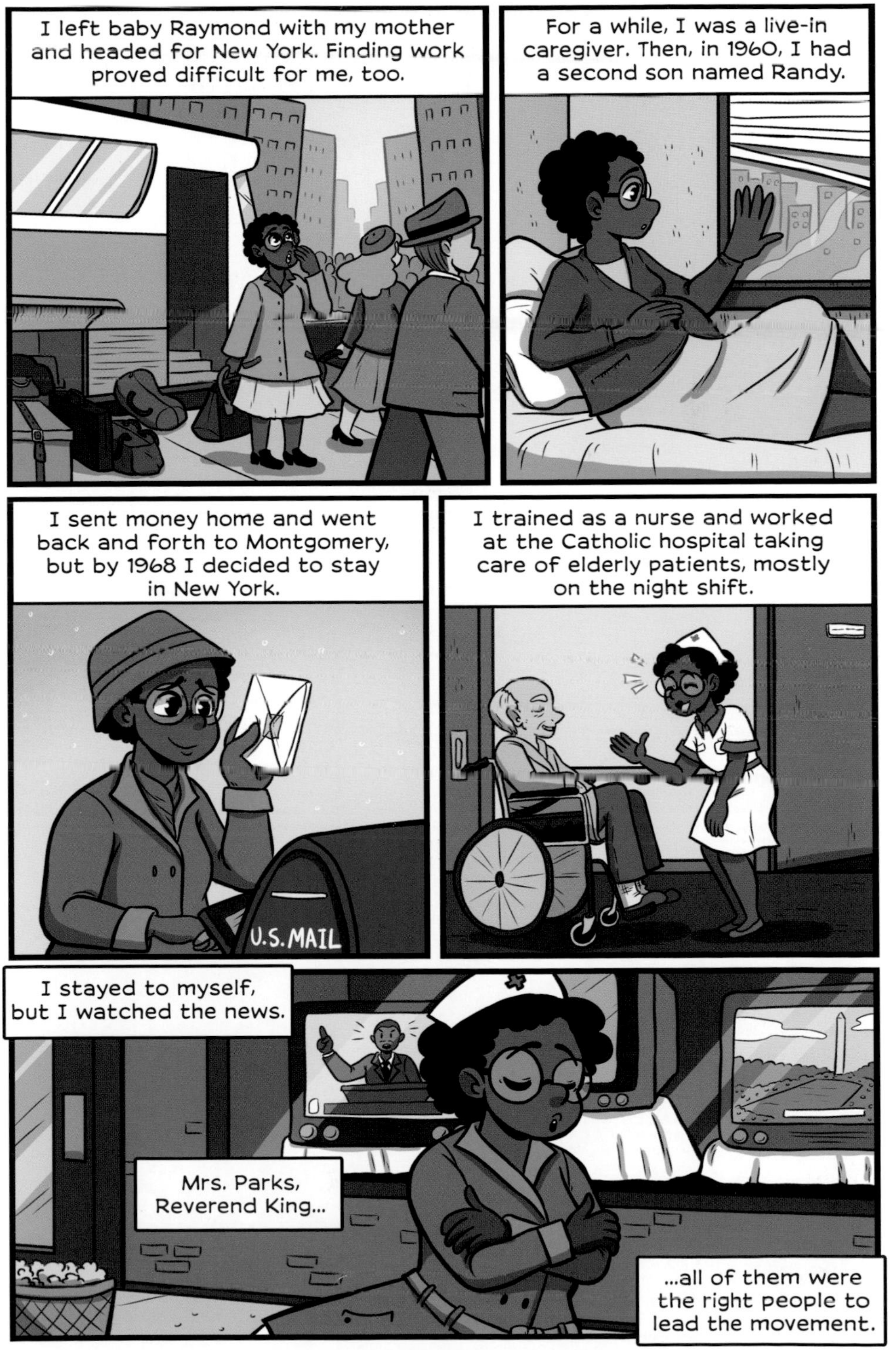

I left baby Raymond with my mother and headed for New York. Finding work proved difficult for me, too.
For a while, I was a live-in caregiver. Then, in 1960, I had a second son named Randy.
I sent money home and went back and forth to Montgomery, but by 1968 I decided to stay in New York.
U.S. MAIL
I trained as a nurse and worked at the Catholic hospital taking care of elderly patients, mostly on the night shift.
I stayed to myself, but I watched the news.
Mrs. Parks, Reverend King...
...all of them were the right people to lead the movement.

In 1975, a reporter called, asking about me.

More people started to reach out to me. Slowly, my story was being told.

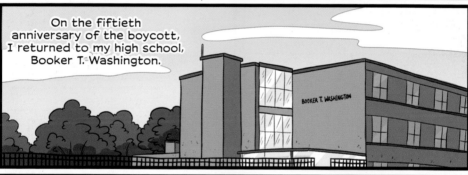
On the fiftieth anniversary of the boycott, I returned to my high school, Booker T. Washington.

BOOKER T. WASHINGTON

FLASH

FLASH

We're so proud that you are a student from our own school!

And you were the same age as us when it all happened.

There are things you will need to stand up for, too.

Don't slide back.

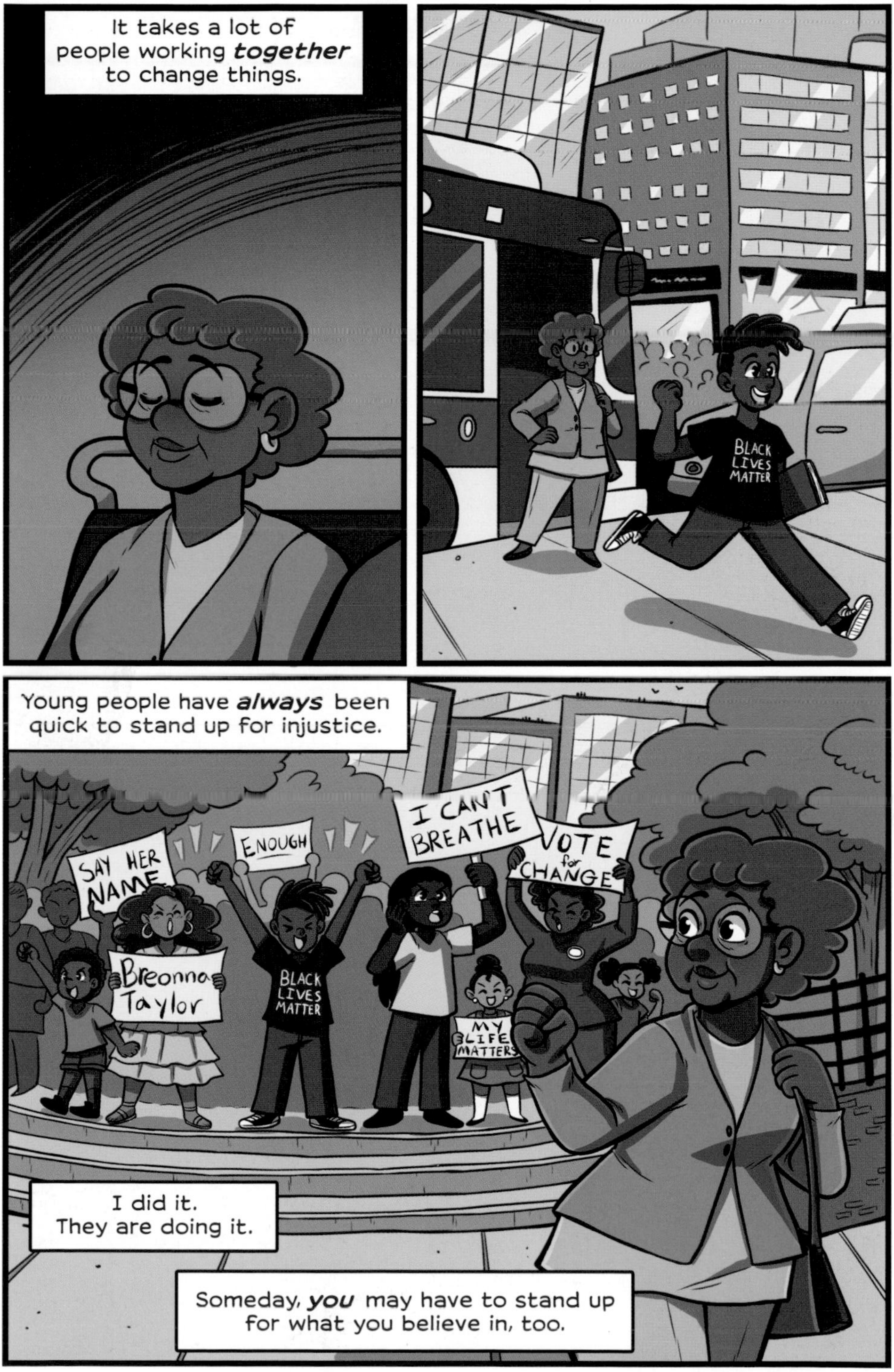

It takes a lot of people working ***together*** to change things.
BLACK LIVES MATTER
Young people have ***always*** been quick to stand up for injustice.
SAY HER NAME
ENOUGH
I CAN'T BREATHE
VOTE for CHANGE
Breonna Taylor
BLACK LIVES MATTER
MY LIFE MATTERS
I did it.
They are doing it.
Someday, ***you*** may have to stand up for what you believe in, too.

Afterword

The thing that struck me most during my research for this book was just how long activism had been happening in Montgomery, Alabama, and how many people were involved. Rosa Parks may have been the "mother of the movement," and it's clear that Claudette Colvin was its spark, but without so many people coming together, this may never have worked.

The idea for the boycott came from Jo Ann Robinson, who was the head of the Women's Political Council (WPC) at the time. She had seen the need for a boycott six years before Colvin and Parks were arrested and had been laying the groundwork for it since then. The boycott came together quickly because Robinson and her associates had long been ready to organize for just such an event. Then it stayed on track because of these same women.

If Colvin's teacher had not instilled in her a sense of the benefits of resistance, Colvin might not have refused to leave her seat. Like Robinson, Parks had a history of activism years before the boycott. In history books, we tend to focus on the moment, not the work that came before or continued after. We profile the biggest names of a movement, but thousands of people are often involved. Robinson credited 52,000 people with supporting the boycott. Each one of them was important in overturning the segregated bus laws.

Sometimes people think they have to make big gestures to be involved in a movement, but this one in particular showed that people don't always have to be on the front lines to help. Some people simply put on their shoes and walked. Some people sent shoes for those walking. All of that mattered. Every gesture, no matter how small, helped to make the Montgomery Bus Boycott a success.

—Tracey Baptiste

While drawing this book, I thought a lot about my grandmother. She was born in South Carolina in 1939. It seems like so long ago, but really she was a young woman during the height of the civil rights movement. Her youngest child, my mother, was a baby when the Civil Rights Act was signed. To me this book is history—a lot of which I've learned for the first time—but, to my mother and my grandmother, it was a moment in their lives. It's very humbling to think how much our world has changed within one lifetime. It's a little sad to think how much more still needs to be done, but I hope every young person is able to learn where they came from and take those lessons to shape a better future. As a Black woman, I am eternally grateful to be able to share this story of Claudette Colvin and Rosa Parks with the world.

—Shauna J. Grant